Invest Yourself

Yourself

The Catalogue of Volunteer Opportunities

Susan G. Angus,
Editor

Published by
Commission on
Voluntary Service & Action

New York, New York

A GUIDE TO ACTION

COMMISSION ON VOLUNTARY SERVICE & ACTION

INVEST YOURSELF Published by Commission on Voluntary Service & Action,
1 Union Square West, Suite 902, New York, New York, 10003
(646) 486-2446 or (877) 867-6150
Editor: Susan Angus
Cover Design by Niberca Polo
Printing by Bind-Rite Graphics
©2010 by Commission on Voluntary Service & Action
Invest Yourself Editions 1946–2010
ISSN: 0148-6802
ISBN: 978-0-9629322-5-0

About the Editor:

Susan Angus has been Executive Director of Commission on Voluntary Service & Action (CVSA) since 1984, and editor of *INVEST YOURSELF* since 1979. She was introduced to CVSA as a staff member of United Methodist Voluntary Service, a unique program created by the Board of Global Ministries of the United Methodist Church, under the leadership of Rev. Randle B. Dew, Executive Director of UMVS, to provide an alternative to the traditional "mission" model. Susan Angus has done volunteer work since her high school years, community work in the Lower East Side of Manhattan in the early 1970s, and was a volunteer organizer in full-time service with associations of the lowest-paid workers in the country for two decades. Still working as a full-time volunteer, her dedication to the promotion—on a local, national and international level—of full-time volunteer activism with non-government organizations serving people in need as a goal-oriented vocational choice has been unbroken for over 40 years.

INVEST YOURSELF is distributed by volunteers. Please contact CVSA for information about how you can help distribute this catalogue. See page 13.

Dedication

"If we fail to make solidarity and a sense of social and environmental responsibility the main driving force behind our human society then, quite simply, we will not survive. The egotism, individualism, greed and exclusive national interests that characterize and drive human behavior today can lead only to the extinction of our species. We are already heading down this path. At some point, it might not be possible to turn back."

"To take a qualitative leap forward, we must give up our quest to become the lords and masters of creation, forgetting that we are not owners but only caretakers, which, after all, is no small thing. Only when we accept the fact that we are caretakers and not owners and that we will one day be held to account for our stewardship will the grandeur of our humanity shine forth."

— **Miguel D'Escoto Brochman** challenged the leaders of the 192 nations of the UN General Assembly with these words in 2009. D'Escoto, who served as President of the 63rd General Assembly of the United Nations, is the former Minister of Foreign Affairs of Nicaragua, a Maryknoll Priest and founder of Orbis Press.

We dedicate this issue of *INVEST YOURSELF*
to those of our readers
who have chosen to invest yourselves
in working with others to create that better world
and allow the grandeur of our humanity
to shine forth through your service to others.

Thanks to our SPONSORS

The businesses, educational institutions, organizations and individuals with displays and messages throughout the pages of these articles and the index sections of this catalogue rallied behind volunteer efforts and helped make this issue of *INVEST YOURSELF* possible. These displays represent their investment in you, the volunteer, future volunteers and the voluntary organizations that are changing how we live.

Please patronize their businesses and their institutions and make the power of the non-government volunteer service movement felt. Please call CVSA at (646) 486-2446 to ask how you can sponsor the next edition of *INVEST YOURSELF*.

CONTENTS

How to Use This Catalogue

INVEST YOURSELF is a catalogue of volunteer opportunities. It provides descriptive text about each organization and their volunteer opportunities along with their contact information so that you can talk with them directly about their needs, arrangements for volunteers and application process. It also provides alphabetical, geographic and skill/interest indexes to guide you. We strongly encourage you to simply browse through all the listings in the book to gain perspective on the scope of the needs and the range of possibilities. Reading the articles in Part 2 written by volunteers about their experiences will give you a variety of insights from people directly involved.

In the sixty-five years of publication of *INVEST YOURSELF*, the numbers and types of projects have changed, as have the problems and needs volunteers devote their time, talent and energies to addressing. *INVEST YOURSELF* continues to serve as the most comprehensive resource directory of non-government volunteer opportunities, both full-time and part-time.

Each listed organization has its own application or placement process. Many provide on-the-job training in the work you will be doing. Many also seek people who can bring specific skills or experience needed in their endeavors. You will find this information and more in the descriptive listings of each organization which are in Part 3 and Part 4.

Volunteer organizations differ as much in what they do as in their reasons for doing it. Some reach out with aid to one person or family at a time. Others organize workers in their community for economic betterment. Some provide urgently needed services to marginalized communities and also organize for change in policies they see at the root of the problems. Others organize in their communities for the collective advancement of those who live there. Some strive to overcome conditions of poverty and injustice for reasons based in religious faith. Many combine these and other elements. The forms these organizations take are just as diverse. Some are community associations, some are membership associations and others are non-profit corporations.

If you have particular interests already in mind, or types of endeavor and goals you seek to pursue, use the indexes in Parts 6, 7 and 8 to match up your aspirations and interests with appropriate availabilities listed herein.

Upon taking an interest in a program listed in *INVEST YOURSELF*, contact the organization directly to obtain more information. Once you apply, take your application and acceptance seriously, and treat your opportunity with respect. If you apply to more than one project, notify the other organizations if you have accepted another assignment.

Please contact CVSA with questions, articles about your volunteer experiences, new organizational listings for the next edition and offers of aid. Thank you.

Part 1

ABOUT CVSA

Commission on Voluntary Service & Action (CVSA) is a consultative and coordinating body of more than 200 non-government volunteer service organizations and agencies that support voluntary service projects or place volunteers with such projects, in all parts of the world. They are primarily based in North America and are engaged in serving the interests of people and communities in need throughout the United States as well as Asia, Africa, Latin America, Europe and the rest of the world.

CVSA seeks to interpret, extend, promote and support the world of voluntary service and involvement programs, and maintain and expand the ability of individuals to donate their time and services to persons and communities in need. Since its inception in 1945, CVSA has acted to protect the fundamental right of individuals to participate in voluntary service activities outside the domain of corporate and government controls. CVSA's functions also include providing assistance to volunteer organizations to upgrade the quality of the training and incorporation of the volunteers.

CVSA has long recognized and promoted the special role of full-time volunteers and independent volunteer organizations in addressing the needs of the world's communities.

CVSA itself is an all-volunteer organization and urgently needs volunteers—full-time or part-time—to advance the crucially important work of the independent, voluntary service movement, and help expand our outreach, educational and advisory work, as well as the year-round work of producing and distributing *INVEST YOURSELF.*

INVEST YOURSELF has gained international renown in over 65 years of publication as the most comprehensive catalogue of full- and part-time volunteer opportunities through non-government organizations. Organizations and programs are listed in *INVEST YOURSELF* completely free of charge.

CVSA does not place volunteers with voluntary service projects, but publicizes the availability of these programs through *INVEST YOURSELF,* such that individuals looking for volunteer placement can make their own inquiries directly to the organizations of interest to them.

CVSA is an entirely voluntary effort, has no paid staff, and accepts no government funds. CVSA is governed by an Executive Committee, and benefits from the input and involvement of the members of its Advisory

Board which is comprised of individuals with a proven track record of leadership in the voluntary service field. Together, these bodies are committed to the expansion and growth of CVSA's activities, and the entire field of non-government voluntary service. CVSA is a not-for-profit corporation with federal tax-exempt status and your financial contributions, as well as your volunteer time, make it possible for us to grow.

How to Become a Member of CVSA

Membership in CVSA is available to volunteer organizations and agencies serving people in need, and to individuals with involvement or interest in the field of voluntary service. Member organizations can be listed in *INVEST YOURSELF,* receive a complimentary copy of each edition of the catalogue and can arrange for reduced rates for multiple or bulk orders. CVSA members also receive the membership newsletter, *ITEMS,* which includes recent developments, achievements and needs within the voluntary service sector, as well as related developments—on the local, national and international level—in government, education and business that affect voluntary service organizations and their missions. Submissions from CVSA members of information, news, advice, experience, needs and concerns to be shared are welcome.

Just as an organization is stronger than any one individual, the collective experience of many organizations with common interests is also more powerful than that of a single individual or a single organization. The problems which volunteer service organizations seek to overcome are larger than any one of those organizations, and meaningful discussions on such subjects with other organizations on a cooperative basis towards the advancement of their ability to meet those needs and solve those problems are extremely important. CVSA works to provide arenas and forums for such discussions. Members can participate in and help organize consultations, seminars and workshops on topics of interest and import to them and other voluntary service organizations through CVSA.

CVSA members are asked to contribute dues of $25 a year. Payment is voluntary and CVSA neither penalizes poorer organizations nor rewards those with greater resources. The level of participation by members in the activities of CVSA varies in relation to the demands and pressures of their own work. CVSA strives to enhance the ability of its membership organizations to carry out their missions, primarily through aiding in the mobilization of volunteers to be involved in their work.

CVSA's History and Purpose

CVSA was founded in 1945 as a coordinating council organizing American volunteers to spend their summers helping citizens of war-torn Europe rebuild their devastated communities. CVSA subsequently grew in scope beyond this initial catalyst to incorporate more organizations serving people who suffer from conditions of poverty, discrimination, disease and distress all over the world, including within the United States. These groupings have frequently been on the cutting edge of progressive change, demonstrating the ability of independent non-government volunteer action to promote lifesaving and life-giving programs and solutions at a grass-roots level.

When CVSA was founded in 1945, the embattled peoples of Europe, ravaged by the armies of the world, were weary. Millions of war victims were starving, diseased and homeless, and had nowhere to turn. A groundswell of volunteer activism developed among members of ecumenical groups, churches and service organizations throughout North America to provide aid to those who needed it most without bureaucratic or political conditions attached. Their interest was to develop international fellowship and reconciliation among the people of these nations, through physically working together to solve common problems.

Many of those service organizations and individuals were horrified with the announced policy of the U.S. government toward reconstruction in Europe. The Marshall Plan would exclude aid to all but a handful of countries, and would condition aid on political, rather than humanitarian criteria. Under the Marshall Plan, citizens of European nations would be required to permit the U.S. government to choose their leaders and direct their foreign and domestic policies as precondition to receiving American government humanitarian aid funds. The Marshall Plan set both trade and political controls over recipient nations and demanded permission for the U.S. to set up military bases and station missiles inside their borders.

One of the founding members of CVSA, the Reverend Ed Schlingman of the United Church of Christ, firmly put forth a principle that has served CVSA since its inception. Schlingman said that religious and ecumenical bodies could exemplify government policies as they should be enacted, rather than blindly follow the promulgations of government. CVSA has been a consistent voice for independence in volunteerism. CVSA maintains that without the freedom and flexibility to develop their own strategies for change, volunteer organizations are reduced to mere extensions of the very same failed government policies from which the need for their volunteer assistance arose.

Progressive church leaders formed CVSA as a council to coordinate and promote opportunities for individuals to volunteer their summers living and working with communities in need in Europe and throughout the world. Under the title of *Invest Your Summer*, CVSA put together a listing of volunteer work camps and service programs being run throughout Europe and the world. These included programs to assist communities in building water and sewer systems, laying bricks for shelters and health centers, distributing food and performing community service of all forms.

In 1965 the catalogue was given a new title and *INVEST YOURSELF* was born. It had expanded to include volunteer needs and opportunities in North America year round, as well as the volunteer camps in Europe and across the world. It became the most comprehensive listing available of full-time volunteer opportunities, short-term and long-term with non-government organizations. *INVEST YOURSELF* serves as CVSA's primary tool for the promotion of volunteer service. This catalogue provides the link between organizations in need of volunteers and those persons seeking meaningful, community-based involvement.

INVEST YOURSELF began to be used not only by church groups, but also high schools, colleges, libraries and civic organizations, to find volunteer service opportunities through non-government organizations offering full-time service placements on both a short-term and long-term basis.

The conditions of intense unmet human need and suffering that prompted the outpouring of volunteer commitment at the end of WWII were also to be found in other parts of the world, including in the U.S. The geographic focus of CVSA's activities changed, moving on to areas of intense poverty in the developing nations and the poorest areas of the United States.

With the explosion of civil unrest and protest in the U.S. against the war in Vietnam and for the civil rights of all citizens, there were many people who opposed what they understood to be imperialist policies of the U.S. government, and wanted to do something positive for the millions suffering under the effects of those policies. They wanted to end the poverty and racism that plagues this nation, other nations, and the relations between nations. Many began to see Americans in voluntary service abroad as a way to end the poverty and famine there. Many began to hope—as the original founders of CVSA did in 1945—that individuals could do what institutions could not, or would not. A growing number of volunteer organizations focusing on domestic problems of illiteracy, hunger, lack of medical care and housing, joined CVSA and began to list in *INVEST YOURSELF.*

Many of them were attempting to address the root causes of the growing needs and promulgating ideas critical of U.S. government policy.

At the same time, thousands of volunteers who had taken part in voluntary service programs in third-world nations had come back frustrated; problems there were getting worse, not better, and the activities of volunteers were not equal to the tasks and goals they set for themselves in the face of a new kind of economic exploitation far more sophisticated in kind and extent than that which existed before the Second World War. The negative ramifications of World Bank and International Monetary Fund (IMF) policies and programs, born out of the 1944 Bretton Woods International Monetary and Financial Conference, were becoming evident in the poor communities of these countries.

Church agencies and voluntary service programs began to deal more directly with the demands of those in need and suffering the effects of poverty and racism in the U.S., including those who were coming to the United States as refugees from the economic and political conflict taking place in Latin America. More and more, those involved in volunteer service began to look at how to effect solutions as well as deal with the rising tide of need—both in the United States and abroad, with an understanding of the global nature of the problems.

INVEST YOURSELF grew with the times. As those involved in volunteer service had begun to understand that poverty is not a precondition of fate but a man-made phenomenon, and that the ability already exists to feed every person on the planet, the role and interrelationship of global corporate and government policies to human deprivation became a looming concern.

In the early 1980's, former President Ronald Reagan slashed the budgets of social service and "safety net" benefits for the poor, elderly and disabled. At the same time he called for a "New Voluntarism," claiming that if every local church congregation took care of one welfare family, he could abolish welfare. His administration proceeded to attack grassroots volunteer organizations looking for real solutions to the massive hunger and poverty that he so easily brushed aside. Every subsequent U.S. Presidential administration has announced "new" efforts to utilize volunteers to fill gaps of unmet needs created by government policies and priorities, while cutting more budgets for basic services. The wages of U.S. workers fell drastically during that period of time, and have continued to fall ever since. While millions of U.S. workers do not earn enough to live above poverty levels, the federal government has established international policies such as NAFTA, encouraging U.S. factories to close, eliminating jobs which then go to cheap foreign labor. "Welfare reform" has eliminated many of the economic and social "safety net" programs for children, elderly, disabled, immigrants and the marginally employed.

Many official voices of church and social agency leaders at that time became advocates for partnerships with these federal programs and their alleged economic benefits. Churches that had run their own food closets for the poor according to their own criteria, for example, were now organized by government officials to instead refer all those requesting help to a government agency for approval and "screening." This usually meant turning away all those found to have gotten emergency food somewhere else any time within the prior one to three months.

CVSA took a stand against collusion between church-sponsored programs of aid and government agencies that deny the voice of those in need. CVSA subsequently became independent of official national church bodies, and more strongly anchored in the grassroots level of the voluntary service field. In the early years of the 21st century, programs such as the federal "Faith-Based Initiative" involving government funding and supervision of church and other charitable community efforts have been proposed and enacted by both major political parties.

For those who have found comfort in a government seal of approval, we in CVSA have found wisdom in the words of Benjamin Franklin, who said that, "They that can give up essential liberty to obtain a little temporary safety, deserve neither liberty nor safety."

CVSA and the United Nations

In the same year CVSA was formed, the United Nations was also established. The founders of the United Nations understood the importance of non-government citizens' groupings participating in the process of national and international policy-setting on behalf of the peoples of the world. The UN allocated a place for them within the UN system as Non-Government Organizations (NGOs). CVSA gained United Nations recognition in 1946 to participate as an NGO through the Department of Public Information. The UN's NGO section designates NGO's to allow an international forum for organizations representing groups holding positions independent of the policies of their governments, or representing peoples without a country.

CVSA works in accordance with the NGO responsibilities to support and uphold the three basic tenets of the United Nations Charter: a) to work to maintain international peace and security; b) to develop friendly relations among nations based on the principle of equal rights and self-determination of peoples; and c) to achieve international cooperation in solving international problems of an economic, social, cultural or humanitarian character, and in promoting respect for human rights and for fundamental freedoms for all without distinction as to race, sex, language or religion.

A significant example of CVSA's efforts to put UN principles into action as a non-government organization was in 1979 when CVSA sponsored an organizational member to present a document of appeal citing subhuman living and working conditions for native Puerto Rican farm workers within the U.S. to the UN's Special Committee on De-colonization. The UN Committee was holding hearings on the colonial nature of Puerto Rico's territorial relations with the U.S. CVSA was instrumental in exposing the conditions faced by 1,500 native Puerto Rican farm workers brought to the U.S. via New York State Department of Labor contracts with the Commonwealth of Puerto Rico. The document cited breaches of the Helsinki Accord on Human Rights and the UN colonial policy. Many of the workers lived in such horrendous poverty, overcrowding and lack of sanitation on farm labor camps that they contracted tuberculosis. Hundreds of volunteers from a local independent organization had worked with the farm workers in gaining access to treatment of the disease and changes in their living and working conditions.

Call to Action

CVSA promotes genuine, independent voluntary service to those in need, with no profit made in the process by any individual, and no strings attached in exchange for the service given. CVSA rejects schemes that exploit volunteers through programs in which "volunteers" are employed by the government as free or cheap labor, replacing former union-wage workers; in which "volunteers" are supplied by public agencies as subsidized labor to private corporations (under the designation "trainee"), to the companies' profit and the "trainees" expense; and in which student "volunteers" work off their loans at minimum-wage jobs which perpetuate conditions of poverty. These have proven to be thinly veiled means of union busting and obtaining free or cheap labor for the benefit of a minority and at the expense of a healthy economy in which we all can work and earn a decent living and build vibrant communities.

The results of government-inspired and funded programs for the poor and disadvantaged in the U.S. or internationally have been less than encouraging, while the results of well-planned volunteer programs rooted in and run by people in the community being served are documentable. On the national level, the billions of dollars spent by the government on its "War on Poverty" now seems to have had the results of a war against the poor. On the international level, hundreds of billions of dollars going to the International Monetary Fund to prop up the international capital markets have not benefited those in need. The predominant international fiscal policies have generated in their wake higher levels of worldwide unemployment, inflation and depressed wages, causing even more suffering and need, not less, as seen again in the most recent financial system collapse. In the U.S., less and less money is made available for education, health care or even food programs for the 13.5 million hungry children, while trillions are given to unscrupulous financiers.

The organizations in *INVEST YOURSELF* desire to share their knowledge, experience and resourcefulness, such that this reserve of aid and assistance can be made available to others seeking to alleviate forever the miserable conditions faced by the downtrodden of our world. Their objectives encompass a wide spectrum of goals, perspectives, endeavors and struggles from a rich history of challenges and achievements. They represent material manifestations of hope for the future for all of us.

CVSA's uninterrupted service of compiling, expanding, promoting and circulating *INVEST YOURSELF* makes it possible for thousands of volunteers to make a difference in the lives of hundreds of thousands, to change the future of whole communities, influence the development of solutions to every major problem facing communities and nations today—health care delivery, hunger, education, methods for economic betterment—every aspect of human and social concern, endeavor and need.

Communities across the nation, and peoples and nations throughout the world, are demanding change and real solutions to the problems of poverty, health care, education, employment, crime, literacy, housing, the poisoning of the environment and more. CVSA needs you to help meet this challenge and provide leadership to change these conditions through the mobilization of volunteers in those communities to eradicate the poverty and injustice that are destroying them.

Volunteering itself is a fundamental rejection of the notion that things are too big and powerful to change. It is a self-aware determination that action can and must be applied to advance and achieve progress.

Please join us!

CVSA needs full-time and part-time volunteers.
See page 68 for more information about
volunteering with CVSA.

HOW to LIST YOUR ORGANIZATION in the next

The Catalogue of Volunteer Opportunities

Listing Copy Form

For organizations interested in being listed in INVEST YOURSELF, please fill out this form, enclose copies of your newsletter or other literature, and send to CVSA/INVEST YOURSELF, One Union Square West, Suite 902, New York, NY 10003.

If you are already listed in IY, please review the information as it was last printed, and update, correct or improve it for the next issue.

Please make copies of the form for others you know who may also want to be listed. Call CVSA for deadlines: (646) 486-2446 or (877) 867-6150.

Organization's Name _____

Address_____

_____

Phone_____Fax _____

E-mail_____Website_____

Contact person/title_____

Your name/position_____ Date _____

PLEASE TYPE THE FOLLOWING ON A SEPARATE SHEET AND ATTACH:

Geographic Area: List areas (cities, states, regions, countries) where volunteers work.

General Information: Describe the work of your organization, the needs it addresses, whom you reach and serve and the role of part-time and/or full-time volunteers, in 225 to 450 words. Indicate any specific time periods for service, application deadlines, or age limits.

Skills: Specify any required and/or desired skills or experience.

❑ I have enclosed a brochure, newsletter and/or other literature about our organization.
❑ Photos and caption information are enclosed.

HOW TO ORDER MORE COPIES OF

ⓧ Invest ⓧ Yourself

The Catalogue of Volunteer Opportunities

The perfect gift idea for high school and college students, graduates, retirees, or for your school, community library, church, club and others looking to invest themselves. Vocation counselors' offices and resource libraries should have multiple copies on hand. To place your order, send this order form to CVSA at One Union Square West, Suite 902, New York, NY 10003, or call us at (646) 486-2446 or (877) 867-6150.

INVEST YOURSELF $10.00

Postage & Handling (for single order) $ 2.50

(for priority mail) $ 4.95

(from overseas) $10.00

Bulk: 10-19 @$8.00

20-49 @$7.50

50-100 @$7.00

101 and up @$6.50

Plus cost of shipping (via most cost efficient means)

Items newsletter subscription (see p. 38) $15.00

Please make checks payable to CVSA and mail your order to:

CVSA, 1 Union Square West, Suite 902, New York, NY 10003

Enclosed $ _____for_____

(Outside U.S. please use U.S. Money Order)

Name _____

Address _____

City/State _____

Country _____ Zip_____

Organization/Occupation _____

Phone _____

HELP DISTRIBUTE

⚇ Invest ⚇
Yourself

The Catalogue of Volunteer Opportunities

and get more people involved

☐ I can sponsor an INVEST YOURSELF table at my school, community center, conference or convention site, place of worship, place of business, or other locations or gatherings of people who would be interested in learning about volunteer opportunities.

☐ I would like information about having a CVSA speaker come to my classroom, club, study group, congregation, community center, professional association or other gathering to hear more about the need for volunteers and the non-government voluntary service and action movement.

☐ I can print a promotional display about the INVEST YOURSELF catalogue in my organization's publication_____.

☐ I can print a review or article about INVEST YOURSELF and voluntary service in_____.

☐ I can include IY brochures in a bulk mailing to #_____ members of my organization, congregation or other mailing list.

☐ I can display _____ color posters about INVEST YOURSELF in my office, school, campus, place of worship or local library.

☐ I would like to be an IY representative and distribute INVEST YOURSELF in my community. Call me today!

Please Send # _____ Free Brochures

Name _____

Address _____

City/State _____

Country _____ Zip_____

Organization/Occupation _____

Phone _____

A Legacy of Service

The Heller Service Corps, one of Furman's largest student groups, demonstrates the university's vigorous commitment to engaging students and serving the community.

Each year, Heller Service Corps places more than 1800 students in community agencies to serve the disabled, work with children, address community concerns, and participate in the medical field.

For more information on the Heller Service Corps or other service opportunities at Furman, visit <www.hellerservicecorps.org> or call 864.294.2000.

 FURMAN

3300 Poinsett Hwy.
Greenville, S.C. 29613
www.furman.edu

CVSA and Volunteer Service Today: Seize This Time to Change the Course of History

Whether volunteering in service to others becomes your life's vocation or simply an important avocation in your life, *INVEST YOURSELF* will help you gain perspective on the scope of the needs and on the many possibilities of organizational hosts for your volunteer involvement and commitment.

The endeavors into which each of us invests our volunteer time are of no small significance in the bigger picture of what future we are forging for mankind.

Over the last several years, as we were compiling this edition of *INVEST YOURSELF,* other CVSA volunteers and I have talked with hundreds of community and volunteer leaders. When the biggest economic meltdown in history hit their communities—and their organizations' budgets—it was like a massive avalanche had descended on them which very few had heard coming. In some areas, unemployment rose from 7% to 18% within 14 months. In that same time, homelessness in many areas jumped by more than 10%. Staff from organizations listed in IY have reported that they have found families living in their cars on the edge of town, or in tents on public campgrounds. Under the current economic conditions, the needs have quickly become greater than ever, while the resources to address these needs have become harder to assemble. This is in large part because the constituencies who have traditionally made up the base of support for the organizations represented in IY—individual donors, local churches and organizations, small businesses—are themselves facing foreclosure, debt, loss of income or donations due to job losses among their own memberships, loss of consumer spending in local economies as workers lose income. These historic support bases now find themselves in need of relief as the economic disaster spreads.

In a single weekend, governments of the wealthiest nations of the world diverted more money to bail out their leading financial institutions than they have invested in the last decade to the ending of hunger, illiteracy and disease in the world. Most community leaders we talked with shared CVSA's view that simply standing by was not an option. Most agreed that simply hoping for change in the decision-making priorities that place greater significance on saving wealthy banks that were "too big to allow to fail" than on the survival needs of the people, was an unsound approach to solving our local, national or global problems. We can look at the history of social movements and progressive change and know that nothing changes for the better until people organize and impel those changes out of necessity. But what do we do with that understanding? We need caring people to step forward with a goal-oriented, professional approach to the work of volunteer service and action, to organize and provide the urgently needed leadership for bringing together those suffering the most under the current set of priorities, to take a real role in changing them.

For decades, CVSA has been describing volunteer service as a process of taking responsibility for the wellbeing of our brothers and sisters, taking responsibility to right the wrongs being done to others, taking responsibility to end injustices and to correct policies that are harmful to people and to the earth which allows us to be alive. These days, volunteer service is also about rebuilding our communities, our country and our world which is suffering greatly under one man-made crisis after another: food, water, energy, climate change, financial collapse. Taking responsibility starts with questioning why certain conditions and problems exist in the first place. The best way to then find the answers is to get materially involved in working for the solutions along with the people whose lives depend on those problems being solved.

The strength of each of our organizations will grow as we share with each other our experience and knowledge of how to do that work successfully. How will we build a society in which health and nutrition for those denied it, sound and affordable housing for those without it, employment at wages people can live on, care for our elderly, safety and education for our children and youth, the end of hunger, the end of exploitation and a reverse in the practices that are destroying the planet —all become the country's and the world's actual priorities?

At the time of the publication of the previous edition of *INVEST YOURSELF,* the 60th Anniversary Edition, non-government organizations and the member nations of the UN General Assembly had just assessed the progress and lack thereof made during the first 5 years of pursuit of the Millennium Development Goals (MDGs). The MDGs, agreed to at the beginning of the 21st Century in September 2000 by all the member nations of the UN, established the goal of eradication of extreme poverty and hunger in the world by the year 2015. They declared this an international priority, with the underlying analysis that the world can never have peace and an end to war until these material conditions of deprivation are ended; they acknowledged that the resources and abilities to make these systemic changes existed—only the political will to do so was missing.

Now, in 2010 we are well past the half way point to that date with destiny.

Yet much of the progress made by many developing nations in the last decade has now been lost in 2009 alone. In September 2009, the UN issued a report titled *Voices of the Vulnerable: the Economic Crisis from the Ground Up* which describes how, just in the past year, there has been an increase of 100 million people suffering from hunger while infant mortality may increase by an additional 200,000 to 400,000 each year from now to 2015 if the current economic crisis continues as it is. The UN Secretary General, Ban Ki-moon, said about the situation, "The global economic crisis is not 'over' as some have begun to predict, but rather it

has just started for hundreds of millions of people around the globe." He admonished that, "The near poor are in danger of becoming the new poor, as the clock is running out on the coping strategies of the vulnerable and poor. Many options, such as dipping into savings and selling assets, have been exhausted by previous crisis or were non-existent in the first place."

According to the UN Special Rapporteur for the Right to Food, Olivier De Shutter, "The right to food is not the right to be fed after an emergency. It is the right to access the means to produce food or the means to an income that enables the purchase of adequate food."

Hunger is a growing specter in the U.S. as well as in the developing nations. Official unemployment rates in the U.S. have reached 15 percent in several rural localities—parts of Washington State, California and Michigan, for example—and, in a handful, have exceeded the 20 percent mark. According to the Bureau of Labor Statistics, the jobless rate for men rose to 10 percent in June 2009, the second highest on record since World War II. When you combine the number of people who are officially counted as jobless with those who are working part-time because they can't find full-time work and those who have stopped looking for work but would take a job if one became available—we have 30 million Americans, or 19 percent of the work force, unemployed.

As you read these pages, the process of an astounding amount of capital being concentrated in the hands of a few major banking conglomerates continues, while a massive concentration of housing and land assets are moving into the hands of a few financial institutions—at the same time millions of homes are being foreclosed on. The crisis is in no way over, and people need answers and help now. The resources to solve these problems clearly exist. They are simply not in the hands of those who need them and who, therefore, are in the best position to determine how they should be used.

Where does CVSA come into this? With your participation and support, CVSA can help strengthen the volunteer organizations that are on the front lines of the growing poverty in communities worldwide, serving those in need, bringing people together and not allowing anyone to be left isolated, misinformed or desperate. CVSA's role is to get more volunteers involved through the distribution of this catalogue, through speaking engagements and by providing independent, non-government organizations who join us with information, training and consultation on tactics, strategies and processes for growth. We can act on the knowledge that using trial and error as a method of work is a waste of time and human energy; we know collective experience is more powerful than that of any single individual or any single organization. We need more volunteers to join us in building mechanisms for aiding each other organizationally, sharing our knowledge and experience in this work.

Calling on the leaders of all the 192 nations that make up the body of the United Nations to take their responsibility in building a new, viable and sustainable international economic order seriously and with vigor, Miguel D'Escoto Brockman of Nicaragua, the President of the 63rd UN General Assembly said, "The main focus of this new step will be life in all its forms, humanity with all its peoples and ethnic groups, the Earth as a mother with all its vitality and an economy that creates the material

conditions for making all this possible. We will need the material capital we have built up, but the focus will be on human and spiritual capital, whose most wholesome fruits are fraternity or brotherhood, cooperation, solidarity, love, economic and ecological justice, compassion and the capacity to coexist happily with all our differences, in the same shared home, the great and generous Mother Earth."

The people involved with the organizations you will find in *INVEST YOURSELF* represent the human capital D'Escoto speaks of as the most important component in building that better future. You will find examples of leadership through action; examples of ordinary people accomplishing extraordinary things through working together. You will find material manifestations of hope that there are better ways to produce and distribute our food in order to end hunger, care for the earth so that it cares for us and tend to the basic human needs of all the world's people.

For all these reasons, we heartily welcome you to the pages of *INVEST YOURSELF.* We urge you to join our ranks with whatever time, skill, experience and desire to learn and to serve that you can bring.

I will end with this warning: Investing yourself may change you, your world view and your future. We are counting on you to take that step to be part of changing the future for all of us through volunteering your time, energy, skills and desire for a better world.

Please contact CVSA anytime with questions, offerings of assistance, feedback and reports on your volunteer experiences that we can share to benefit others.

Susan G. Angus
Executive Director
Commission on Voluntary Service & Action

A nationally recognized, residential liberal arts college—one of the few located in a major city—118-year-old **Occidental College** is at the forefront of interdisciplinary, intercultural education that integrates the classroom with community-based learning. Our small size and strong sense of community, rigorous curriculum, superb faculty, diverse student body, and access to the resources of **Los Angeles** make Occidental the best of both worlds: intimate in scale, but infinite in scope. Contact us for more information by phone (800-825-5262), e-mail (admission@oxy.edu), or online (**www.oxy.edu**).

Part 2

HOW VOLUNTEERS CHANGE OUR WORLD

The articles that follow are a few of those we have received from volunteers speaking about their own experience with endeavors of organizations listed in *INVEST YOURSELF.* These stories are presented as examples of the wide range of volunteer work available to those seeking involvement, not an editorial position on the part of CVSA as to the relative merits of any voluntary service program over another.

How Best to Invest Yourself

by Melissa Crane Draper

What qualities are necessary to be an effective volunteer?

Although my volunteer experience is primarily international, the advice I can offer is quite basic and useful to keep in mind wherever you are—whether volunteering down the street or a hemisphere away. These guiding principles have navigated me through some tricky—and equally rewarding—situations, from my native Santa Fe, New Mexico to the town of Mhaswad in western India, and the rural villages of the Tapacarí province in central Bolivia.

Three characteristics should guide you as you enter a new volunteer position. These principles are regular traits to some, and for others it may take a little digging. That's the beautiful flip side of the volunteer coin—not only are you contributing to a cause you believe in, but you can also learn a great deal about yourself in the process. First, and this one rings as clearly as a freshly-hit gong in an ashram: *be humble.* No matter how many skills or experiences you think you are bringing to your host organization, remind yourself that you are new to that space and that the local context (the political, social or cultural nuances unique to that place) are going to be different from your own. In some instances, you may have far more formal education than some of the people you are working with. Keep in mind that formal education has its limits, especially in foreign and/or rural settings where local knowledge far outweighs any economic formula or business model. When you *invest* yourself remember that it may require that you *divest* yourself first. That may mean letting go of an attachment to the way you think things should work. Once you can do that, you are ready to fully engage in your new environment.

Second, *be curious.* Chances are, if you've opened this book you have some level of curiosity as well as a willingness to give to others—two key pillars of volunteerism. The key is to remain curious—about the local situation you are working in, about the people you interact with, and about how you can best merge your skills and experience with your host organization. Even when you think you know the ropes, keep that curiosity refreshed so you can keep learning and innovating with whatever tasks or work you may have.

Third, *be willing to listen.* This characteristic is closely linked to both humility and curiosity. The action of listening is an expression of humility. It is also a vehicle for curiosity. And it is the means by which you can learn about the complexities of that sometimes perplexing local context that defines the how-when-where and with-whom of your volunteer work.

I can still remember the hours I sat on the floor in a corner of a packed room every Sunday in a small town in Bolivia. I listened and watched as a meeting of the local household worker's union would unfold. I took in the way they spoke, how they addressed one another, how they brought up problems and dealt with differences. The local politics were charged, and

People helping people
is not just a slogan,
it is a way of life.
Congratulations to CVSA.

Paul O'Brien

In support of all the
volunteers who dare to care
and do the needed work to
build change.

Martha Davis

"Never doubt that a small group
of thoughtful, committed citizens
can change the world; indeed, it is
the only thing that ever has."
—Margaret Mead

In honor of Björn S. Grund

*Lotus
Garden
Club*

being a foreigner amidst a gathering of Quechua and Aymara women was new for me. It was only after being a good observer and listener for several weeks that I felt I could become a participant.

So how do these qualities translate into action? We can think about it in two phases—the "before you go" and the "once you are there."

Before you go, make sure you've done your homework. This is a part of the curiosity piece that is key to prepping you for your new environment. This might be informal research, like having a conversation with someone connected to the organization (or a previous volunteer or intern) or it may be more formal, like taking a particular class—perhaps in a language, some topic related to your work, or even consult with CVSA about some on-the-job training in basic organizing skills you can gain in advance.

If you're going abroad, it's always good to be familiar with local history and geography. You can read up in your history book or on-line. Reading the local papers on-line gives a good sense of current events and pressing issues that may soon become a part of your volunteer reality. Especially for those volunteering in politically-charged environments, familiarize yourself with perspectives from all points in the spectrum by reading or talking to people who know about the issues. Novels based in your country of destination can sometimes be quite revealing, giving you a window into your new world about the life, culture and history of the place.

Once you're familiar with the larger context of your new setting, make sure you also have a sense of what your volunteer work will entail. This is all about expectations—yours and your host organization's. Do they know how long you're coming for? Have you committed to doing certain tasks or is it a come-and-we'll-see type of situation? Are you working with a specific task or team of people and are you expected to produce a final product? Do they know your skills (or limitations) with the local language? If possible, spell these out before you arrive, or at least soon upon your arrival. If expectations are off on either side (too high or too low) it can make for a difficult reckoning once you actually get to work.

Then when you actually are on-site, keep up the communication. Identify who supervises your work, whether formally or informally. Set up time to check in with that person periodically to ask for feedback and to offer feedback on what you're seeing or doing. That will open a healthy channel of commuication through which you can deal with adjustments to expectations, or even challenges that may come up down the line.

In the village of Mhaswad in the drought-prone region of western India, my first challenge was the language. I felt like I had fallen out of the sky into my volunteer position with this local microfinance group in rural

Maharashtra. Unlike my experience in Bolivia, where I had a chance to buckle down and spend three months learning Spanish intensively, I had just three months to work at this site in India—and not a single word of Marathi or Hindi to share with the women's group. Communication was difficult since I could only really speak with the head supervisor of the project. My relief—and a friend—came in the form of a young Indian student who had just started working for the organization. She was eager to practice her English and I was thirsting for a chance to communicate with the incredible women that surrounded me. She opened up that world to me, and I offered back impromptu English lessons and a friendship.

With this set of tools, you're ready to go. Watch, listen and be ready to share with and learn from your fellow volunteers and colleagues. Open yourself to the experience and celebrate your decision to be a committed volunteer.

Melissa Crane Draper has made volunteering a central part of her experience abroad over the past ten years. She is co-editor and an author of Dignity and Defiance: Stories from Bolivia's Challenge to Globalization *(University of California, 2009).*

PITZER COLLEGE
A MEMBER OF THE CLAREMONT COLLEGES

Pitzer College, a member of The Claremont Colleges, is a nationally recognized residential liberal arts and sciences college. Our emphasis on interdisciplinary learning, intercultural understanding and social responsibility distinguishes us from most other colleges in the country. Interdisciplinary learning encourages you to explore how different academic fields intersect and draw on each other's wisdom and ideas; intercultural understanding enables you to see issues and events from cultural perspectives different from your own; and social responsibility shows you how to transform knowledge into action as you strive to make the world a better place to live for yourself and future generations.

If you would like to learn more about Pitzer, please call us at 1-800-PITZER1, visit our web site at www.pitzer.edu, or email us at admission@pitzer.edu.

Mentoring at Hour Children: Love Makes the Difference

by Denise H. Sutton

In my early forties, I found myself wanting a child. For various reasons, it didn't look as if that was going to happen. In an attempt to find an outlet for my desire to nurture a child, I turned to mentoring. I chose Hour Children because of Sister Teresa "Tesa" Fitzgerald's (founder and executive director) reputation. And, to be honest, even though I'm not Catholic—or even particularly religious—I wanted to work for a nun because of a previous experience. I had taught at a Catholic women's college in New York and the director of my program was a nun. What I admired about her was her complete and utter devotion to the program's mission; her selfless commitment inspired me and I wanted to work with other women who embodied the ideal of service. Sister Tesa is dedicated to helping incarcerated women and their children—a population I knew practically nothing about. What I learned in my mentoring interview and orientation was revealing and painful. I had to address my own preconceived notions of who incarcerated women are and what leads them to prison. And it was difficult to think about what their children endure, through no fault of their own.

Hour Children, a non-profit agency in Long Island City, New York, almost directly across the East River from the United Nations, provides prison-based services to incarcerated women as well as community-based services once women are released and are transitioning back into society. Some of these services include mentoring for their children while they are in prison, educational services, counseling, day care while newly released mothers are working or attending classes, housing for the entire family and job readiness training.

Surprisingly, these services are not available to formerly incarcerated women by federal, state or local government agencies. In fact, some government regulations actually work against the availability of basic necessities. If a woman has a criminal record, for instance, she is not eligible for public housing. The Vera Institute of Justice reports that only 12.5 percent of employers would be willing to interview someone with a history of incarceration, making employment opportunities rare. Many women are left with no choice but to go back to the destructive environment that contributed to their criminal activity in the first place.

The ten year old girl I mentor is fortunate to live with her older sister and grandmother. She does well academically and was recently accepted into a talented and gifted school, quite an accomplishment considering the upheavals in her relatively short life. My mentee's grandmother, however, is loving and strict; she sets expectations and boundaries for her granddaughters. Children in foster care may not have such devoted caregivers and I shudder to think what it must be like for those children. But even children who do end up with relatives when their mother is incarcerated are at risk emotionally and psychologically.

Incarcerated mothers face different challenges than incarcerated fathers. The vast majority of fathers who go to prison are able to leave their children in the care of the children's mother. Only 37 percent of children whose mothers go to prison are taken in by the father, so most incarcerated women must leave their children with other family members or in foster care (The Sentencing Project Report). When a mother goes to prison, her children enter a parallel prison.

In a country that locks up more people than any other industrialized nation (according to a study by the nonpartisan Pew Center on the States), the well-being of children of incarcerated women has become an issue too often overlooked by the criminal justice system. In addition,

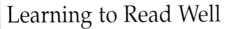

services that help former prisoners adjust to life outside prison walls are practically nonexistent.

For most women, serving a prison sentence is only the start of a long uphill battle to becoming a productive member of society. Once released, formerly incarcerated women face a mountain of challenges beyond their criminal record and the associated social stigma. These women, for instance, generally have weak job skills, little education and few, if any, financial resources. An estimated 50 percent of incarcerated women have been victims of domestic violence, and many of these women are still recovering from childhood physical and sexual abuse (Hour Children website). And, of course, if she is a mother, she has yet another challenge: reuniting her family.

Fifty-one percent of the women that Hour Children serves are first-time offenders; 75% are incarcerated for non-violent, drug-related offenses (Hour Children website). The mentoring coordinator I worked with is a Hour Children resident. As she interviewed me, she told me about her own experiences in the criminal justice system and what led her there. My notion of an ex-offender and this woman sitting across from me didn't quite mesh because what I saw was an intelligent, hard-working, dedicated and loving mother. The only difference between this woman and other women who may be dealing with a drug addiction is simply a matter of resources: a person with resources could hire a good attorney with connections, perhaps evading prison time. Furthermore, a person with resources could go off for a few months to an expensive drug rehab center (hence preventing the spiraling down to more dangerous drugs or other criminal activity).

In 2007 there were 1.7 million children in America with a parent in prison, more than 70% of whom were children of color (The Sentencing Project Report). More than 11,000 children in New York State have a mother in prison (Hour Children website). These children live in a prison

of their own where uncertainty, fear, trauma, and confusion reign. Many are sent to live with relatives or foster families, and are shunted from household to household and school to school, often living in at least two residences. The absence of their mother leaves them vulnerable to an increased risk of involvement with crime, substance abuse, truancy and other anti-social behaviors. Without proper care and attention, they become victims of the prison system—for the second time.

My mentee and I meet for at least four hours a month and our commitment is to continue meeting for a year. Often this commitment lasts longer at Hour Children because of the bond that develops between mentor and mentee. Two of the most important aspects of my mentoring experience have been the attention paid to the match and the incredible amount of support that I receive from the mentoring coordinators. I now work as a writer and was formerly a college professor. I spent many years (more than I care to remember!) going to college to prepare to teach, research and write. I love reading and going to the movies, though I'm not particularly athletic. The mentoring coordinators paid attention to those details. They matched me with a girl who is academically gifted and who has dreams of going to college.

One of our first activities was going to see the Hannah Montana movie. In the movie, one of the songs Hannah Montana sings is called "The Climb," which is about the beauty of the process of achievement, the climbing of the mountain, the testing of one's inner strength and determination. And as she started to sing this, my mentee turned to me and said "that's my favorite song!" As I sat there listening to the song's message, I got goose bumps and struggled to hold back tears. Despite all the personal challenges this little girl faces because of her family situation, she still has dreams and she wants to work hard to achieve her goals. She also knows that once she achieves one goal, there will always be another "mountain to climb." I thought that for a ten year old, that was pretty amazing. Where is the mercy in the U.S. court system for little girls and boys like this?

Denise H. Sutton, Ph.D., is a writer who lives in Brooklyn, New York. Her book *Globalizing Ideal Beauty: How the Female Copywriters at the J. Walter Thompson Advertising Agency Redefined Beauty for the Twentieth Century* (Palgrave Macmillan) was published in 2009.

Mindful of the Bigger Picture
While Doing the Day-to-Day Work

by Maggie Page

I am an idealist, but even I knew when I decided to spend a year volunteering as a full-time advocacy counselor with Project PLASE (People
Lacking Ample Shelter and Employment) that I wouldn't be able to end
homelessness or drug addiction in Baltimore in that year. I knew that I
would not single-handedly eradicate urban poverty or relieve people of
addiction. But I did think that I would be doing important, meaningful
work; the term "advocacy counselor" gave me visions of myself in court
and at social service agencies, standing up for justice and demanding
adequate services for my homeless clients, all while inspiring hope and
confidence for them to stand up for themselves.

It didn't take long for me to learn that this is not exactly what an advocacy counselor does. It isn't that the work is not important or meaningful, because it is both of those things. Make no mistake, though, it is not
glamorous and I rarely, if ever, feel very heroic. Project PLASE is a nonprofit agency serving homeless adults in Baltimore, Maryland. There are
several facilities operated by the organization, and I was assigned to work
in a co-ed transitional housing facility with space for 14 adults for my
year of service, which I am doing through the Mennonite Voluntary
Service. Project PLASE provides food, housing, case management,
addiction recovery services and life skills training, among other things.
We also work to connect our clients with outside agencies and services
for medical and mental health care, substance abuse treatment, financial
assistance, and ultimately, permanent housing.

Day to day, for me, this means a lot of filing. It also means I spend a
lot of time on the phone on 'hold' with Social Security or the Department
of Housing. I spend a lot of time entering urinalysis results from drug
testing or medical appointments or Narcotics Anonymous meetings into
the computer. There are also exciting times; the first week I was here I
called 911 three times for three different medical emergencies. There are
some very busy days (filled with both good and bad events), but the bulk
of my work is still done at a desk.

It is important to be mindful of the larger picture of what we're working towards. Project PLASE's vision is simple: to eliminate homelessness. I love that about this organization, that it unapologetically seeks to
solve what many would declare an unsolvable problem. The groundwork

for solving this problem, and the basis of volunteer work, is found in patiently executing the small tasks that make up the larger resolution.

As I gain experience and confidence I am able to do more direct service with and for our clients. I've been here for seven months, and have been a counselor/case manager for anywhere between one and nine clients at a time. I have gone with clients to look at apartments, taken them shopping, helped fill out housing and SSI applications, and started a weekly therapeutic art group. I've helped mop up sewage when the toilets backed up, baked cookies and sung Christmas carols with clients, and listened to some of the most heartbreaking stories I've ever heard. I've seen clients get their lives together and move into permanent housing and I've seen clients either walk out or be asked to leave due to relapse into substance abuse. I've seen parents rebuild relationships with their children and I've watched a mother weep as she was told she had permanently lost all parental rights. There are some boring days at this job, but there are also terrifying days, frustrating days, incredibly sad days, and once in a while, days full of joy.

The most valuable thing I've learned so far about volunteering is that I can't single-handedly end homelessness or cure addiction, but that working together through effective organization, we can make a big difference.

Sure, if I had the power I would provide housing, health care, and a sustainable, livable income for all of my clients, and for everyone who struggles with cycles of poverty and addiction. That is not in my power to do right now. What I can do right now is treat my clients with dignity and respect and work with them to fight for what they need. I can be a listening and supportive ear and provide what direction and guidance I can. I can help navigate difficult and confusing applications and connect clients with services to which they might not otherwise have access.

My work here is about ending homelessness, but that goal is composed of many smaller tasks. Loving and serving people doesn't need to be large-scale or heroic in order to matter. The point isn't being a hero or fixing everything immediately; the point is diligence and faithfulness in meeting people where they are and providing concrete solutions for their needs as they arise. Mother Theresa said, "we cannot do great things, only small things with great love." That's what we do as volunteers at Project PLASE, and what we will continue to do until the great things are accomplished, piece by piece.

Maggie Page graduated from St. Olaf College and after her year serving as a volunteer with Project PLASE, she plans to serve as a volunteer in Belgrade, Serbia with the Mennonite Central Committee.

Local Food Systems and the Social Economy

by Brad Masi, Executive Director, The New Agrarian Center

Citizens increasingly recognize how their food choices impact health, the environment, community and local economies. A range of issues have motivated shifts in consumer trends, from rising incidents of food-borne illnesses to concerns about the impact of method of food production on climate change or water quality. The increasing incidence of health problems such as Type II diabetes, heart disease and obesity can all be linked to the foods people have access to, can afford and choose to consume in the current predominate U.S. food industry.

In my work and travels, I have seen the significant impact that local food systems can have on communities. Food is something that we all share that has the power to connect us across diverse communities and re-engage us with the good work of growing sustainable local economies.

Northeast Ohio, as with many so-named rust-belt regions of the Great Lakes, has struggled with a wide range of environmental and economic challenges. The burning of the Cuyahoga River propelled national concern about environmental issues in the 1970's. Many cities in Northeast Ohio, such as Cleveland and Youngstown, have received national attention for record home foreclosures and the decline of the industrial economy. Cleveland's population has dropped from almost one million residents in the 1950's to about 470,000 today. Cleveland faces what many old industrial cities struggle with: high rates of poverty, unstable economies, environmental pollution and aging infrastructure.

For a region like Northeast Ohio, engagement in local food systems enables citizens to begin to re-weave the fabric of their own communities and create an economy rooted in community. No issue demonstrates the power of this more than the problem of healthy food access confronting many urban residents.

In Cleveland, residents have to travel a 4.5-times greater distance to reach a full-service grocery store than a fast food establishment (compared to just a 2-mile distance for the average suburban resident). A drive through many Cleveland neighborhoods will reveal the boarded up storefronts of old grocery stores, many of which have stood empty for more than 10 years. In some of these neighborhoods, over half of the residents do not own a vehicle and cannot easily access locally grown foods.

The challenge of access to healthy food in these communities has stimulated a new level of social innovation. Community gardens and market gardens are being established on vacant and foreclosed properties, turning them from overgrown lots and dumping grounds into sources of healthy food. In many cases, these initiatives involve the leadership and involvement of local youth. Today, there are more than 200 of these gardens in Cleveland, with an estimated 40 additional garden spaces in development. The City of Cleveland itself has acknowledged the importance of gardening to re-making the city, having recently passed garden zoning and legislation to make it easier for residents to keep their own chickens and bees. The city even offers grants to seed new garden projects on vacant land as a way to both address public health and to create new entrepreneurial opportunities for residents.

Of course, these gardens did not sprout up on their own. They come through the careful attention and collaboration of thousands of residents. They come through public institutions such as hospitals or schools who open up their land for gardening and volunteer activity.

In one example, the Huron Hospital in East Cleveland has begun to convert its turf-lawn into growing space for the community. The hospital collaborated with City Fresh, a community-based initiative founded by the New Agrarian Movement to install the gardens as a means to improve food access in urban neighborhoods. On one pleasant Friday morning in May, City Fresh organized a community dig-in at the hospital. About 50 volunteers converged on the site and in two hours built two large raised beds for vegetable production. The volunteers included doctors and staff of the hospital, neighborhood youth, mothers and volunteers from across the city. The volunteers took the food waste from the hospital's dining hall, shredded office paper, leaves, wood mulch, cardboard and other wastes to build the raised beds. At the end of the two hours, the beds were planted with seedlings and a small patch of turf-lawn became a beginning place for creating food access in a food-desert neighborhood.

Urban gardens and food distribution are an example of a growing "social economy" around food. At a time when access to resources is tight, many communities are beginning to value their own assets and realizing that through shared work and common vision for a healthier community, many of the solutions to our larger problems sit right beneath our feet, in the house next door, and in the neighborhood down the way. Through these voluntary relations, we can begin to sow the seeds for a truly green economy rooted in the very communities in which we live.

The good news is that anyone can be involved and the more we work across communities, the more we will gain traction on the larger national issues of our day.   ⊕

Volunteers Bring Access to Clean Water For Rural Nicaragua

by Anders Olson

Access to clean drinking water is a crucial factor for dramatically improving people's health in developing countries. Globally, contaminated water is the second greatest cause of infant deaths. An estimated 1.8 million children die each year as a result of illnesses linked to consumption of polluted water. In Nicaragua more than two-thirds of rural communities lack access to clean drinking water. In developed countries like the U.S. it is difficult to imagine how a child could die from diarrhea and dehydration caused by consuming contaminated water. Diarrhea-induced dehydration will cause a child to go into shock and die. In Nicaragua, access to clean water and proper sanitation has been found to reduce the risk of diarrhea in children by up to 30%.

In June 2009 I volunteered with an El Porvenir work brigade to participate in a reforestation program outside of San Lorenzo in a village called La Pita. I learned that since 1950 Nicaragua has lost 50% of its natural forest cover. Unequal access to land rights in Nicaragua remains a core issue causing high levels of deforestation and poverty. The expansion of subsistence agriculture along forest frontiers, turning forests into pastures, is considered to be a primary cause of deforestation in Latin America as small farmers who do not have enough money to obtain titles to land with rich soil are forced to plant in frontier areas on steep slopes. Nicaragua is struggling to change ineffective land rights policy and improve the situation for a deeply impoverished population. The government has constructed nurseries for five million trees, while allies in the business community, including the sugar industry have also produced 14 million more trees for reforestation. Reversing the deforestation is critical

to solving the water crisis; deforestation reduces rainfall, rainwater infiltration and aquifer recharge rates, as well as causing soil erosion and deadly landslides.

I first found out about El Porvenir through the International Studies department at the University of Denver shortly after I graduated. El Porvenir (The Future) assists rural villages to improve the standard of living through community initiated well projects, sanitation projects, reforestation projects and health education projects. What interested me in particular was the organization's attention to sustainability and devotion to a bottom-up development model. After working in El Porvenir's Denver office for a few months as a volunteer I decided to experience the organization's work in the field first hand.

El Porvenir was born in the 1980's during the United Nations International Drinking Water Decade. The majority of communities El Porvenir is working with consist of subsistence farmers or day laborers who live in extreme poverty, surviving on less than $50 a month. On the national level an estimated 80% of the population lives in poverty, surviving on less than $2 a day.

We worked side-by-side with local families. The on-site program directors first met with and listened to what people struggle with the most within the community. All development projects are initiated by a proposal drafted by villagers desiring access to El Porvenir resources. The community provided the labor and worked together on projects; El Porvenir provided the training, education, and construction resources. The El Porvenir staff remain in contact with the community for years after the project's completion, to ensure villagers have help whenever there might be problems with new infrastructure or need for an expanded project.

The hands-on work I did with El Porvenir gave me a direct understanding of the crucial importance of addressing international health issues, human rights, sustainable development and environmental protection and insight into how I can prioritize my time and energy towards helping solve problems that are critical to the quality of people's lives. ☺

"If you have knowledge, let others light their candles in it."
— *Margaret Fuller*

In Memory of
Ruth Gordon Fisk
1919 – 2009
Dorothy Rosemary Gordon
1915 – 2009

Part 3

ORGANIZATION LISTINGS

The organizations listed here offer volunteer opportunities for direct involvement with their urgently needed work. In addition to part-time volunteer opportunities, many have full-time (short- or long-term) opportunities as well, whereby volunteers receive room and board or other means of subsistence. Arrangements, requirements, access to resources and size of operation vary from organization to organization. Contact them directly for more information.

AKWESASNE FREEDOM SCHOOL

PO Box 290   (518) 358-2073
Via Mohawk Nation   Fax: (518) 358-2081
Rooseveltown, NY 13683   office@akwesasnefreedomschool.org

Area: Mohawk territory of Akwesasne which straddles the international border between the United States and Canada. The territory lies in parts of New York State and the provinces of Quebec and Ontario.

General Information: Akwesasne Freedom School (AFS) is an independent elementary school founded in 1979 by Mohawk parents who were concerned with the potential loss of the Mohawk language and culture, as well as how poorly their students fared in the regular public schools. Students in grades pre-K to six are immersed in the Mohawk language and culture to form Mohawk identity, citizenship, and nationhood, reversing the assimilation process. English is taught in grades seven and eight to facilitate the transition from the Akwesasne Freedom School to the off-reserve public school.

AFS is a community effort, involving the support of all of the Mohawk nation's governments and their citizens. This commitment by the parents, community, and Mohawk Nation Council to run a school independently ensures continuity and common goals in educating all of the nation's youth. The school has been generating a cadre of knowledgeable Mohawks as well as building more self-determined Mohawk institutions, including the Handenousaunee Environmental Task Force.

Volunteers in solidarity with these goals and interested in working with the Mohawk community to advance this program are needed in various capacities and welcomed. English teachers are needed for the higher grades in the school, as well as people who can assist with grounds maintenance, construction and other aspects of our work. On

AKWESASNE FREEDOM SCHOOL

Photos: Akwesasne Freedom School

Volunteer college students provide English and Math tutoring to 6th, 7th and 8th grade students. A former AFS student (woman standing in the middle) is now a volunteer tutor while also attending college.

AFS students work together to improve their school and grounds. Students participate in decorating a vegetable oil-powered bus used in the community.

a case-by-case basis, we can organize room and board for full-time volunteers who make a long-term commitment. We primarily need part-time volunteers.

Skills: We need people with experience in teaching, fund-raising, proposal writing, event organizing, building repairs and in agriculture (organic), environmental and yard work.

Contact: Terri Day

ALABAMA COUNCIL ON HUMAN RELATIONS, INC.

PO Box 409
319 West Glenn Avenue
Auburn, AL 36831

(334) 821-8336
alma.gholston@achr.com
www.achr.com

Area: Lee and Russell Counties, Alabama

General Information: Alabama Council on Human Relations (ACHR) carries out programs to improve economic conditions, education and racial relationships for all people, resulting in increased self-sufficiency and overall improvement in the quality of lives. ACHR is a statewide private nonprofit organization committed to equality and opportunity for the citizens of Alabama. Founded in 1954 as a forum for discussion and action on issues of racial and economic justice, ACHR's first efforts were directed toward voting and school desegregation. In 1965 ACHR began one of the first Project Head Start programs in Alabama. Originally housed in basements and churches, the ACHR Head Start program now is housed in three centers in Lee and rural Russell counties. In 1998 ACHR began an innovative Early Head Start program, which offers either home-based services or a multi-age center-based program, depending on the needs of the family. These two programs serve over 500 children and their families. The ACHR is both an advocate and a service delivery program to aid low-income children and their families.

ACHR administers Head Start, Early Head Start and Family Services Center in Lee/Russell and a wide range of other federally funded programs (WIC, energy assistance, housing counseling, low-income housing). Because the center serves children, volunteers must have a criminal background check and a medical physical.

Skills: Volunteers with skills in a variety of areas, such as preschool and adult education, administration, clerical, maintenance and/or organizational experience are welcome.

Contact: Janet Burns, Administrative Coordinator

ALDERSON HOSPITALITY HOUSE

Alderson Hospitality House volunteers provide friendly and supportive hospitality to visiting relatives and loved ones of prisoners in the nearby women's federal penitentiary.

ALDERSON HOSPITALITY HOUSE

PO Box 579
Alderson, WV 24910

(304) 445-2980
aah@suddenlinkmail.com

Area: Alderson, West Virginia

General Information: Alderson Hospitality House offers lodging, meals, transportation and support to families who must travel, sometimes long distances, to visit loved ones at the nearby federal women's prison. The House has been operating independently since 1977, run by a volunteer community in the ecumenical catholic tradition.

In recent years, as the population of the prison has grown, Alderson House has expanded to three houses, including space that a local Catholic church has made available, to accommodate increasing numbers of visitors. The House is not government-operated nor part of the federal prison system. In addition to providing an essential way for prisoners and their loved ones to stay connected (there is only one hotel in town, and it is unaffordable to many), the Hospitality House community advocates on behalf of families of prisoners; is committed to alternatives to incarceration; and promotes social and economic justice in the community and society. The House also produces a quarterly newsletter that includes news and information about the incarcerated population at Alderson and nationwide, as well as news and needs at Alderson Hospitality House.

Volunteers are provided room and board and a small monthly stipend. Duties include listening to guests, providing transportation, working in the community, office work, as well as house maintenance such as cooking, cleaning and gardening. Concerned volunteers of any faith are welcome. Full-time volunteers are urgently needed. Commitments of six months or a year (or more) are most desirable, but we are flexible.

Skills: Volunteers must be flexible, open to strangers who come to the House in difficult situations and willing to share living quarters. The staff lives as a community, rooted in faith and commitment to serve others. Knowledge of Spanish language and driver's license are helpful. We are interested in mature volunteers with life experience, and in people who have cared for a house before, have good judgement and are good communicators.

Contact: Tina Marquart, Manager

ALL STARS PROJECT, INC.

543 West 42nd Street
New York, NY 10036

(212) 356-8431
gelberg@allstars.org
www.allstars.org

San Francisco, CA	Chicago, IL	Newark, NJ
(415) 986-2502	(773) 624-2848	(973) 622-5506
cdonnola@allstars.org	jlenner@allstars.org	cdevlin@allstars.org

Area: Oakland and San Francisco, California; Chicago, Illinois; Newark, New Jersey; New York City, all five boroughs

General Information: The All Stars Project creates outside of school, educational and performing arts activities for thousands of poor and minority young people. Our innovative approach—performance as a tool for growth—is the foundation for all of our breakthrough programs around the country. Our performing arts and youth development center in New York City is a hub for creative activity. Volunteers are a driving force in all the programs of the All Stars Project. They work side by side with young people, help produce community talent shows and recruit and teach young people to perform in Youth Onstage, organize special events, and work in the theatres on

ALL STARS PROJECT, INC.

All Stars Project helps over 20,000 inner-city young people produce and perform in neighborhood talent shows yearly to create something positive in their communities.

costumes, sets, tech, managing house staff, audience development, marketing, and fund-raising. In our Development School for Youth, volunteers teach young people how to give a good interview and hold a relevant conversation. Additionally, volunteers participate in administrative work in public relations and volunteer management.

Short-term and long-term projects as well as group and corporate volunteering are welcome. Hours are varied and flexible. Contact us to schedule an Introduction to Volunteering session.

Skills: The All Stars Project needs volunteers of all ages and from all walks of life who want to donate their time, energy and talents.

Contact: Gail Elberg (New York), Christina Devlin (Newark), Julie Lenner (Chicago), Caroline Donnola (Bay Area)

ALZHEIMER'S ASSOCIATION
225 North Michigan, 17th Floor
Chicago, IL 60601

(312) 335-8700
(866) 699-1246
jan.hann@alz.org
www.alz.org

Area: The Alzheimer's Association is a national federation of 77 chapters covering the United States with over 300 points of service.

General Information: The Alzheimer's Association's mission is to eliminate Alzheimer's disease through the advancement of research, to enhance care and support for individuals, their families and caregivers and to promote brain health. While the number and titles of volunteers needed may vary, each of the 77 chapters depends on volunteers to work with families and caregivers, to advocate on issues related to those suffering with Alzheimer's disease at local, state and federal government levels, to be educators and public speakers, to help with fund-raising events, to manage resource centers, to answer information and referral requests and to serve on the governing board and its committees. Consult www.alz.org, In My Community or call our office to learn the specific volunteer needs in your community. Assignments may be weekly, monthly or every so often.

Skills: Grassroots advocacy, public speaking, understanding of geriatric health concerns, education, writing for newsletters, web sites, fund-raising, computer skills, language translation, management skills, library, effective listening skills and ability to work with a diverse client population are just a few of the skills needed. Volunteers work closely with staff and can expect to receive a job description and appropriate training before beginning their assignments.

Contact: Jan Hann, Director Leadership and Training

AMERICAN VETERANS ALLIANCE (AVA) AND SOCIETY OF HISPANIC VETERANS

1923 SW 8th Street (305) 883-3133
Miami, FL 33135 (305) 213-5496
www.wesupportvets.org

Area: Miami, Florida at headquarters

General Information: The American Veterans Alliance (AVA) and its affiliate, Society of Hispanic Veterans, are advocacy groups that assist veterans and their dependents in the struggle to obtain their rightful benefits that have been arbitrarily denied by U.S. government agencies. We focus on advocating for homeless and underserved men and women veterans and their dependents.

One of the most serious challenges the nation faces today is providing services for troops returning from Iraq and Afghanistan, as the government provides scant resources to aid veterans with the transition back into civilian life. We help with their reintegration into the community by securing mental health services through partnerships with counselors who specialize in the treatment of PTSD, creating real employment opportunities by directly hiring veterans for AVA construction projects and assisting them with vocational training, aiding them with the development of job readiness and overall life skills, and working to eliminate discrimination against veterans. Through our community outreach, we serve as a lifeline for many Florida-based veterans who would otherwise have no place to turn.

We also provide information and referrals to members of Florida's veteran community in the areas of housing assistance, employment, job training, education, legal assistance and general benefits. AVA is registered as a national Veteran Service Association (VSO).

We are not funded by the government and rely on volunteers from the community. We need volunteers who can assist with day-to-day administrative and community outreach work, expand our information and referral, advocacy and other program services.

Skills: While anyone concerned can volunteer in whatever capacity they are able, we also need volunteers with writing skills, particularly in the areas of public relations, marketing and grant writing.

Contact: Waddell McGee

APPALACHIAN SOUTH FOLKLIFE CENTER

PO Box 10 (304) 466-0626
Pipestem, WV 25979 the_folks@folklifecenter.org
www.folklifecenter.org

Area: Mid-Appalachia

General Information: Appalachian people have struggled with poverty, isolation and a demanding environment since they climbed the mountains and created community nearly 280 years ago. We strive to help people overcome obstacles and become self-reliant. Our housing program offers help to families so children don't have to worry about being warm, safe and dry while doing homework. Elderly folks can stay in their homes once they have been fixed up and in some cases made more accessible. On top of the benefit to our community, folks from all over the country learn about our unique culture while giving their time to perform the repairs.

Each summer certified teachers give nearly 60 children extra educational attention during our Learning Day Camp. At-risk children from two of West Virginia's poorest counties get experiential educational time and parents are invited to participate. Putting learning in a setting away from the traditional structure of a school system gives a child an opportunity to think it's fun. Full- and part-time volunteers are needed to assist with various activities, from daily chores and maintenance to secretarial and library work, and to help with our events and functions. Residential volunteers who live and serve in this rustic setting can apply to stay for a weekend, a month or longer.

Skills: Applicants need to be sensitive to our philosophy of being a place where people of all ages, races, faiths and origins can share community work and creativity.

Contact: Shelli Osborne, Director

ARISE FOR SOCIAL JUSTICE

467 State Street   (413) 734-4948
Springfield, MA 01105   arisesocialjustice@yahoo.com

Area: Western Massachusetts

General Information: Arise for Social Justice is a member-based and multiracial low-income rights organization. Most of our members are poor. We believe we have the right to speak for ourselves on the issues that affect us. We promote organizing, empowerment, involvement with electoral process and fighting oppression on all fronts. We do advocacy and organize around issues such as housing, homelessness, and run an anti-violent peace group.

Volunteers are needed in any of these areas, as well as research, developing literature, advocacy and outreach.

Skills: Experience is not as important as openness to all kinds of people, patience, a non-judgmental attitude and an interest in the whole political system.

Contact: Ellen Graves, Organizer

BIG CREEK PEOPLE IN ACTION, INC.

HC 32 Box 541   (304) 875-3418
Caretta, WV 24821   Fax: (304) 875-3518

Area: McDowell County, West Virginia

General Information: Big Creek People in Action (BCPIA) was founded in 1990 to address family, community and economic concerns in the area. McDowell County is the seventh poorest area in America, has the fifth highest child poverty rate, the sixth worst health status, more than triple the national rate of unemployment and the highest

BIG CREEK PEOPLE IN ACTION

Photos: Big Creek People in Action

College student volunteers take time out from their work project for a tour of the local coal mine. McDowell County is the seventh poorest county in America, with thousands of unemployed coal miners and their families struggling to survive.

A Bluegrass band performs for the volunteers and local youth after a day of service together.

illiteracy rate in adults in West Virginia. A great deal of timbering and other excavation of the land in the mountains around us is done by gas, coal and paper companies leaving environmental destruction that harms our communities. Reconstruction of homes in the area is still going on since severe flooding that occurred in 2002. Official aid from state and national agencies has been scarce.

BCPIA's mission is to strengthen the community in which people learn, work and grow together and prepare it for success in the 21st century. BCPIA strives to make it possible for people to be self-sufficient and live in communities that are economically vibrant, democratic and socially just. We believe the best people to address a problem are those who are most directly affected by it. Education is fundamental and we have a Youth Program based on youth/adult partnerships to promote building leadership skills through their involvement in working for community change.

Groups are needed for short-or long-term commitments to help with home repairs, renovations and other community needs and programs. Dorm housing is provided, but BCPIA does not have the resources for other materials and will work with you on what you need to bring.

Volunteer attorneys are also urgently needed for assistance with the rights of disabled children in school and other problem areas with the education system, as well as legal advocacy for residents and home-owners for their right to stay on their land.

Skills: All skills are welcome. Carpentry, general building, painting, residential renovation, plumbing or electrical work are especially needed. We also need attorneys.

Contact: Marsha Timpson, Volunteer Coordinator

BOOKS-FOR-CHINA FUND

c/o Mr. John T. Ma
138-10 Franklin Avenue #3-D
Flushing, NY 11355

(718) 886-4687
johntajenma@att.net
www.booksforchina.org

Area: United States

General Information: The main purpose of the Books-for-China Fund is to collect books from individuals, libraries, publishers and other institutions in America and to donate them to universities in China. Established in 2005, it has already sent three full containers of books to China. A score of Chinese universities have received the books. By making many American publications available to China's college students and professors, we believe that our project helps, not only modernization of China, but also betterment of U.S.-China cultural relations. We need volunteers to give us information about available gift books, to pick up books from donors and deliver them to our storage in Brooklyn, New York and Millbrae, California, and to help us raise funds to cover the costs of collecting books. Contributions to the Fund are tax-deductible.

Skills: No special skill or experience is required.

Contact: John T. Ma

BUILDING GOODNESS FOUNDATION

PO Box 4325 (434) 973-0993
Charlottesville, VA 22905 volunteer@buildinggoodness.org
www.buildinggoodness.org

Area: Gulf Coast Mississippi, Central Virginia and Mattaponi Indian Reservation (near Richmond, Virginia); Guatemala, Haiti, Honduras

General Information: Building Goodness Foundation (BGF) is a nonprofit organization powered by skilled volunteers from the construction trades and surrounding communities. Bringing together volunteers from every part of the construction industry and using donations of time, money, materials and expertise, we build clinics, schools, shelters, community centers, specialized housing and other structures for communities in need. BGF builds for the local community in Charlottesville, Virginia, for impoverished and disaster-stricken areas such as the Gulf Coast and in developing countries. (See page 200 for BGF's international projects) Instead of focusing solely on individuals in need or residential projects, Building Goodness seeks out ambitious projects with the greatest potential to help the larger community. Our projects create and nurture the connections between people which helps produce prosperity and peace for the entire community. You don't have to be a carpenter, mason or designer to make a difference. Other ways to volunteer include working on a committee, preparing mailings, event support and representing BGF in outreach activities. Beyond the bricks and mortar of a new structure, BGF volunteers build lasting relationships with the people they are helping, profoundly improving the lives of all involved.

Skills: Building, design and construction volunteers are the most needed. Anyone interested in participating in construction projects is welcome; a cooperative, positive attitude and willingness to contribute to the goals of the team is a must.

Contact: Ethan Tate, Program Coordinator

CAMP VICTOR MINISTRIES

1515 Government Street
Ocean Springs, MS 39564

Camp: (228) 875-0313
Reservations: (228) 282-3754
www.campvictor.org

Area: Ocean Springs and Jackson County, Mississippi

General Information: On August 29, 2005 over 64,000 homes along the Mississippi Gulf Coast were destroyed by Hurricane Katrina and over 78,000 left uninhabitable. Within days of the storm, Christus Victor Lutheran Church in Ocean Springs, Mississippi became a hurricane disaster response center. During the months that followed, the church's walls were stretched to provide housing, food and case management for thousands, while continuing to accommodate regular church services and activities. In June of 2006 the disaster operations were moved to Camp Victor, where an old factory was turned into a volunteer camp, distribution center and construction warehouse under one roof. Since the hurricane we have hosted over 14,000 volunteers, worked on the reconstruction of more than 1,800 homes and given assistance to over 28,900 families at our distribution center. Volunteers have served from each state in the U.S. and from over 30 foreign countries.

Short-term volunteers, staying one to two weeks, work on rebuilding, help in the distribution center, or assist with cooking and camp maintenance. Volunteer construction crews go to the sites Monday–Friday and perform a variety of tasks: framing, roofing, siding, building porches and handicap ramps, hanging and finishing drywall, installing doors and windows, installing laminate flooring and tile, and painting the interior and exterior of homes. Our distribution center provides hurricane survivors with food and supplies.

Long-term volunteers are needed to help with case management, volunteer management and construction supervision. Each person interested in volunteering for three weeks or more should submit a purpose statement, detailing their motivation to serve with Camp Victor, and two reference forms to the volunteer manager.

Skills: The requirement is a willingness to learn and serve others.

Contact: Kendall Gordon, Volunteer Manager

CAMP VICTOR MINISTRIES

Photos: Camp Victor Ministries

A volunteer helps rebuild one of the 142,000 homes destroyed or left uninhabitable by Hurricane Katrina. Every week, Camp Victor Ministries hosts volunteers who come from every state and over 30 countries to rebuild homes and help run the Ministries' distribution center.

College students transform a damaged building into a usable public space. Reconstruction continues more than five years after the hurricane.

CAMPAIGN FOR LABOR RIGHTS

1247 E Street SE
Washington, DC 20003

(202) 550-7025
clr@clrlabor.org
www.clrlabor.org

Area: Washington, DC

General Information: Campaign for Labor Rights mobilizes grassroots activists throughout the U.S. in support of anti-sweatshop campaigns through action alerts, speaking tours, a monthly bulletin and other events and activities to educate the public and press for change in policy. Our Economic Literacy Campaign seeks to educate U.S. residents about global economic issues. We prioritize campaigns which have the goal of worker empowerment through union recognition and collectively bargained contracts. We operate on the solidarity model, taking our lead from the workers whose livelihood and lives are at stake. Volunteers are needed at our office and we also welcome those who can work on campaigns in their local communities around the country.

Skills: Organizing experience, research and strong writing skills and a strong commitment to labor and human rights is required. Spanish, computer proficiency, web and video abilities are desired.

Contact: James Jordan, National Coordinator

CAMPHILL ASSOCIATION OF NORTH AMERICA

PO Box 152
Philmont, NY 12565

(518) 610-3179
lauren@camphill.org
www.camphill.org

Area: California, Minnesota, New York, Pennsylvania; British Columbia, Ontario

General Information: Camphill is an international social movement of intentional communities where children, adolescents and adults with developmental disabilities, mental illness and social disadvantage can be supported in community to unfold their potential.

There are over 100 Camphill communities worldwide, ten of which are in North America. The Camphill approach honors the spiritual integrity of every human being, regardless of ability or circumstances, and recognizes the individual's need and right to lead a full life that includes material, emotional, social and spiritual needs. This approach is a practical expression of the holistic worldview introduced by Rudolf Steiner, Ph.D. It brings together education, science, healing, agriculture, the arts and civil society. Most Camphills are in rural settings, providing opportunities for agricultural and horticultural work supporting a sustainable world ecology. In each Camphill community people live together in house communities and share in the daily life and tasks of the house. They engage in work at school, on the land, in one of the craft workshops or other services. Celebration has a central place in the life of the community through arts, festivals and honoring special events and milestones in people's lives. Care for the earth is highly valued and considered an essential component to the well-being of people and the community. Minimum age for volunteers is 19. Here are brief descriptions of each North American community:

Camphill Communities California: Located in Soquel, California, a residential care community for adults with developmental disabilities. (831) 476-7194, www.camphillca.org

Camphill Communities Ontario: On 300 acres of land in Canada, with a biodynamic garden, sugarbush, beef and poultry farm and forests. Volunteers must acquire a Canadian visa. Contact Diane Kyd. (705) 424-5363, www.camphill.on.ca

Camphill Soltane: In Glenmoore, Pennsylvania, a community for young adults with developmental disabilities, ages 18-25. (610) 469-0933, www.camphillsoltane.org

Camphill Special School: Outside of Philadelphia, Pennsylvania, a residential community of 150 people, almost half of whom are developmentally disabled children and adolescents living with trained curative educators and their families. Contact Anne Sproll. (610) 469-9236, www.beaverrun.org

Camphill Triform Community: In Hudson, New York, a therapeutic/educational program for young adults in need of special care, helping them find meaning and direction in their lives through its Education and Apprenticeship Training Program. (518) 851-9320, www.triformcamphill.org

Camphill Village Kimberton Hills: In Kimberton, Pennsylvania, a residential community for adults with developmental disabilities, on a 430-acre farm in Kimberton. Both resident and nonresident volunteers are needed. (610) 935-3963, www.camphillkimberton.org

Camphill Village Minnesota: An intentional community of approximately 60 people, including adults with developmental disabilities. Located on a 360-acre working farm. Contact Phil Drake. (320) 732-6365, www.camphillvillage-minnesota.org

CAMPHILL ASSOCIATION OF NORTH AMERICA

Photo: Camphill Association of North America

A bell choir consisting of adult residents and co-workers perform during the community's tenth anniversary celebration.

Camphill Village USA: In upstate New York, 100 miles north of New York City, an international community of 250 people, about 105 of whom are adults with mental disabilities. Three-year training course in Social Therapy available. Must speak English. (518) 329-7924, www.camphillvillage.org

Cascadia Society: Cascadia Society is a life-sharing community that includes adults with special needs. Cultural, artistic, and therapeutic experiences are provided through residential home care and day activities within the urban setting of Vancouver's North Shore. Contact Patricia Smith. (604) 987-3407, www.cascadiasociety.org

Ita Wegman Association of British Columbia: Located in Glenora Farm, a rural and agriculturally based community for adults with special needs, the community operates a biodynamic farm. Contact Lynne or Katrin. (250) 715-1559, www.glenorafarm.com

Skills: Flexibility, a willingness and interest in living and working with people with a developmental disability are needed. In some cases, office skills, farming experience or skill in handcrafting are especially helpful. Practical skills in crafts, arts, household/cooking, gardening and farming are also helpful in many communities.

Contact: Lauren Wolff at Camphill North America, or contact any of the individual communities directly

CAPITAL AREA FOOD BANK

645 Taylor Street NE   (202) 526-5344
Washington, DC 20017   cruzm@cfoodbank.org

Area: Washington, DC and northern Virginia

General Information: The Capital Area Food Bank is the largest distribution center for donated food in the Washington, DC metropolitan area, with an annual distribution of over 20 million pounds of food. Our mission is to feed those who suffer from hunger in the Washington, DC area by acquiring food and distributing it through our network of 740 community member feeding programs, as well as to educate, empower and enlighten the community about the issues of hunger and nutrition.

Volunteers sort food or assist with our other programs and special events, at both our Washington DC and northern Virginia locations. They help to collect food donations at pickup points that are announced during public service announcements on the radio, as well as assist families in getting food stamps via advocacy programs. Volunteers also go with staff members to speak on Capitol Hill. Volunteer chefs and nutritionists are needed to teach classes about how to make healthy meals. Some volunteers work at Claggett Farm, a cooperative venture with The Chesapeake Bay Foundation located in Upper Marlboro, just outside DC.

Skills: Skill requirements may vary, according to the work to be performed. The most important thing to have is a serious commitment to do what you can to eliminate hunger.

Contact: Oye Omorogbe, Director of Volunteer Programs; Myra Cruz, Volunteer Coordinator

THE CARING COMMUNITY

20 Washington Square North   (212) 777-3555 Ext 112
New York, NY 10011   Fax: (212) 353-9690
david.mcgillan@thecaringcoßmmunity.org
www.thecaringcommunity.org

Area: New York City (Greenwich Village neighborhood)

General Information: The Caring Community is the longest running and largest private, nonprofit service organization in Greenwich Village and Lower Manhattan that is dedicated to improving the quality of life for older adults. We offer a wide range of services and programs to seniors 60+ at a number of sites. Volunteers shop for or with a senior or accompany a senior to appointments. The Shopping & Escort program

THE CARING COMMUNITY

Volunteers help make it possible for seniors to continue living in dignity in their own homes and are very much appreciated.

Photo: Caring Community

is vital for seniors who are unable to shop or attend appointments on their own. This is a valuable service which volunteers find interesting and rewarding.

Friendly Visitor volunteers make weekly visits to a senior living in Greenwich Village who has limited social contact due to illnesses and/or impairments associated with older adulthood. Friendly Visits provide an invaluable service to these seniors, allowing them to have social interaction. Volunteers have the opportunity to develop a lasting friendship and learn from a senior's life experiences.

Skills: All we need is your time and patience.

Contact: David McGillan, Operations Manager

CATHOLIC WORKER/ISAIAH HOUSE

316 South Cypress   (714) 835-6304
Santa Ana, CA 92701   www.occatholicworker.org

Area: Orange County, California

General Information: Isaiah House is a Catholic Worker community near Disneyland. We provide a consistent, caring presence for the poor and homeless. We are a hospitality house, not an agency. We serve 3,000 nutritious meals each week, in seven servings, and through our food pantry for the neighborhood needy. We encourage

CATHOLIC WORKER/ISAIAH HOUSE

Photos: Catholic Worker/Isaiah House

Volunteers who serve the daily free meals take time to play with children who are there with a parent.

The number of families who are becoming homeless in Orange County is growing. Isaiah House volunteers help parents get needed food and other assistance.

each other and our 75 weekly volunteers to personally attend to the needs of our brothers and sisters and to each day practice the corporal works of mercy: Feeding the hungry, sheltering the homeless, clothing the naked and visiting the sick and imprisoned. We practice witness against war and the death penalty and for needs of homeless children.

Located in a Latino barrio, we are open to people in need from 6 am to 10 pm daily. We offer long-term shelter for up to 110 homeless women and families (much to the chagrin of local authorities) and always a friendly ear and kind words of support. No TV or alcohol. Voluntary poverty and 18 hour days are the easy part. We celebrate Mass each week in our home. One- to three-month, or longer internships are available. All volunteers receive shared room, use of car, special diet (kosher, vegan, etc.) if needed and stipend.

Come and practice your Spanish in this multilingual community. Meet Jesus in His most unfortunate disguise. Become a Good Samaritan. Show Mercy.

Skills: Experience cooking, housekeeping and working with children is a plus, not a requirement.

Contact: Dwight Smith, Director

CATHOLICS SPEAK OUT/QUIXOTE CENTER

3502 Varnum Street   (301) 699-0042
Brentwood, MD 20722   cso@quixote.org

Area: Washington, DC metropolitan area

General Information: Catholics Speak Out works to give progressive Catholics a place to speak out for justice in the world and in the Roman Catholic Church. Issues include women's ordination, a married clergy, greater lay participation, democratic modes of decision-making, gay and lesbian rights and dialogue on issues of sexuality and reproduction. Volunteers or interns should be college age or older. Time periods for service are flexible and negotiable. Work would include office-based projects, occasional research, setting up events and telephone organizing. Quixote Center is an exciting venue for anyone—a place to learn about justice ministries in general.

Skills: Clerical and computer skills are helpful. Ability to meet the public in person or on the phone is needed. Any theological knowledge can be acquired on site.

Contact: Dolly Pomerleau, National Coordinator

CHICAGO LEGAL ADVOCACY FOR INCARCERATED MOTHERS (CLAIM)

Photo: CLAIM

Mothers with children under the age of 18 are the fastest growing segment of the prison population in the U.S. Eighty one percent of women in prison in Illinois are mothers separated from their children. CLAIM works to keep mothers and their children in contact and advocates for alternative sentences, residential and day programs, and better visiting programs.

CHICAGO LEGAL ADVOCACY FOR INCARCERATED MOTHERS (CLAIM)

70 East Lake Street, Suite 1120   (312) 675-0912
Chicago, IL 60601   zenaidaalonzo@yahoo.com
                                         www.claim-il.org

Area: Greater Chicago area

General Information: CLAIM helps women prisoners and their children maintain contact. We provide legal aid to mothers in jail, prison, work release and on parole. We assist mothers in appointing relatives as guardians for their children to keep the family intact whenever possible, and we help women regain child custody after a period of transition and adjustment. CLAIM is the only agency that provides legal services on family law in Illinois correctional centers. Most women are charged with minor, nonviolent offenses. They need help providing stable homes for their children until they can get their lives on track. Without such assistance, their children are more likely to suffer worse consequences due to the mother's incarceration.

We need volunteer lawyers and licensed law students for CLAIM's Panel Program and Jail Clinic. We provide free training and our programs have been approved for CLE credit in Illinois. We provide malpractice insurance and case coaching for our cases. Volunteers must commit to serve for one year. Jail Clinic volunteers visit the Cook County Jail once a month; they may schedule their visit any day or evening to fit their own schedules. Jail Clinic volunteers conduct extensive intake interviews, give legal advice, and may negotiate on behalf of clients, but they do not need to take on cases for representation in court. Panel Program volunteers provide representation in Probate or Domestic Relations court, and must commit to take at least one case per year. Cases range from simple, uncontested minor guardianships that require only one court appearance, to contested child custody matters that may take two years or more to resolve.

Skills: Must be licensed as an attorney or Section 711-licensed law student. Excellent communication skills, dependability and promptness. Must have a deep concern for social justice and a desire to work with women from different backgrounds and life experiences.

Contact: Zenaida Alonzo, Staff Attorney

CHRIST HOUSE

1717 Columbia Road NW
Washington, DC 20009

(202) 328-1100
shepler@christhouse.org
www.christhouse.org

Area: Washington, DC

General Information: Christ House is a 33-bed medical recovery facility for men and women who are homeless and sick. Our mission is to provide comprehensive health care to sick, homeless men and women and assist them in addressing critical issues to help break the cycle of homelessness. Patients receive 24-hour medical care, case management, addiction counseling, housing placement assistance, nutritious meals and other supportive services in a safe, welcoming and nurturing community. Year-long volunteers fill staff positions and work 40 hours per week. Positions include Nurse, Nursing Assistant, Community Builder (formerly called Patient Activities Coordinator), Social Work Assistant, Medical Unit Assistant and Generalist (a multi-department assistant role). Year-long volunteers must be at least 21 years old and receive a stipend of $100 per month, health insurance and reasonable transportation costs. Short-term volunteers (one month minimum) perform a variety of tasks depending on their skills and our

CHRISTIAN OUTREACH WITH APPALACHIAN PEOPLE (COAP)

Volunteers with COAP build and repair houses in the Appalachian region while also learning about Appalachian history and culture.

Photos: COAP

High school students reflect on a week of building houses in Appalachia. COAP invites groups and families to volunteer for a week making a difference and gaining an understanding of a culture different from their own.

needs at the time. They must be at least 18 years old. All full-time volunteers are provided with room and board. All volunteers are involved in direct service. Christ House volunteers live in an intentional community at Emmanuel House, our residence for full-time volunteers. Applications for year-long volunteers are accepted on a rolling basis. Early application is encouraged (before March 1) but not required. Applications for short-term volunteers should be received at least two months in advance of available date.

Skills: Skills vary by job. Desire to work with men and women who are homeless and live in an intentional community are a must.

Contact: Shannon Hepler, Director of Volunteers

CHRISTIAN OUTREACH WITH APPALACHIAN PEOPLE (COAP)

Box 1617   (606) 573-9853
Harlan, KY 40831   jessnorthlewis@yahoo.com

Area: Southeastern Kentucky

General Information: Christian Outreach with Appalachian People (COAP) is a nonprofit, ecumenical housing construction and repair organization. We invite groups to work with us year-round. Week-long work camp groups provide unskilled or semi-skilled work opportunities. During the week you work with us, programs are also available involving local history, side trips, music and tours to augment the understanding of Appalachia in a fuller way. COAP accepts any adult or high school group. Volunteers participate from Florida, Chicago, Wisconsin, Connecticut and many other areas. We need volunteer groups all year-round, especially in the spring and fall months. Minimum age is fourteen, except for families. We ask a fee of $195 per person, for the week to cover housing and materials.

Skills: Hard workers who are flexible, open-minded, and willing to serve. Any type of construction experience is helpful, but not required.

Contact: Jessica N. Lewis, Volunteer Program Coordinator

CLARETIAN VOLUNTEERS

205 West Monroe Street   (312) 236-7782 Ext 479
Chicago, IL 60606   www.claretianvolunteers.org

Area: Stone Mountain, Georgia; Chicago, Illinois; Springfield, Missouri

General Information: The Claretian Volunteers welcomes women and men united in spirit with the Claretian Missionaries of the Eastern U.S. For over twenty-five years the Claretian Volunteers have joined the Claretians in service to many different communities in need. Rooted in the Roman Catholic tradition, we strive to live the values of the church and community. Service and ministry placements are arranged individually based on applicants' skills and interests and needs of the communities where we serve. Opportunities include working with youth and children, young adult mentoring and ministry, community and neighborhood development, housing and social services, teaching and nontraditional education and tutoring, Hispanic and Spanish speaking ministry, peace and justice advocacy and parish/pastoral ministries, working with the elderly and immigrant and refugee services. Specific positions are added each spring and early summer.

Volunteers serve one year at a time for up to two years. Benefits vary from AmeriCorps Education Awards and loan deferments up to room and board, monthly stipend, transportation and basic health insurance. Volunteers can be single women and men or married couples with no dependents who are willing to participate in community living with other volunteers. Each prospective volunteer completes the online application, screening and interview with the program and the placement site. Minimum age requirement is 21 years, and up to 30 years old. College education is preferred, but each case will be looked at individually. Placements normally begin in August. Preference is given to applications received by June 15.

Skills: Spanish is helpful but not necessary.

Contact: Deana Brewer

COALITION OF CONCERNED LEGAL PROFESSIONALS (CCLP)

25 Chapel Street, Suite 601   (718) 522-1619
Brooklyn, NY 11201

Area: New York State

General Information: Coalition of Concerned Legal Professionals (CCLP) is an all-volunteer association of lawyers, law students, paralegals, court reporters, law librarians as well as concerned people with no law background at all. Volunteer legal professionals and lay volunteer advocates work in teams with those in need of legal help to meet some of the most pressing needs for legal recourse for members of organizations of low-paid workers, including workfare recipients,

COALITION OF CONCERNED LEGAL PROFESSIONALS

Photos: John Leschak

A volunteer attorney addresses farm workers and other low-income workers on "What to do if you are cheated out of your wages." CCLP volunteers attending the presentation assist with individual interviews and advocacy afterwards.

A CCLP volunteer attorney provides advice to a member of an organization of low-income workers; a volunteer advocate assists with follow-up.

the unemployed and the elderly and disabled in these communities. They share a long-term goal of ending the injustice manifested in the fact that 99% of the U.S. population is served by only 5% of our nation's attorneys. CCLP maintains an ongoing program of education and information coupled with lay advocacy that aggressively seeks any available resource—with no strings attached—to fill a request for legal assistance. CCLP volunteer attorneys conduct "Know Your Law" presentations on topics like what to do when your civil rights have been violated; health care law; landlord-tenant problems; what to do when arrested or stopped by the police; employment law; and job discrimination.

Individual legal problems are often manifestations of larger systemic causes. CCLP promotes involvement and provides leadership to those seeking organizational, legal and systemic solutions to the complex problems faced by our poorest and most oppressed communities. This can involve coordination of major civil rights and other litigation through a team approach. CCLP teaches grassroots organizing skills and fights government policies that abrogate constitutional principles and public accountability.

CCLP volunteers can participate in the writing, production and distribution of CCLP publications and literature and contribute to CCLP's newsletter, *The Gavel.*

Skills: No experience necessary, only a commitment to the struggle for meaningful access to the courts and a willingness to learn, although attorneys, paralegals, law students, clerks, etc. interested in organizing the profession are essential.

Contact: Susan Prensky, Operations Manager

COALITION OF CONCERNED MEDICAL PROFESSIONALS (CCMP)

1023 Church Avenue, Second Floor   (718) 469-5817
Brooklyn, NY 11218

Area: New York metropolitan area and Long Island

General Information: Coalition of Concerned Medical Professionals (CCMP) is an all-volunteer association of health care professionals, students, low-income workers, clergy and other concerned citizens fighting for the right to comprehensive health care for all, regardless of ability to pay. More than 80 million Americans have no medical coverage and millions more cannot afford their deductibles, co-pays or the cost of treatment. Treatable but untreated diseases like TB and asthma are on the rise among the working poor and minorities while silent killers such as diabetes and hypertension reach epidemic proportions in our society. CCMP volunteers work under the supervision of experienced CCMP organizers who teach volunteers how to build a winning fight through organization to overcome the political and economic barriers to good health.

Health care professionals volunteer their skills and resources to organize medical education information sessions, which offer presentations on

COALITION OF CONCERNED MEDICAL PROFESSIONALS

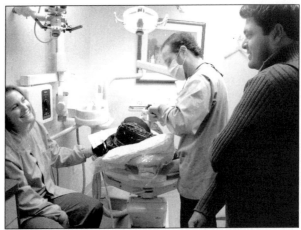

Photos: CCMP

CCMP's volunteer dentists include endodontists who provide treatment otherwise unavailable to low-income, uninsured patients. Medical students volunteer as patient advocates and help remove obstacles to care.

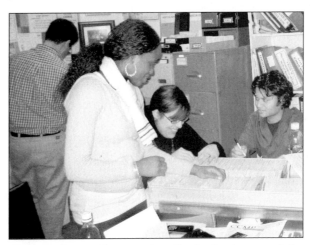

Students from colleges and medical schools around the country volunteer full-time with CCMP over their winter, spring, and summer breaks. Seasoned organizers provide on-the-job training and demonstrate how to fight for comprehensive health care.

topics of interest to maintaining good health for the low-income community. Through CCMP's general medical sessions volunteer doctors examine CCMP patients, who are uninsured low-paid service and farm workers, and treat them without charge. Together with lay medical advocates, the doctor works with each patient to realize a treatment plan. This can involve procurement of donated lab tests or medications; specialist referral; advocacy with government agencies or insurance plans; or procurement and distribution of nutritious foods.

CCMP volunteers also learn how to fight for access to health services through on-the-job training in individual patient advocacy as well as organizing campaigns to defeat laws and policies detrimental to New York's growing number of poor workers. CCMP publishes *Vital Signs* to provide our constituency with facts and analysis not available through the established press.

Because poverty is the leading cause of ill health, CCMP volunteers also collect and distribute donated food and clothing as part of its preventive medical care program, and actively work to advance conditions of low-income workers.

Skills: A commitment to learn leadership skills to advance the fight for access to comprehensive health care. Volunteers can learn and then teach, patient advocacy. We need individuals with publication production skills and foreign language translators, as well as licensed physicians, dentists, nurses and other health care professionals. However, no special skills or previous experience are required to become a volunteer; a willingness to learn and serve is.

Contact: Middy Mincer, Operations Manager

COMMISSION ON VOLUNTARY SERVICE & ACTION (CVSA)

1 Union Square West, Suite 902   (646) 486-2446
New York, NY 10003   or (877) 867-6150

Area: New York City or on field assignments anywhere in the country

General information: Commission on Voluntary Service & Action (CVSA) is a consultative and coordinating body of non-government, voluntary service organizations that serve people and communities in need, based primarily in North America but also working with volunteer efforts in other parts of the world. CVSA works with organizations endeavoring to reverse such devastating conditions as hunger, lack of access to health care, unemployment, lack of access to legal recourse,

COMMISSION ON VOLUNTARY SERVICE & ACTION (CVSA)

CVSA volunteers produce the membership newsletter, ITEMS, *the catalogue,* Invest Yourself, *maintain communication with member organizations and organize speaking engagements and other outreach to promote voluntary service across the country and around the world.*

Photo: Celeste Tandy

decent housing and many other areas of need, including environmental concerns, sustainable food production programs, education for youth and care for the elderly.

CVSA is dedicated to making it possible for more people to volunteer their time and services to people and communities in need and strengthening the independent, non-government volunteer service and action movement. We publish and distribute the *INVEST YOURSELF* catalogue and conduct year-round outreach to potential volunteers through speaking engagements in college classrooms, presentations to retiring professionals and information tables at volunteer and career fairs. CVSA has also developed a benefit program of assistance for member organizations on a voluntary mutual-assistance basis, through which we can provide consultations, training and information and referral by drawing from the experiences of all the organizations involved and from CVSA's own 65-year history and experience.

CVSA volunteers compile, produce and distribute *INVEST YOURSELF* year-round; learn to conduct speaking engagements and other outreach to promote *INVEST YOURSELF* and the urgent need for volunteers on behalf of the organizations listed in these pages; coordinate consultations for member organizations on methods to increase volunteer participation and other issues of concern to volunteer organizations; produce CVSA's membership newsletter, *ITEMS*, which provides a forum for national and international news and analysis, as well as practical matters of method and organizational strategies relevant to those involved in non-government voluntary service and action projects.

CVSA's staff is made up entirely of full-time and part-time volunteers. Volunteers learn the practical skills of organizing and the history, methods and strategies of service organizations and movements for social change on the national and international scene. In addition to working from CVSA's base office, volunteers can participate from communities anywhere in the country or the world by being *INVEST YOURSELF* Representatives.

Skills: No previous experience or specific skills required; but skills in all aspects of publications, writing, photography, design are always needed. We provide on-the-job training for all aspects of our organizing and outreach. Willingness to learn and take responsibility is essential.

Contact: Susan Angus, Executive Director

COMMON GROUND HEALTH CLINIC (CGHC)

1408 Teche Street   (504) 365-8800
New Orleans, LA 70114   www.cghc.org

Area: New Orleans, Louisiana

General Information: The Common Ground Health Clinic (CGHC) is a nonprofit organization that provides free quality health care for the greater New Orleans community, and develops and provides programs to address community health care needs through collaborative partnerships. The CGHC offers primary health care, social work, acupuncture, herbalism, health care education for preventative self-care, HIV testing, referrals for specialty care and works to undo racism within its walls and beyond.

CGHC started on September 9, 2005, just days after Hurricane Katrina devastated the Gulf Coast, in response to the humanitarian disaster and lack of governmental response. Two community activists, Sharon Johnson and Malik Rahim, put out a call for healthcare workers and began a first aid station operating out of donated space in a mosque with volunteer "Street Medics." Nurses, physicians, herbalists, acupuncturists, EMTs, social workers and community activists came from around the world to volunteer, and the clinic was established. CGHC now relies mostly on volunteers from the local area, while still welcoming volunteers from around the country. The clinic is also serving the growing Latino population in New Orleans through the Latino Health Outreach Project (LHOP) which is a mobile clinic that exemplifies patient advocacy and helps to decrease barriers to accessing care.

CGHC is now implementing an Electronic Medical Record system, requiring more time to train and orient volunteers. We do welcome non-clinicians who can volunteer at least six weeks during the summer for front desk duty, data entry and programs support.

Skills: Interest in community organizing and outreach. Transcription, computer/IT and other office skills are helpful.

Contact: Antor Odu Ndep, Executive Director

COMMON GROUND RELIEF

1800 Deslonde Street   (504) 312-1729
New Orleans, LA 70117   www.commongroundrelief.org
                              commongroundvolunteers@gmail.com

Area: New Orleans, Louisiana, primarily in the Lower 9th Ward

General Information: Common Ground Relief (CGR) was formed in the wake of Hurricane Katrina to provide immediate aid to residents in the Gulf Coast area and provide long-term support in rebuilding the communities in just and sustainable ways. Because of the historic lack of investment in public infrastructure in this area, poor Black, Asian and Native American communities were the hardest hit by the storms. Hurricane Katrina brought to light the failures of government and official relief organizations to meet the basic needs for shelter, food and health care, exposing the long-standing injustices of racism, inadequate health care, education and housing, ill-designed levees, and police harassment and brutality in these communities.

CGR has had an average of 150–300 volunteers on the ground at any given time since the week of the storm, and has created a network of over 14,000 "Common Grounders" across the country, who continue to support CGR's programs from wherever they are.

CGR's goal is to rebuild sustainable communities in the Gulf Region by providing opportunities for displaced citizens to return to their homes through a broad range of volunteer projects including construction projects (gutting, deconstruction and rebuilding), free legal counsel offered in areas of contractor management, eviction and demolition prevention and civil and human rights, education initiatives that provide information about minimizing health risks associated with soil toxicity (offering free soil testing and reduced price bioremediation of contaminated sites), and educating the community about the importance of protecting and replanting the coastal ecosystem. We also have a mowing project to provide low cost grass cutting and maintenance to protect homes from being fined, condemned or confiscated, a gardens initiative to develop community and backyard gardens, a media collective which provides grassroots media coverage of events and activities to inform and inspire people in constructive social action, and the Common Support Crew (which runs the kitchen and maintains the grounds, facilities and vehicles).

We need volunteers who can make long-term or short-term commitments. Individuals and groups interested in our project areas are encouraged to apply online.

Skills: Volunteers with skills in construction and the legal fields are especially needed, but everyone is welcome.

Contact: Volunteer Coordinator

COMMUNITY DEVELOPMENT OUTREACH MINISTRIES (CDOM)

900 Washington Street, East   (304) 342-0029
Charleston, WV 25301

Area: Charleston, West Virginia and surrounding areas

General Information: Community Development Outreach Ministries (CDOM) is a United Methodist affiliated mission project. Our programs include housing rehabilitation (work teams); New Life Camp for young single mothers and their babies; Community Development through both Avesta Drive and Coal Branch Heights Community Centers, which provide after school programs for children and youth; and Heart and Hand House, which houses a food pantry, low-priced clothing store and an emergency bill payment program. We seek to work with people on a grassroots level and provide a connection between church and community. Volunteers could work with one or several programs.

Skills: Housing repair and rehabilitation skills are especially needed.

Contact: Executive Director

COMMUNITY FOR CREATIVE NON-VIOLENCE (CCNV)

425 2nd Street NW   (202) 393-1909
Washington, DC 20001   ccnv@erols.com

Area: Washington, DC

General Information: Community for Creative Non-Violence's (CCNV) Federal City Shelter is one of America's largest transitional homeless shelters and recovery communities. Located just blocks away from the U.S. Capitol in Washington, DC, the 1,350 bed shelter and its on-site service providers offer one free meal a day, social services, medical and legal clinics, job training and educational programs for residents of the building. The CCNV staff receive no salary and many are formerly homeless. Volunteers work in all shelter departments: the residents' floors, front desk, mail room, administrative office, clothing room, donations, special projects and events. CCNV welcomes international volunteers who are able to obtain proper visas and permits. Volunteers interested in progressive ideas and activism come to work with us from all over the world. Minimum age for volunteers is 18.

Volunteers receive room and board. Full-time summer internship placements are available for a three month period, or regular internship placements for six months.

Skills: Volunteers will complete a 3-week rotation orienting them to the facility and on-the-job-training in their work area.

Contact: Rico Harris

CONCERNED CITIZENS OF TILLERY

PO Box 61   (252) 826-3017
Tillery, NC 27887   tillery@aol.com

Area: North Carolina

General Information: Concerned Citizens of Tillery (CCT) is a grassroots organization established in 1978 committed to the struggle in the Black Belt South for social change, economic justice and political empowerment. CCT promotes the social, political and economic welfare of the citizens of Tillery, NC and the surrounding area to keep the community from dying out and to eradicate dependency on a system which has been created to keep African-Americans and other ethnic groups at the mercy of the traditional power structure. It offers assistance in organizing community groups and provides a support system for their survival, without destroying the groups' own autonomy.

CCT's established auxiliaries include Black Land Loss Fund/Black Farmers and Agriculturists Association, Halifax Environmental Loss Prevention (HELP), Health Committee, CCT's Youth Group and the Grown Folks Group. We emphasize the need for sustainable economic development and truly empowering education for youth, adults and senior citizens alike. Room, board and stipend (negotiable) are provided. Two month minimum commitment required. This job requires a great deal of cultural sensitivity, a commitment to social change and patience. Interns must be personable, flexible, mature and able to connect with people with a wide variety of backgrounds. Additionally, interns must be prepared to work in some isolation and to encounter racism and sexism in many forms. The transition from college life or "middle class status" to this community is extreme; a visit is required before making a final commitment to the job.

Skills: An intern's primary goal should be to educate and empower community members to define issues of concern for them and develop ways to address them.

Contact: Gary Grant, Director

CONNECTING TO ADVANTAGES (CtA)

61 East 4th Street, Ground Floor   (646) 226-3259
New York, NY 10003   connectingtoadvantages@gmail.com
www.connectingtoadvantages.org

Area: New York City (all boroughs)

General Information: Connecting to Advantages (CtA) was founded in January 2007 as an empowerment model for how organizations that serve low-income people can more effectively refer people to the government benefits for which they are eligible. We train low-income people who have accessed Public Assistance, SSI, Medicaid and Food Stamps, to do the referral work and become community leaders. The peer relationship of former clients, now volunteers, to new consumers empowers both groups. We seek social justice through this process, working to increase needed benefits for low-income and unemployed people and making them more accessible to people in need. We show people how to apply for food stamps, WIC, school meals, tax refunds, utility and rent subsidies, reduced telephone rates, day camps for their children and other needed services. We have seven sites throughout the five boroughs of New York City where CtA volunteers post themselves in areas where low-income people congregate for assistance and need advocacy help, such as in employment centers, medical clinics, food pantries and legal aid offices.

CtA teaches the volunteers the screening/application processes, rules and regulations of specific benefits, and effective client interaction.

CtA needs at least two 20 hour/week volunteer interns to fill particularly critical roles: a Site Coordinator, who would travel to each of the seven sites throughout NYC's boroughs to coordinate the volunteers that work at each site; and a Volunteers Coordinator, to recruit, train and supervise the growing staff of needed volunteers.

Skills: A certain level of computer, public speaking, writing, and reading comprehension skills are necessary. Volunteers are also needed who have Chinese and Spanish bilingual skills.

Contact: Judith Rubenstein, Project Director

THE COUNCIL OF CHURCHES OF GREATER BRIDGEPORT

1100 Boston Avenue, Building 5-A (203) 334-1121 Ext 243
Bridgeport, CT 06610 www.ccgb.org

Area: Greater Bridgeport, Connecticut

General Information: The Council of Churches of Greater Bridgeport is a faith-based, ecumenical social service agency with a 64-year history of working in partnership with local congregations and other community partners to educate children, feed the poor, support youth and families in crisis, guide ex-offenders to productive lives and build bridges of understanding and respect.

Volunteers are needed for these programs: CO-OP Center which assists between 500 and 600 persons as they transition from incarceration to the community each year. Volunteers work with experienced case managers drawing upon a diverse set of resources to help men and women with legal identification, secondary and higher education, learning a vocation, employment, and referrals for material and medical needs.

Project Learn is a neighborhood-based network of learning centers in partnership with local churches and community organizations. Volunteers work with elementary school age children from Bridgeport's most under served neighborhoods. Our after-school program emphasizes academics, offering homework help and tutoring, as well as healthy snacks, and positive recreational activities. The Kids for Kids Initiative adds a winning dimension to Project Learn. It engages inner city teenagers, often graduates of a Project Learn Center, to serve as

THE COUNCIL OF CHURCHES OF GREATER BRIDGEPORT

Photo: The Council of Churches of Greater Bridgeport

A volunteer works with children at Project Learn, an after-school program that provides homework help, tutoring, healthy snacks and positive recreational activities.

mentors for the younger children, offering teens a productive, mutually beneficial alternative to simply "hanging out" after school.

The Janus Center for Youth in Crisis assists youth in serious conflict with their families, schools or the juvenile court. Its mobile intervention team supports the program's 57-site Safe Place network, responds to the 24-hour Youth in Crisis Hotline, and provides counseling and connection to necessary services. Temporary respite care is a critical component of Janus Center services. Volunteers conduct periodic Safe Place audits at the 57 safe place sites, and do outreach at community events.

Skills: Experience in tutoring, computer instruction, art or music are each helpful.

Contact: Dan Braccio, CO-OP Center; Sean Campbell, Project Learn; Dale Holder, The Janus Center for Youth in Crisis

CUMAC/ECHO, INC.

223 Ellison Street
Paterson, NJ 07509

(973) 742-5518
volunteer@cumacecho.org
ww.cumacecho.org

Area: Paterson, New Jersey

General Information: CUMAC/ECHO works to alleviate hunger and its root causes for those in need in Paterson, Passaic County and northern New Jersey. CUMAC began in the late 1970s under the name of Center of United Methodist Aid to the Community Ecumenically Concerned Helping Others, when a Paterson schoolteacher recruited his church congregation to collect food for his obviously ailing students. As they met that need, a greater need in the city of Paterson became apparent, and a small pantry was born to provide emergency food to the local community. In our 30 plus years of operation, we have shortened our name to CUMAC/ECHO, but we have grown to a staff of 13, with our own 28,000 square foot facility and 2,000 volunteers annually. Wages for working people have continued to not keep up with cost of living in northern New Jersey, forcing increasingly more people to seek food assistance to make ends meet.

CUMAC heavily depends on its volunteers. During the Food Drive in October our volunteers helped sort over 26 tons of food. Volunteers also help with annual events and with day to day duties. We work with groups, individuals, churches and organizations.

Skills: Ability to work with a wide range of people. Warehouse experience appreciated.

Contact: Stephanie Ames, Volunteer Coordinator

DAMAYAN MIGRANT WORKERS ASSOCIATION

c/o Metro Baptist Church (212) 564-6057
406 West 40th Street, 3nd Floor contact@damayanmigrants.org
New York, NY 10018 www.damayanmigrants.org

Area: Jersey City, New Jersey; New York City

General Information: DAMAYAN Migrant Workers Association is an independent grassroots organization that upholds and promotes the rights and welfare of Filipino migrant workers, raising awareness and organizing around issues of migrant workers, particularly domestic workers. Damayan is a Filipino word that means helping each other. At the core of DAMAYAN is the leadership of highly committed Filipino domestic workers. Volunteers have the opportunity to learn step-by-step community organizing by working directly with experienced domestic worker organizers. Committed individuals can integrate into the Filipino community and take on various projects that broaden, build and strengthen our movement for dignity, justice and lasting peace. The work includes outreach to members and the community at large, coordinating follow-up to legal cases with volunteer attorneys, coordinating the network of volunteer health care advocacy volunteers, production of our membership newsletter, and many other areas of organizing. The out-migration of Filipinos who end up as overseas workers has its roots in the political and economic crisis in the Philippines—a crisis that causes poverty for 88% of the nation's population. The Filipino domestic workers in the U.S. often face economic exploitation, isolation and mental, physical and emotional abuse. DAMAYAN and its members believe that we must educate, organize and mobilize.

Skills: Interest in social justice; willingness to learn the skills of organizing; reliability. Ability to speak and understand a Filipino language is a plus, but not required.

Contact: Ana Liza Caballes, Program Coordinator

THE DES MOINES CATHOLIC WORKER COMMUNITY
PO Box 4551   (515) 282-4781
Des Moines, IA 50305   frank.cordaro@gmail.com
www.desmoinescatholicworker.org

Area: Des Moines, Iowa (Contact us for information about the 180 Catholic Worker communities in the US and other countries)

General Information: The Des Moines Catholic Worker Community, established in 1976, responds to the Gospel call to compassionate action as summarized by the Sermon on the Mount. In the spirit of the Catholic Worker tradition, we are committed to a simple, nonviolent lifestyle as we live and work among the poor. We directly serve others by opening the first floor of the Bishop Dingman House to those in need of food, clothing, bedding, a shower, a cup of coffee and conversation. We also engage in activities that foster social justice.

Dorothy Day and Peter Maurin founded the Catholic Worker movement in 1933 in New York City to effectuate the gospel teachings by living their promise of mercy, compassion, justice and love. Grounded firmly in believing in the God-given dignity of every person, the movement is dedicated to nonviolence, voluntary poverty and the Works of Mercy as a way of life.

The Des Moines community has four houses in the River Bend area of Des Moines. The houses are a stone's throw apart and include the Bishop Dingman House, where we do hospitality, day time drop in

THE DES MOINES CATHOLIC WORKER COMMUNITY

Volunteers set up the Saturday morning free produce store. Meals, showers, clothes and bedding are available to people in the community at the Bishop Dingman House.

Photo: Des Moines Catholic Worker Community

center for street people (homeless) and those in need, and the Phil Berrigan House, our peace and justice center.

We need all types of volunteers: people to help on a weekly basis for a few hours, short-term interns who live and get room and board and folks to actually join our community full-time. The best way to find out what is best for both any prospective volunteer and for the DMCWers is for a person to come visit us for a few days to see how it feels.

Contact: Frank Cordaro

DISABLED AMERICAN VETERANS

807 Maine Avenue SW
Washington, DC 20024

(202) 554-3501
cmoos@davmail.org
www.dav.org

Area: There are 172 locations in all states; contact headquarters or the website to find the hospital nearest you.

General Information: The Disabled American Veterans (DAV) has one sole purpose, building better lives for America's disabled veterans and their families. During the 1980s, travel benefit cuts left many veterans with no way to get to Department of Veteran Affairs (VA) medical facility treatment centers. Many were men and women who answered our country's call in times of war and lost limbs, sight, hearing, or good health. They often lived far from a VA hospital and existed on a small, fixed income, finding the cost of transportation to the hospital just too high. Many veterans were faced with choosing between going without needed treatment and skimping on food or other necessities to pay for transportation. Disabled Veterans in our nation should never face such options. Many who are hospitalized have no family or friends. Others are so far from home they rarely get visitors. DAV volunteers bring a touch of home, a personal contact with the world outside the hospital walls, giving the feeling that patients are remembered and that they are still a part of the community. You can help as a volunteer driver or office helper. We welcome anyone who would like to give themselves to improve the lives of our disabled veterans.

Skills: Volunteer assignments vary across the nation based on the needs at the local VA Medical Center. Requirements/skills will be based on your selected assignment and an orientation will be provided. Some facilities have a minimum age requirement for youth volunteers. If you wish to learn the types of assignments in your area, please contact us with your interests in mind.

Contact: Edward E. Hartman, National Director of Voluntary Service

E/THE ENVIRONMENTAL MAGAZINE

28 Knight Street
Norwalk, CT 06851

(203) 854-5559 Ext 109
info@emagazine.com

Area: Norwalk, Connecticut

General Information: E Magazine is a bimonthly, nonprofit environmental magazine dedicated to giving the environmental perspective on local, national and global issues. Founded in 1990, E Magazine is sponsored by Earth Action Network, a nonprofit organization located in Norwalk, Connecticut. Volunteers are needed year-round. Volunteer internships for students are available in the editorial and advertising departments. Hours vary from 10 to 40 per week, and internships usually last three months (often coinciding with the academic calendar). College credit is available.

Skills: Good command of the English language required for editorial internship; working knowledge of environmental issues and sense of humor desirable.

Contact: Brita Belli, Editor

EAGLE EYE INSTITUTE

14 Chapel Street
Somerville, MA 02144

(617) 666-5222
nature@eagleeyei.org
www.eagleeyeinstitute.org

Area: Massachusetts and in selected areas nationally through partner organizations running programs developed by Eagle Eye

General Information: Eagle Eye Institute (EEI), was founded in 1991 by MaJa Kietzke and Anthony Sanchez to provide access to hands-on exploratory learning programs on environmental topics, and a career-bridge to natural resource fields for urban people, with an emphasis on under-served urban youth and youth of color.

EEI uses the power of nature to transform urban youth through learning, stewardship and career-bridging programs that build awareness, develop responsibility and cultivate leadership in urban youth who traditionally do not have access to the natural world. Eagle Eye's core learning program is a one-day Learn About Forests™ program, which includes hands-on exploration, stewardship and teamwork. The Green Industry Career Pathway (GICP) career-bridging program introduces youth to careers in the natural resource fields and the green industry, after experiencing the Learn About Forests and Stewardship Days. Champions are the individuals or organizations who deliver Eagle Eye's programs to under served youth throughout the nation. They run Learn About Forests™, by bringing together natural resource professionals, natural sites and youth development organizations. Champions are located throughout Massachusetts, in Ithaca, New York and in Columbus, Georgia. We have various year-round and seasonal opportunities for volunteers of all ages.

Skills: Concern for and/or experience with youth and the environment are vital, as well as office/administration, technology, marketing, fund-raising/grant writing, event planning, education and editing.

Contact: Renee Toll-DuBois, Executive Director

EAST END COOPERATIVE MINISTRY

250 North Highland Avenue
Pittsburgh, PA 15206

(412) 361-5549
eecm@eecm.org
www.eecm.org

Area: Inner-city Pittsburgh, Pennsylvania

General Information: East End Cooperative Ministry (EECM) is made up of 47 congregations, including both Christian churches and Jewish synagogues. EECM is best known for its adult homeless and hunger programs such as a men's shelter, soup kitchen, food pantry, drop-in, Bridge housing and elderly services. In 2009 EECM faced a 22% increase in people thrown into homeless situations due to job and home loss. These programs depend on part-time volunteers. Full-time volunteers are critical to our children and youth programs, which serve individuals age 5 to 19. These projects include recreation, drug and alcohol prevention, gang prevention, high school intervention for students at risk for academic failure and drug or alcohol use. During the summer we run a large Summer Day Camp program with over 500 children. Volunteers receive training and work under the supervision of paid staff members.

Skills: Ability to work with youth.

Contact: Paul DeWalt

EASTERN FARM WORKERS ASSOCIATION (EFWA)

58 Beaver Dam Road   (631) 286-8004
Bellport, NY 11713

Area: Suffolk County, New York

General Information: Once featured in Edward R. Murrow's documentary, *Harvest of Shame*, Long Island's farm workers toil 12 hours a day in the hot sun, 7 days a week to produce our most essential commodity—food. Suffolk County, New York is known for its upscale summer resort towns and its great agricultural wealth, generating over $250 million annually in farm products. Yet despite their backbreaking labor, the vast majority of farm workers and their families cannot afford sufficient food, clothing or housing, and they lack access to health care and legal representation due to low wages and no benefits, resulting in hunger and ill-health. Although national statistics document that the life expectancy of a farm worker had dropped from 49 years of age to 41 years of age in the 20th century, overall conditions for farm workers in Suffolk County have improved due to EFWA's presence.

EFWA has garnered national renown throughout its 37-year history by using a proven method called "systemic organizing" that unites seasonal and migrant farm workers together with concerned citizens in the historic effort to build a strong, independent membership organization to fight for the political and economic advancement of farm workers and other low-income workers. The systemic method breaks down the work of the organizing drive into its component parts, such

EASTERN FARM WORKERS ASSOCIATION (EFWA)

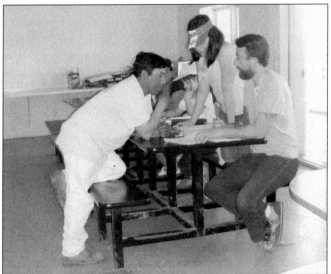

A team of volunteers visiting a farm labor camp explain the benefits of being an EFWA member and sign up a migrant worker. Volunteers also take benefit requests to fill workers' needs for medical and dental care and bring food, clothing, work boots and other necessities for distribution to EFWA members on the labor camps.

that volunteers can receive training on-the-job and take on an area of responsibility immediately. EFWA needs volunteers willing to make full-time or part-time commitments. Volunteers receive an orientation, training and classes by certified professional volunteer organizers.

Volunteers are needed for all aspects of organizing, including participating in Operation Camp Crew visits to the migrant farm labor camps; membership canvasses in low-income communities where seasonal farm workers live; newspaper production; organizing legal advice and preventive medical and dental benefit sessions; public speaking engagements; food and clothing distributions and more.

Skills: All skills are helpful and will be utilized, but no experience is necessary. Only a willingness to work and learn are required.

Contact: Joel Biddle, Operations Manager

EASTERN SERVICE WORKERS ASSOCIATION (ESWA)

1518 South Street   (215) 545-9055
Philadelphia, PA 19146

Area: Philadelphia, Pennsylvania

General Information: The all-volunteer organizing drive of Eastern Service Workers Association (ESWA) has led the fight for jobs with living wages and benefits, while opposing such destructive, anti-labor policies as workfare, enterprise zones, managed care and the privatization of our public health care resources. Association members have led successful efforts to stop mass evictions of low-income residents and have won victories against the municipal utility company to reduce and prevent life-threatening rate increases. ESWA provides on-the-job training in organizing the lowest-income workers and others concerned with the plight of the lowest income workers so that, united, we can attack the root causes of poverty, while helping one another survive. ESWA's 11-Point Membership Benefit Program for its constantly growing membership includes emergency food, clothing, preventive medical care, non-emergency dental care, "Know Your Law" sessions, job information and more.

The "City of Brotherly Love" offers no love, and no way to survive, for its poorest citizens. Philadelphia has lost over a quarter of a million production jobs in the last 30 years. Eighty-seven percent of the labor force does service work, with wages running 37% less on average than former manufacturing jobs paid, and the overwhelming majority have no access to health care.

The association publishes the *Philadelphia Service Worker* newspaper to keep members and friends informed about these struggles. Volunteers contact current and potential members through door-to-door canvasses in low-income neighborhoods; speak in schools, churches and community groups about how they can help; run food and clothing drives and distributions; help with our newspaper; and learn to build a strong organization of low-income workers and concerned residents working together to fight for living wage jobs and real solutions to the problems of hunger and poverty. Full-time and part-time volunteer organizers are needed immediately.

Skills: No previous experience is necessary. Learn organizing on-the-job, taught by professional volunteer organizers. Volunteers with skills in desk-top publishing and other graphic arts are also needed

Contact: Freyda Kornblum, Operations Manager

EDUCATIONAL CONCERNS FOR HUNGER ORGANIZATION (ECHO)

A volunteer works alongside an experienced staff member on ECHO's Florida test farm. On the farm, new agricultural techniques that can be used to increase food production in developing countries are demonstrated and tested.

EDUCATIONAL CONCERNS FOR HUNGER ORGANIZATION (ECHO)

17391 Durrance Road
North Fort Myers, FL 33917

(239) 543-3246
macton@echonet.org
www.echonet.org

Area: South Florida

General Information: Educational Concerns for Hunger Organization is an interdenominational Christian organization that seeks to provide sustainable hunger solutions for those working with the poor overseas. Those solutions include agricultural problem solving, providing seeds of nutritious plants, and an extensive training center in Fort Myers.

ECHO's 50-acre global farm demonstrates practical ideas for growing food under difficult conditions in tropical climates. The unique "living classroom" is visited by over 15,000 guests each year who either take a guided tour or stay for longer-term training at ECHO for overseas assignments with thousands of organizations from the Peace Corps to World Vision.

Currently over 350 volunteers work alongside staff and students in jobs that vary from planting, harvesting, cleaning, packaging and mailing seeds overseas to taking care of the farm animals (goats, rabbits, ducks, chickens, bees and fish). Many volunteers who live in the Southwest Florida area devote a half day per week. Some volunteers spend 3-6 months each year and come 3-5 days per week.

Skills: Because this is the global headquarters for ECHO, many talents are needed including data input, graphic design, library research skills, farm equipment repair, golf cart and vehicle maintenance, irrigation installation, fruit tree grafting, nursery workers, landscaping skills, cleaning, general household repairs, painters, plumbers, and even good cooks would be a blessing to prepare meals for students.

Contact: Marilyn Acton

EL CENTRO DE LA RAZA

2524 16th Avenue South
Seattle, WA 98144

(206) 957-4602
volunteer@elcentrodelaraza.org
www.elcentrodelaraza.org

Area: Seattle, Washington

General Information: As a voice and hub for the Latino community, El Centro de la Raza provides child and youth programs with a holistic approach to build self-sufficiency. Founded in 1972 through a peaceful community occupation, El Centro's philosophy centers on principles that help community members empower themselves, advocate for positive social change and struggle together for civil and human rights for all persons. We build unity across all racial and economic sectors, to organize, empower and defend our most vulnerable and marginalized populations, and to bring justice, dignity, equality, and freedom to all the peoples of the world. We serve over 18,000 children, youth, adults, families and seniors each year. Participants include low-income individuals from a variety of racial and ethnic backgrounds, many of whom speak English as a second language. El Centro provides 24 bilingual/multicultural programs and services, including child and youth programs, human services, education and skill-building programs, and community building and development opportunities.

We have several long-term volunteer opportunities available with Americorps Vista, Lutheran Volunteer Corps, Just Serve Americorps, and Jesuit Volunteer Corps. These positions are filled in the spring/summer, start in the fall and include working in the development office, in youth programs, and homeownership center. These positions are great for someone interested in learning about nonprofit development and fund-raising, events, volunteer coordination, community action, advocacy, social justice work and supportive services for low-income communities. We also have part-time, events-based volunteer positions to support our special events throughout the year.

Skills: An interest and commitment to providing service to communities of color, ability to work collectively in a team as well as independently and a completed Bachelor of Arts degree by the time position starts. Some positions may require Spanish proficiency.

Contact: Sarah Haywood, Volunteer Coordinator

EL COMITÉ DE APOYO A LOS TRABAJADORES AGRÍCOLAS (CATA)
The Farmworker Support Committee

PO Box 510   (856) 881-2507
Glassboro, NJ 08028   catanj@aol.com
www.cata-farmworkers.org

Area: New Jersey, Pennsylvania and the Delmarva Peninsula (Delaware and Maryland)

General Information: El Comité de Apoyo a los Trabajadores Agrícolas (CATA), The Farmworker Support Committee, is a migrant farm worker organization that is governed by and comprised of farm workers who are actively engaged in the struggle for better working and living conditions. CATA's mission is to empower and educate farmworkers through leadership development and capacity building so that they are able to make informed decisions regarding the best course of action for their interests. Since 1979, CATA has been committed to facilitating the organizing of farm workers, based upon the belief that only through organizing and collective action will farm workers be able to achieve social, economic and environmental justice.

CATA's program, based on the Popular Education Methodology, develops leadership skills and capacity building among farm workers. CATA works in coalition with many groups including labor, environmental, religious, academic/student, and progressive organizations on a local,

EL COMITÉ DE APOYO A LOS TRABAJADORES AGRÍCOLAS (CATA)
The Farmworker Support Committee

Photo: CATA

Volunteers, supporters and members of CATA fight for better working and living conditions for vulnerable and marginalized populations. By taking the day off from work and refusing to spend money, immigrant communities demonstrate their contribution to the local and national economy.

regional, national and international level. CATA provides opportunities for young people to be exposed to social justice issues.

Full and part-time volunteers contribute to CATA's mission by sharing their talents and developing new skills along the way. CATA matches up the interests and abilities of the person with the needs of the organization so that both can benefit from the experience.

Skills: Possess a strong commitment to working alongside farm workers as they strive to improve their working and living conditions. Be culturally sensitive and have some experience with multicultural issues. Spanish language skills, newsletter production, organizing experience, research skills, and secretarial skills are helpful. Training provided as needed.

Contact: Nelson Carrasquillo, Executive Director

EMMANUEL HOUSE/HOME FOR THE ELDERLY

475 Evergreen
Ann Arbor, MI 48103

(734) 669-8825
Fax: (734) 669-8261

3341 Hillside Drive
Ypsilanti, MI 48197

(734) 528-9031
ehypsi@juno.com

Area: Ann Arbor, Michigan

General Information: Emmanuel House is a ministry to older adults who are not able to live alone and who may have no other housing options. Our society often does not value seniors, especially those who find themselves alone, ill or living in poverty. Emmanuel House seeks to extend God's love to those in greatest need by providing a home where they can live comfortably and with dignity, viewed as a source of blessing to those who have the privilege of serving them— not a burden. The home is the result of a vision and desire on the part of the Servants of God's Love, a Catholic Religious Community in Ann Arbor, to bring God's love to those in greatest need. In collaboration with the Roman Catholic Diocese of Lansing and Hope Medical Clinic of Ypsilanti, the sisters lead an all-volunteer staff in the care of residents. The staff consists entirely of volunteers. The residents are not charged for the services they receive at Emmanuel House.

Volunteers do everything needed to care for the residents and the household: cooking, cleaning, yard work, personal care and maintaining the positive atmosphere of unconditional love for those in need. The length of service may vary from two to four weeks, to a year or more. Volunteers receive room and board in exchange for 40 hours of service per week. A family from the community volunteers to act as a sponsor for every live-in volunteer, and provides guidance and support.

Skills: No special skills are needed. The level of care provided to residents by volunteers is the same they would receive from a family member if they were able to provide it.

Contact: Sister Mary Zielinski

EMMAUS HOUSE/HARLEM

160 West 120th Street
New York, NY 10027

(212) 749-9404
Fax (212) 749-5363

Area: Harlem, New York City

General Information: Founded in 1965 by Father David Kirk, Emmaus is a healing and empowering faith-based community that seeks to build new lives through the goals of personal change, social action, works of mercy and education for the disenfranchised. Our current focus is on outreach services to the Harlem poor community and building a strong network with other services in the city as gentrification and our economic climate is making life more and more difficult for people with little means. We do not accept government monies and rely on donations from individuals, churches and grants.

We welcome volunteers who believe that supporting others can make a difference in all of our lives. Volunteers need to be open minded, tolerant, kind and patient. We welcome both men and women, religious or lay, people who believe that hope can be infused into any abject situation. You would come to help with our weekly Food Pantry that serves poor neighbors, to help with Outreach Referrals to other service agencies, to join in on the Traveling Kitchen that serves hot soup and blankets to those people on the streets from our van, to help with weekly Fellowship Meals and to share Literacy Skills. You might just come to listen to someone's life story. We are open to ideas for developing new services and are looking to give more attention to the elderly, the environment and animal care.

Skills: The main "skill" we are looking for is an open heart and knowing that we are our brothers' and sisters' keepers.

Contact: Julia Demaree

EPISCOPAL URBAN INTERN PROGRAM

260 North Locust Street
Inglewood, CA 90301

(310) 674-7700
euip@euip.org
www.euip.org

Area: Los Angeles, California

General Information: The Episcopal Urban Intern Program (EUIP) invites young adults from all over the country who wish to serve those in need, to be involved in working for justice and to live in an intentional Christian community. EUIP interns work in various social service agencies in and around Los Angeles. Placements can include working with a homeless service project, a food distribution center, assisting in schools for students with special needs, as well as work doing advocacy and other organizing for change. The program runs for a full year from August to August. Interns work a full 40 hours per week and are also expected to participate in building a strong community with one another and their host church. Interns are provided with housing, health/dental insurance and a monthly sustenance stipend.

Skills: College degree preferred. Dedication to social service and spiritual growth, hold a valid driver's license, be between the ages of 21 and 30, in good physical and emotional health.

Contact: The Reverend Ruth Monette

EQUAL JUSTICE USA

20 Jay Street, #808   (718) 801-8940
Brooklyn, NY 11201   info@ejusa.org

Area: New York City

General Information: Equal Justice USA launched Moratorium Now! in 1997 seeking to foment a grassroots dialogue on how unjustly the U.S. death penalty is applied, and to organize grassroots pressure to stop executions. Our goals are: to bring about a national moratorium on executions, and to deepen public understanding about how the death penalty is applied and abuses human rights. As of April 2007, over 4,600 organizations have signed on to the call "not one more execution," including 142 local governments. Many have held an educational debate about how the death penalty is applied before passing a formal moratorium resolution. Momentum builds as people become activated. Grassroots organizing to get resolutions passed will serve to strengthen and enable state moratorium activist networks, working toward enacting legislation or executive orders imposing a moratorium on executions.

Skills: Good written and verbal communication skills are necessary. Flexibility; ability to work in a team dynamic; organizing and fundraising skills are helpful.

Contact: Volunteer Coordinator

EVICTION INTERVENTION SERVICES (EIS)

1233 Second Avenue   (212) 308-2210 Ext 207
New York, NY 10065   development@eisny.org
                                 www.eisny.org

Area: New York City

General Information: The mission of Eviction Intervention Services (EIS) is to prevent homelessness in New York City by promoting and supporting housing for low-to-moderate income tenants, many of whom are the elderly and families with children. EIS programs include: legal and social services, tenant education, housing maintenance assistance, elder abuse prevention, Mitchell-Lama conversion

EVICTION INTERVENTION SERVICES

Photo: Eviction Intervention Services

A volunteer prepares for a demonstration to promote affordable housing for low-income families.

assistance, and our telephone housing hotline. There is a vital necessity for homelessness prevention, tenant advocacy, the protection of affordable housing stock, housing advocacy and education on behalf of New York City tenants. EIS is the only focused housing organization on the Middle and Upper East Side of Manhattan. The homelessness prevention programs that EIS provides save taxpayers millions of dollars annually. In the past year EIS attorneys prevented the homelessness of 550 families, including 1,200 children. We believe that prevention is the most economically and humanely sound strategy to save the affordable housing stock.

EIS volunteers are responsible for much of what we, as an organization, are able to accomplish. Qualified volunteers have founded and headed new projects, helped clients to navigate the housing court process, organized special events and much more.

Skills: Lawyers, paralegals and law students are needed. Social workers and students are particularly needed for community organizing and canvassing and the Anti-Eviction Team, including phoning, home visits and advocacy. Artists and photographers are also needed. Other helpful skills include writing, researching, organizing events and general office work.

Contact: Audrey Tanner, Executive Director

FAMILY FARM DEFENDERS (FFD)

1019 Williamson Street #B   (608) 260-0900
Madison, WI 53703   familyfarmdefenders@yahoo.com
                         www.familyfarmdefenders.org

Area: Madison, Wisconsin and other areas of the Midwest

General Information: We are a organization with national and overseas membership, with most of our members located in the Midwest. The mission of Family Farm Defenders (FFD) is to create a farmer-controlled and consumer-oriented food system based upon democratic institutions that respect and empower local people in their quest for justice and dignity. To this end, FFD supports sustainable agriculture, farm worker rights, animal welfare, consumer safety, fair trade, and food sovereignty. It is FFD's belief that healthy, safe, accessible food is a basic human right and that all communities should be able to control their own food system.

FFD addresses the ongoing dairy crisis; challenges neoliberal "free trade" agreements and the global corporatization of the organic industry; educates and activates the public about the threats posed by the National Animal Identification System (NAIS); and campaigns against the commercialization of genetically modified organisms (GMOs) and other dangerous food technologies (nanotech, irradiation, cloning). We also promote a global moratorium on agrofuel development, and support grassroots initiatives to relocalize food/farm economies through: farm fresh atlases, local food/fair trade directories, alternative exchange networks (time banks, local currencies), land trusts, community garden expansion, food policy councils, farm to school and buy local programs. Our members are family farmers and our major outreach is to consumers to gain their support in our fight for food sovereignty. We also work closely with labor activists, indigenous communities, global justice activists, and faith-based organizations.

FFD volunteers assist with tabling at public events, mailings to members, doing research for fact sheets and policy papers, writing grants and press releases, as well as helping to represent the organization at forums, conferences, and so forth. We can easily accommodate flexibility in volunteer time commitment.

Skills: Especially desirable skills include ability to speak and/or translate other languages (Spanish, French, Portuguese), computer programming, website design, grant writing, and media experience.

Contact: John E. Peck, Executive Director

FARM LABOR ORGANIZING COMMITTEE (FLOC)

1221 Broadway Street   (419) 243-3456 Ext 3
Toledo, OH 43609   bmaya1@floc.com
       www.floc.com

Area: North Carolina, Ohio, Mexico

General Information: The Farm Labor Organizing Committee (FLOC) is a labor union for farm workers. Since its inception in 1967, it has fought to improve working and living conditions for migrant farm workers. FLOC has negotiated unprecedented multi-party contracts among workers, growers and major processing companies, including Campbell Soup Co., Heinz, Vlasic and Dean Foods. In 2004, FLOC won an unprecedented agreement with the North Carolina Growers Association after a five-year boycott of Mt. Olive Pickle Products. The agreement covers 8,000 guest workers and about 1,000 farms in North Carolina. Intensive leadership development, organizing and educational activities with farm workers and recent immigrants are handled by the Ohio and North Carolina office year-round. FLOC is also a leading force in the struggle for the rights of new immigrants in the U.S. Full-time or part-time volunteers are welcome for organizing and/or administrative organizing duties. Training provided. Work related expenses covered. Stipend negotiable.

Skills: A heart and spirit to create change in the lives of farm workers, ability to communicate well with a variety of people, e.g., labor, religious groups, educators and media. Basic computer literacy and conversational Spanish useful. Strong commitment to farm workers obtaining just wages, benefits and decent living conditions. Good organizational skills are helpful.

Contact: Beatriz Maya, Secretary Treasure

FARM SANCTUARY

PO Box 150   (607) 583-2225
Watkins Glen, NY 14891   intern@farmsanctuary.org
       www.farmsanctuary.org

Area: New York and northern California

General Information: Farm Sanctuary is a farm animal protection organization, incorporated in 1986, that works to expose and stop cruel practices of the "food animal" industry through research and investigations, legal and institutional reforms, public awareness projects, youth education, and direct rescue and refuge efforts. Farm

Sanctuary shelters in Watkins Glen, New York and Orland, California provide lifelong care for hundreds of rescued animals and we educate visitors about the realities of factory farming.

The Volunteer Internship Programs at Farm Sanctuary's New York and California Shelters provide individuals with unique opportunities to advocate for and connect with farm animals, establish community with like-minded people, and acquire valuable knowledge of the various facets of animal protection. Housing is provided for all interns who work at our California and New York Shelters. Occasionally, off-site internship opportunities may be available; in these special cases, housing is not provided. Internships require a one to three month commitment. All applicants must be 18 years or older and committed to Farm Sanctuary's goals and programs. Intern space is limited; early application is recommended. Housing provided. Internships are available year-round. 8 hours a day, 40 hours per week.

Skills: No experience necessary for most positions; see individual listings for full details about each position. Qualified applicants will be 18 years or older with a strong personal commitment to Farm Sanctuary's goals and veganism. Interns live a vegan lifestyle for the duration of their internship.

Contact: Don Walker, Intern Coordinator

FOOD FIRST/INSTITUTE FOR FOOD AND DEVELOPMENT POLICY

398 60th Street
Oakland, CA 94618

(510) 654-4400
foodfirst@foodfirst.org
www.foodfirst.org

Area: Oakland, California; translators can be located elsewhere

General Information: Food First is a nonprofit, membership supported, people's think tank and education-for-action center. Our work highlights the root causes and value-based solutions to hunger and poverty around the world, with a commitment to establishing food as a fundamental human right. Food First/Institute for Food and Development produces books, reports, articles and DVDs, plus interviews, lectures and workshops for public policy makers, activists, the media, students, educators and researchers. Interns assist with research, publicity, book production, clerical and fund-raising work. Minimum is 15 hours per week for a minimum of eight weeks. Current projects include: sustainable agriculture success stories, campaign

THE FOOD PROJECT

Photos: The Food Project

With The Food Project, over 3,000 youth and adults work together to grow over 250,000 pounds of vegetables each year that will go to local soup kitchens, shelters and farmers' markets to help feed hungry people.

A young volunteer learns how to plant vegetables on one of The Food Project's farms.

The Food Project engages young people in personal and social change through sustainable agriculture by placing them in responsible roles. Participation in the project leads to building inspired, diverse and productive youth communities.

against agrofuels, campaign against the Gates/Rockefeller funded "a green revolution for Africa (AGRA)," debunking the myth that genetically modified organisms can feed the world, advocating food sovereignty, demystifying international banking and trade institutions and pushing for greater transparency and democratic process in decision making within those institutional structures.

Skills: Internet and library research skills; self-motivated and well organized; excellent communication skills. Ability to translate from and into French, Spanish and Portuguese helpful, but not required.

Contact: Marilyn Borchardt, Development Director

THE FOOD PROJECT

10 Lewis Street
Lincoln, MA 02130

(781) 259-8621 Ext 30
participate@thefoodproject.org
www.thefoodproject.org

Area: Beverly, Boston, Lincoln, and Lynn, Massachusetts (Greater Boston & North Shore)

General Information: Our mission is to grow a thoughtful and productive community of youth and adults from diverse backgrounds who work together to build a sustainable food system. We produce healthy food for residents of the city and suburbs, provide youth leadership opportunities and strive to inspire and support others to create change in their own communities. Since 1991, The Food Project has built a model of engaging young people in personal and social change through sustainable agriculture. Each year, we work with over a hundred teens and thousands of volunteers on over 35 acres of farmland and urban food lots in and around Boston, Massachusetts. To build a new generation of leaders we place teens in unusually responsible roles, with deeply meaningful work.

We grow over 250,000 pounds of vegetables each year and that requires a lot of hands. The Food Project depends on over 3,000 youth and adults to assist us in growing that food. Volunteers are essential to helping us achieve our goal of providing sustainably and locally-grown food for hungry people in shelters and residents of Boston's inner city and suburbs.

We need volunteers on our farms in Lincoln, Boston and on the North Shore during the months of April–June and September–November. We work on the land on regularly scheduled mornings, rain or shine (an up-to-date calendar can be found on our website). Groups normally spend one morning on the farm, but have been scheduled to stay and work with us for as long as two weeks in the past. Individuals often join us once a week for the entirety of the growing season. The work varies with each season, but includes planting, transplanting, weeding, soil preparation, harvesting and clean-up. The vegetables that you help to grow will feed hungry people at soup kitchens and shelters in Greater Boston, supply our inner city farmers' markets, and be distributed through our Community Supported Agriculture program.

Skills: No specific skills or prior experience with farming is required. Training provided on site for field work.

Contact: Outreach Coordinator

FORTUNE SOCIETY

29-76 Northern Boulevard
Long Island City, NY 11101

(212) 691-7554 Ext 329
jkefalas@fortunesociety.org
www.fortunesociety.org

Area: New York City

General Information: Staffed primarily by ex-prisoners, the Fortune Society is a not-for-profit community-based organization dedicated to educating the public about prisons, criminal justice issues and the root causes of crime. We also help ex-prisoners and at-risk youth break the cycle of crime and incarceration through a broad range of services. Tutors are needed and are asked to make a minimum commitment of two one-hour sessions a week for six months. There are also many other volunteer opportunities. Volunteer positions available include counselor assistant, clerical assistant in court, advocacy department or counseling services unit, IT support assistant and assistance in publication of *Fortune News*.

Skills: If you have special talents, we can find a way to use them. Willingness to learn is essential.

Contact: John Kefalas or Denise Dalton, Volunteer Coordinators

FOURTH WORLD MOVEMENT/USA

7600 Willow Hill Drive
Landover, MD 20785

(301) 336-9489
nationalcenter@4thworldmovement.org
www.4thworldmovement.org

Area: Washington, DC and Maryland; New York City; New Orleans, Louisiana; Appalachia, southwest Virginia

General Information: Fourth World Movement fosters partnerships with families in persistent poverty and other members of society to recognize each person's efforts and the role they play in overcoming social exclusion. This work includes cultural and educational projects in disadvantaged neighborhoods; long-term research into poverty and the efforts made to combat it; public information campaigns, including the regular publication of *Tapori Children's Network,* which encourages friendship among children from different backgrounds, and *Fourth World Journal.* Experimental internship projects serve as an introduction to the work of the Fourth World Movement. Interns may participate in activities with families and children living in poverty in New York City, New Orleans, Appalachia or Washington, DC. Group living with full-time volunteers at Fourth World Movement/USA centers is part of the internship experience. Interns must be at least 19 years old, have a high school diploma or GED and one year of college or work experience.

Skills: Applicants should be ready to learn from the experiences of the very poor and each other.

Contact: Volunteer Coordinator

FRANCISCAN CENTER

85 Mattis Road
St. Helena Island, SC 29920

(843) 838-3924
franctr@islc.net
www.islc.net/~franctr

Area: St. Helena Island area in South Carolina

General Information: Franciscan Center is a service center founded 22 years ago by two Franciscan Sisters of Philadelphia, who continue to provide the leadership for the center, along with over a hundred volunteers from around the region. Strongly rooted in the community, it is dedicated to serving the needs of the economically poor, the marginalized and the oppressed. A wide variety of programs aid a rich mixture of the area's traditional black Gullah, white and growing Hispanic communities, in addition to the seasonal farm workers in the vast tomato fields. The Center runs a benefits program including emergency food, clothing, household items and bedding. They also assist the community through providing help with immigration problems, adult English classes, academic assistance for children from kindergarten through high school, and emergency transportation, as well as advocacy for medical care, schooling, doctors' offices and jail visits, and other services. The center partners with families to repair and modify their homes for accessibility. Volunteers are needed to work with the educational programs, the transportation program, the food and clothing distribution program and all other aspects of the Center's work.

The Center also needs a volunteer with writing skills for a special assignment to record and write the history of how the Center was founded and its accomplishments to date.

Skills: Teaching, driving and other skills are needed; none required.

Contact: Sister Sheila Byrne, Co-Director

FRANCISCAN VOLUNTEER MINISTRY

PO Box 29276   (215) 427-3070
Philadelphia, PA 19125   fvmpd@aol.com
                                         www.franciscanvolunteerministry.org

Area: Inner cities of Wilmington, Delaware; Camden, New Jersey and Philadelphia, Pennsylvania

General Information: The Franciscan Volunteer Ministry provides a setting for volunteers to grow in faith, love and hope by serving the poor and working for social justice. We aim to foster Gospel-based communities as a witness to our faith through prayer and a simple lifestyle. We encourage our volunteers as lay people to work with Franciscan Friars and Sisters in various ministries with the poor and marginalized.

Must be 18 years or older, with a desire to share the mission of St. Francis of Assisi by bringing a spirit of love and care to those in need. Acceptances are on a rolling basis, so please apply early. Room and board, medical insurance, stipend, loan deferment and partial loan forgiveness are provided. Volunteers live in community with other volunteers, four to six volunteers per site, approximately 15 volunteers total. The program term is mid-August through mid-July of the following year. Ongoing, hands-on training is provided at each site.

Skills: No special skills required.

Contact: Katie B. Sullivan, Program Director

FRIENDS OF SEASONAL AND SERVICE WORKERS (FSSW)

1400 East Burnside Street   (503) 231-4826
Portland, OR 97214

Area: Northern Oregon

General Information: Friends of Seasonal and Service Workers (FSSW) is a free and voluntary support effort that, since 1982, has assisted organizations of low-income workers and their families from the perspective that those in need know best how those needs should be filled. If the lowest-paid workers are assured of an income and access to services adequate to meet their daily needs, then all workers will benefit. FSSW's support network generally reaches throughout the northwestern U.S., including Alaska. However, in times of emergency or special needs, FSSW has extended its support to grassroots efforts nationwide. FSSW is responsive to the needs of the membership of organizing drives of seasonal workers, farm workers, temporary and service workers and other low-income workers who have built their own organizations to seek solutions to poverty conditions.

The primary form of assistance to these organizations is to bring together low-income workers and their families with students, professionals, clergy, homemakers, business owners and other concerned community residents working towards the eradication of poverty. FSSW does not accept government funding, leaving it free to serve the interests of the lowest-income workers in the community without influence by funding sources with "strings attached." Volunteers receive training in arranging and conducting speaking engagements in churches, community organizations, and schools; producing newspapers; teaching classes in labor history and more.

Volunteer organizer trainees learn to take charge of specific areas of responsibility and are taught by experienced full-time labor and community organizers who have run such activities as informational picket lines, emergency disaster relief services, transportation and distribution of resources to organizations of low-income workers and testimony at public hearings. Be part of the action.

Skills: A desire to learn how to help rebuild our communities from the ground up is the only requirement. All skills are welcome; needed skills are taught through on-the-job training.

Contact: Volunteer Coordinator

FRIENDS OF THE THIRD WORLD, INC.

611 West Wayne Street   (260) 422-6821
Fort Wayne, IN 46802   fotw@igc.org
         www.friendsofthethirdworld.org

Area: Sierra Vista, Arizona; Bloomington and Peoria, Illinois; northeast Indiana

General Information: Friends of the Third World started in 1972

with a group of students and teachers who wanted to address hunger and poverty, and grew to an organization concerned with educating ourselves and others about the root causes of poverty and possible solutions. We operate a recycling center, purchase directly from cooperatives of low-income persons in 35 countries, provide employment training in five areas and sponsor a graphic arts training center. Most work is done by full- and part-time volunteers with the support of several long-term staff.

We operate nonprofit fair trade shops marketing crafts, clothing, gourmet foods such as coffee, tea, nuts and chocolate. We have also begun a project to produce a northeast Indiana ethnic directory that lists organizations, businesses and people that provide services or goods needed by low-income people from other parts of the world such as doctors who speak their language, translation services, ethnic grocery stores and a wide range of any other needs. Full-time volunteers are asked to commit at least three months and are provided room and board in a house with several other staff.

Skills: Newsletter editing, researching products and producers, printing press operator, marketing of crafts, computer entry/publishing, accounting software, building repair, painting, mechanics and carpentry, driving recycling truck, graphic design and artwork, event organization including international fairs and researching for an upcoming directory.

Contact: Mary Ann Waltz, Volunteer Coordinator

GI RIGHTS HOTLINE

c/o Center on Conscience & War   (877) 447-4487
1830 Connecticut Avenue NW   www.girightshotline.org
Washington, DC 20009

Area: Nationwide, with offices in Fairbanks, Alaska; Arcata, Oakland, San Diego, San Francisco and Santa Cruz, California; Storrs, Connecticut; Gainesville, Florida; South Bend, Indiana; Amherst and Cambridge, Massachusetts; New York City; Fayetteville, North Carolina; Portland, Oregon; Austin, Texas; Salt Lake City, Utah; Seattle, Washington; and Washington, DC. Branches expected to start soon in Albuquerque, New Mexico; Oklahoma City, Oklahoma; and El Paso, Texas.

General Information: GI Rights Hotline Network is a cooperative effort of nonprofit, non-governmental counseling agencies who provide information to members of the military about discharges, grievance and complaint procedures and other rights under military law. A majority of our callers are seeking to get out of the military. Primarily, the Hotline does phone counseling, but e-mail and face-to-face counseling also occurs. In the last several years the Hotline Network has received over 40,000 calls a year. Calls to the toll free number are routed to the various offices based on the area code of the caller. GI counselors answer phones, call people back, do follow-up, make referrals, send out material and assist callers in submitting appropriate paperwork to their military command. Counselors get initial training, day-long or longer, and continue training by pairing up with an experienced counselor for mentoring. Working together with other counselors allows the sharing of both information and support, the main things we also offer to callers. An Advisory Committee, with the assistance of other working committees, coordinates the work of the network.

Skills: Ability to listen empathetically, work with others in an office situation, consistency, responsibility and attention to detail. Familiarity with the military, as a veteran for example, is an asset, but not essential.

Contact: Bill Galvin

GLOBAL EXCHANGE

2017 Mission Street, 2nd Floor   (415) 255-7296
San Francisco, CA 94110   interns@globalexchange.org
                                          www.globalexchange.org

Area: San Francisco, California and worldwide

General Information: Global Exchange is an International Human Rights Organization and operates from an education and action resource center. We work to ensure our members and constituents are empowered locally and connected globally to create a just and sustainable world. Global Exchange takes a holistic approach to working for international human rights; we realize in order to advance social, environmental and economic justice we must transform the global economy from profit-centered to people-centered, from currency to community.

Global Exchange tackles critical issues, such as: the War in Iraq, oil consumption and global climate change, the exploitation of the global economy, and creation of local green economies. Acting in alliance with partner organizations, our local and national campaigns help build strong mass movements for global change. Global Exchange campaigns include Fair Trade; Fair Treatment & Sweatfree Communities; Freedom from Oil; Peace: Stop the Next War Now; Local Green Economy; Mexico, Trade & Migration; Rights Based Organizing; and Reality Tours: Experiential Travel. Global Exchange operates a fun yet structured internship program during the summer; interns work closely with program staff on campaigns and programs, develop skills while working, and learn on the job. Interns should be able to offer 20–40 hours per week from June–August. Interns will work directly with a Global Exchange staff person.

Skills: We expect interns to bring some knowledge and experience to the organization. Self-motivated, creative and willing to make a set time commitment based on project needs; able to assist with basic office work.

Contact: Internship Coordinator

GLOBAL INFORMATION NETWORK

146 West 29th Street #7E
New York, NY 10001

(212) 244-3123
newsdesk@mindspring.com
www.globalinfo.org

Area: New York City

General Information: Global Information Network, a nonprofit, non-partisan news organization that spotlights Africa and the developing world offers internships to both students (undergraduate, graduate and doctoral) and recent graduates. The starting date is flexible based on the intern's schedule. Interns work closely with our editors to discover, research and write stories that provide a more diverse picture of Africa—its achievements; community organizations; interactions with western countries; new authors and political leaders; and its arts and culture. We strongly encourage interns to develop their own story ideas which are sent to subscribers in the U.S. and abroad.

Skills: A good grounding in world history, strong news-writing skills and be familiar with issues impacting minorities. We encourage international candidates to apply. Spanish speakers are welcome to write for our Spanish wire. Volunteers with marketing or development skills needed.

Contact: Volunteer Coordinator

GOOD SHEPHERD VOLUNTEERS

25-30 21st Avenue
Astoria, NY 11105

(718) 943-7488
www.gsvolunteers.org
gsv@goodshepherds.org

Area: Domestic: Los Angeles, California; New Jersey; New York City; International: Paraguay, Peru

General Information: Good Shepherd Volunteers (GSV) collaborates

GOOD SHEPHERD VOLUNTEERS

Photo: Good Shepherd Volunteers

A volunteer in Los Angeles, California plays with children whose parents participate in a community domestic violence prevention program.

with the Sisters of the Good Shepherd to provide full-time volunteers with the opportunity to work in social service ministries and to use their God-given talents serving women, adolescents, and children affected by poverty, violence, and neglect. Developing relationships with the marginalized of our world empowers volunteers to grow in knowledge and faith that inspire them to lead a life of seeking justice. The basic elements of the GSV philosophy are the value of the individual, simplicity, social justice, community and spirituality. GSV requires one-year commitments for domestic placements and two years for international. Applicants of all races, ethnic backgrounds and orientations are encouraged to apply. Must be at least 21 years or older, be a high school graduate and have some college education or work experience. (See page 212 for international program.)

Skills: International placements have a language requirement of conversational Spanish.

Contact: John Alvarez, Program Coordinator

GREATER CLEVELAND HABITAT FOR HUMANITY

6920 Union Avenue   (216) 429-1299
Cleveland, OH 44105   volunteer@clevelandhabitat.org
                                www.clevelandhabitat.org

Area: Neighborhoods in the Greater Cleveland area

General Information: Greater Cleveland Habitat for Humanity is a Christian-based organization, which develops opportunities for all God's people to act out their faith. By working in partnership to eliminate substandard housing, we enable families and volunteers to improve lives. We help by building homes, strengthening neighborhoods and reweaving communities. We rely upon volunteers to participate in all areas of our mission. Volunteers help build new houses, organize donated items for our ReStore, assist with office projects, work in our wood shop and facility, and help get other individuals and groups involved. We welcome mission groups throughout the year, and host a summer high school mission program, called Inward Bound. Cleveland Habitat provides a "hand up" rather than a "hand out" opportunity to many families and individuals.

In the city of Cleveland over 23,000 families live in what the federal agency, Housing and Urban Development (HUD), considers worst case housing situations. Since 1987, Cleveland Habitat has helped to reshape communities that had not seen any new development in over 50 years and make the dream of homeownership a reality for many.

Skills: Volunteers 14 and older welcome. Construction volunteers must be at least 16 years of age to participate on a live job-site. We are always looking for skilled construction volunteers particularly with carpentry, drywalling, electrical, plumbing, heating, or siding experience.

Contact: Melissa M. Frei, Volunteer Programs Manager

GREEN AMERICA

1612 K Street, NW, Suite 600   (202) 872-5307
Washington, DC 20006   internships@greenamericatoday.org
                             www.greenamericatoday.org

Area: Washington, DC

General Information: Green America is the nation's leading green economy organization. Green America works with individuals, businesses, and investors to build a more co-operative and socially responsible economy. We strive to educate our members to use their buying power more effectively to create social and environmental change. Green America serves as a link between socially conscious consumers and responsible businesses by providing multiple resources to our members: National Green Pages, a directory of products and services for people and the planet; *Green American Magazine*, discussing the social and environmental issues of our times; and *Real Green*, a newsletter full of easy ways to green all aspects of your life. Internships are available in Marketing, Publications, Member Services and Development Programs, Climate Action, Fair Trade, Responsible Shopper, Web Design, Green Business Network and Media. Our internships are designed for college students and graduates seeking to gain practical work experience.

Skills: Interns are involved in developing programs, researching and writing, and general organizational strategy; experience in any of the above is helpful.

Contact: Volunteer and Intern Coordinator

HABITAT FOR HUMANITY OF GREATER MIAMI

3800 NW 22nd Avenue (305) 634-3628
Miami, FL 33142 carlos.beron@miamihabitat.org
www.miamihabitat.org

Area: Homestead, Overtown and Liberty City in Miami-Dade County, Florida

General Information: Founded in 1989, Habitat for Humanity of Greater Miami is an ecumenical Christian ministry striving to build decent, affordable homes for low-income families and to eliminate poverty housing in Miami-Dade County. Volunteers help construct the homes for the families selected or help with various other opportunities. Every year, approximately 35 low-income families build their own Miami Habitat homes with the help of volunteers. Unlike other builders who rely on government support, we rely on the concern of the community for the poor and their willingness to share themselves and their time to help break the cycle of poverty housing. Miami Habitat also helps to restore displaced victims in the aftermath of devastating natural disasters by rebuilding houses in impacted communities.

Volunteers bringing a group must schedule ahead of time. All prospective volunteers are required to attend a volunteer orientation meeting, generally held twice a month. We welcome volunteers of all skills and interests; opportunities exist for site hosts, workshop leaders, legal

HABITAT FOR HUMANITY OF GREATER MIAMI

Photos: Habitat for Humanity of Greater Miami

Over 2,000 volunteers came together during Blitz Build 2008 to build ten homes in two weeks. Here, volunteers, including the future owner, help to raise the walls of the home.

Volunteers work with future residents to help them build their own homes. Habitat for Humanity's goal is to eliminate poverty housing in Miami. All skill levels are welcome in this effort. All that is needed is a willing heart and willing hands.

experts, clerical assistants, congregational liaisons and fund-raisers.

Skills: To work on the construction site, only a desire and the patience to learn the skills are necessary. For all other work, we welcome willing hearts and willing hands of every skill and interest.

Contact: Carlos Beron, Volunteer Coordinator

HEIFER INTERNATIONAL LEARNING CENTERS

c/o 55 Heifer Road   (501) 889-5124
Perryville, AR 72126   lcvol@heifer.org
                            www.heifer.org/volunteer

Area: Heifer Ranch, Perryville, Arkansas; Hidden Villa, Los Altos Hills, California; Overlook Farm, Rutland, Massachusetts

General Information: Heifer International, since 1944, has worked to combat hunger and poverty. By providing livestock and training, Heifer assists people in achieving sustainable income and food security in an environmentally sound manner. In the U.S., Heifer International's education programs use full- and part-time volunteers to help increase understanding of issues related to hunger and poverty. Volunteers at our three Learning Centers hold major responsibilities and perform tasks such as: facilitating team-building activities, global village programming, leading tours, hosting the visitors' center, livestock care, gardening, facilities maintenance and administrative support. Age limitations and time commitment vary, according to each Learning Center.

Skills: Volunteers of various backgrounds and skills are essential in all facets of the Learning Center operations. Training and supervision are provided in each assigned area. Residential volunteers live on-site and dedicate months, even an entire year to full-time volunteering.

Contact: Learning Center Volunteer Manager

HOMES OF HOPE

3 Dunean Street   (864) 269-4663
Greenville, SC 29611   Fax: (864) 269-6235
                            www.homesofhope.org

Area: Upstate South Carolina

General Information: Homes of Hope provides safe, affordable housing for low-income or homeless families and individuals while also providing job training and mentoring for men overcoming drug and alcohol addictions. We serve Greenville County and focus most of our housing construction within the city of Greenville's special emphasis neighborhoods as identified by city hall, and in coordination with each neighborhood association to ensure that we match each community's vision for sustainability.

Homes of Hope works with participants to create personal housing stability and homeownership road maps for all housing recipients and for the men in our mentoring and construction trade training internship. We provide training in financial literacy, education opportunities, and increased job skills. Families identified as low-income households who need affordable housing are housed in a safe, quality Homes of Hope home first, and their finances are stabilized through affordable rent. Our Asset Development and Property Management team works with each family on their individual road map to housing stability, all the while working to prevent a cycle of constant risk of chronic homelessness through financial stability and improved life skills. Classes and training offered for all housing participants include classes taught by community professionals on personal budgeting, credit repair, healthy grocery shopping on a budget, preparing for a mortgage, and tips for daily living. These individual efforts, along with our work alongside entire neighborhoods, help to uplift communities who are striving for economic stability and pride.

Volunteers at Homes for Hope help the men in our program to build our homes. This work includes painting, putting up sheet rock/siding, laying carpet, landscaping etc. We also have a donated Mobile Home Project. These homes are renovated on site in Greenville. We welcome groups who schedule with us in advance, as well as individuals.

Skills: No previous experience required.

Contact: Tonya McCutchen, Community Relations Director

H.O.M.E.S., INC. (HOUSING ORIENTED MINISTRIES ESTABLISHED FOR SERVICE)

65 Bentley Avenue
Whitesburg, KY 41858

(606) 632-1717 Ext 304
greggjhawkins@bellsouth.net
www.homesneon.com/pages

Area: Letcher, Knott and Floyd Counties, southeast Kentucky

General Information: Our mission is to expand opportunities available to residents to obtain adequate affordable housing accommodations by constructing new homes and rehabilitating, reconstructing and repairing existing homes to provide decent, safe, sanitary, affordable, owner-occupied and rental housing in Letcher, Knott and Floyd Counties, for low-income individuals and families who otherwise would not be able to find or afford a suitable place to live.

We host volunteer groups of up to 70 for one week service mission trips in the spring, summer and fall. We ask you to work with us, not for us, as we try to eliminate sub-standard housing in our part of the Appalachian mountain poverty zone. Short- and long-term opportunities are available.

Skills: Skilled volunteers, especially carpenters, plumbers, electricians, masons and painters, are always welcome, but you don't have to be skilled, we will teach you.

Contact: Greg Hawkins, Volunteer Coordinator, Donald Profitt, Executive Director

HOUR CHILDREN

36-11A 12th Street (718) 433-4724
Long Island City, NY 11106 lmanzione@hourchildren.org
www.hourchildren.org

Area: Long Island City (LIC), Queens, New York

General Information: Hour Children is committed to compassionate and loving care of children of incarcerated women. Our outreach includes support and empowerment for mothers upon reunification with their families. We serve 100–145 women and their children through the course of the year. Our programs include supportive housing for mothers and children; post release services; day care services; job development and training; mentoring for children of incarcerated parents; advocacy, parenting classes; domestic violence programs; food pantry and community outreach program; family reunification counseling program; and a thrift shop/furniture outlet for the community.

Each month more and more women are released from correctional institutions and more children are uprooted to rejoin their mothers. These families must cope with family reunification and the search for housing and employment with very little support. Hour Children is continually challenged to meet the demands for its services resulting from the increasing numbers of women in prison. In the past decade, the female prison population escalated by a third. The number of women in state and federal prisons is over 63,215 and 76% of women in prison have one or more children. The majority will return as primary caregivers. The name of the organization was chosen to reflect the children's lives which are dictated by the "hour" of the mother's arrest, the "hour" they have for a visit with her and the "hour" of her return.

Volunteers provide core services to the organization, both in prison and in the community, enabling Hour Children to limit full-time staff to about 25. Aspects of our volunteer programs include: Mentoring a child, ages 7 to 17, who has a parent in prison; assisting in our day care center; working in our thrift shops; tutoring children or adults; assisting with office work; providing legal assistance; counseling and connecting employment trainees to employment; driving families/children to visit moms in NY State prisons in Westchester County.

Skills: Useful skills: maintenance skills, computer skills, administration, child care, arts/crafts, tutoring, sales, and mentoring. Attorneys are also needed.

Contact: Linda Manzione, Program Director

HOWARD AREA COMMUNITY CENTER
7648 North Paulina
Chicago, IL 60626

(773) 262-6622
(774) 262-6645
sloellbach@howardarea.org
www.howardarea.org

Area: Chicago, Illinois, specifically the Rogers Park neighborhood

General Information: The Howard Area Community Center (HACC) assists low-income individuals and families to stabilize and develop their lives and the skills necessary to become productive community members. HACC programs provide full-day care and early childhood education; after-school academic enrichment; workshops on life and social skills; employment-related services; recreational activities; a full-day summer camp; and a second chance for youth who dropped out of high school to earn a diploma. HACC also assists adults to increase their reading and math skills, earn a GED, or become more proficient in English; and provides emergency services, case management, and other support services.

The Howard Area Community Center is located in Rogers Park, one of the most racially, ethnically, and economically integrated communities in Chicago and the nation. Rogers Park contains pockets of severe poverty, with more that 22% of all households reporting annual incomes of less than $15,000. Close to 95% of the children who attend our two neighborhood elementary schools come from low-income families.

HOWARD AREA COMMUNITY CENTER

A volunteer tutor works with children in the computer lab at one of HACC's after-school programs. Tutors are just one of the many types of volunteers at HACC.

Volunteers are needed to work with kids in our Family Center or Youth Programs; help teachers with lessons, lead an art or music project; provide after-school mentoring or tutoring for a child. Additionally, volunteers are needed to provide Adult Literacy tutoring; help with resume workshops and mock interviews; work as a receptionist and greet clients. Volunteer tutors require a commitment to two 6-hour training sessions and a 6-month commitment to tutor once a week for 2 hours. Volunteer drivers are also needed. Volunteers must be at least 18 years old.

Skills: People with all educational and experience levels from high school students through retired Ph.D.s are needed. If you are willing to work and have fun, you are qualified.

Contact: Sue Loellbach, Volunteer Coordinator

IFCO/PASTORS FOR PEACE

418 West 145th Street
New York, NY 10031

(212) 926-5757
ifco@igc.org
www.pastorsforpeace.org

Area: New York City; Caribbean; Central America; Mexico

General Information: The Interreligious Foundation for Community

Organization (IFCO), was founded in 1967 as an ecumenical agency to advance the struggles of oppressed people for justice and self-determination. IFCO initiates its own grassroots projects and provides technical support, networking, training and fiscal agency services for progressive community-based organizations working on projects that range from education and advocacy to urban youth activism, protesting police brutality, supporting improved healthcare and more.

Pastors for Peace is an action/education project of IFCO that offers concerned U.S. citizens an opportunity to demonstrate and enact an alternative foreign policy based in justice and mutual respect. Since 1988 IFCO/Pastors for Peace has organized humanitarian aid caravans and human rights delegations to Chiapas, Mexico; Nicaragua; El Salvador; Guatemala; Honduras and Cuba—delivering life-giving aid and organizing at home for a more just policy toward our neighbors in the hemisphere. With our Caravans to Cuba, we reject the unconstitutional and immoral law that requires a license for acts of common humanity. Our faith and international law do not permit us to behave in such an immoral, unjust and inhumane way. The Declaration of Independence and the First Amendment of the Constitution were written by men and women who refused to submit their conscience to licensing.

Skills: We seek interns with computer skills and ability to work in a busy office and with diverse communities.

Contact: Lucius Walker, Executive Director

ILLINOIS STEWARDSHIP ALLIANCE
401 West Jackson Parkway   (217) 528-1563
Springfield, IL 62704   www.ilstewards.org

Area: Illinois and midwestern United States

General Information: Illinois Stewardship Alliance promotes ecologically sustainable, economically viable, socially just local food systems through policy development, advocacy and education. Founded in 1974 as the Illinois South Project, the organization was created to oppose the unfettered strip mining that was occurring in much of the state, and now a 34-year-old statewide membership organization works to promote environmental stewardship throughout the state. ISA is primarily working with small and independent farmers who utilize sustainable and organic practices, to educate the public and a new generation of farmers about the benefits and opportunities of local food systems.

Eighty percent of Illinois is farmland, including some of the most fertile soil on earth. Most of the farmland in the state is currently enrolled in the federal farm subsidy program to grow corn and soybeans, industries dominated by large agribusiness corporations. Over the last 50 years the decline of rural towns and villages throughout the state parallels the decline of the local farmers' share of the food consumer dollar, from over 40% to less than 20% according to the USDA.

There are over 467,000 Illinois households categorized as "food insecure" within veritable "food deserts," or pockets of scarcity, extending from inner city neighborhoods to rural communities, surrounded by bountiful farm fields.

Volunteers are needed in all aspects of ISA's work including community outreach. Internships can be arranged for a summer, or from six months to a year; a monthly stipend may be available. Interns can work full- or part-time with staff in a specific program area and share administrative responsibilities. Duties may include research, writing, working with constituents and participating in organizational management.

Skills: Good communications and research skills, some background in natural resources, agriculture, economics or political/social science studies and issues, interest in working with an agricultural-based organization and at least one year of college.

Contact: Lindsay Record, Executive Director

INTERFAITH VOICES: A PUBLIC RADIO SHOW

3502 Varnum Street   (301) 699-3443 Ext 111
Brentwood, MD 20722   maureen@interfaithradio.org
                                    www.interfaithradio.org

Area: Brentwood, Maryland (Washington, DC metro area)

General Information: Interfaith Voices, a public radio show promoting tolerance and respecting diversity, is a weekly hour-long "magazine" show. It covers religion as news, including the many ways religion intersects with public policy, culture and foreign affairs. It does not proselytize or try to convert, but seeks to inform, educate and foster a spirit of dialogue. Programs deal with the full range of faith traditions. It is heard on more than 40 public and community stations in the U.S. and Canada, and is growing rapidly. The workplace is fast-paced, with a democratic office environment where volunteers/interns truly make a difference. Those who apply should have a high learning curve, dedication, good humor and an interest in progressive religious issues, broadcasting and social justice.

Skills: A range of skills can be used: computer skills and web page management, help with producing the show and booking guests, assisting with fund-raising and grant-writing, outreach to potential new stations, clerical skills, database management. A talented volunteer can get airtime to do interviews.

Contact: Maureen Fiedler, Host

INTERRELIGIOUS FELLOWSHIP FOR THE HOMELESS

479 Maitland Avenue
Teaneck, NJ 07666

(201) 833-8009
nwoods@irfhomeless.org
www.irfhomeless.org

Area: Bergen County, New Jersey

General Information: Interreligious Fellowship for the Homeless (IFH) shelters working families who have lost their homes and helps them return to independent living. Families receive transitional housing for a period of 18 to 24 months when apartments are available and case management to help restore their financial stability and improve their credit rating. IFH also serves a full meal every day for about 150 individuals, provided by the congregations in Bergen County. We run a two week summer camp for the children who are or have been in our programs. Bergen County is an extremely affluent area, where most people cannot believe there are any homeless individuals or families. We discriminate against nobody. Founded in 1986, IFH is the only organization in Bergen County helping working homeless families to overcome personal crisis.

Volunteers are needed in all the areas of our work, including after-school activities with children at the shelter, staffing the shelter and the kitchen work for the meals program, as well as administrative work, outreach and support work for the organization.

Skills: Experience in any of the above work is helpful, but not required. Any specialized skills volunteers bring to us will be put to use.

Contact: Nancy S. Woods, President of the Board of Trustees

INTERRELIGIOUS TASK FORCE ON CENTRAL AMERICA

3606 Bridge Avenue
Cleveland, OH 44113

(216) 961-0003
irtf@igc.org
www.irtfcleveland.org

Area: Cleveland, Ohio

General Information: The InterReligious Task Force on Central

America (IRTF) is a Cleveland-based, interfaith group that promotes peace and human rights in Central America and Colombia. People of faith and conscience founded IRTF after the 1980 execution of four U.S. church women in El Salvador by U.S.-trained soldiers. The work of IRTF exposes and transforms the root causes of injustice as a tribute to the dreams of the church women—for peace and a just society. IRTF educates, advocates and organizes for peace and human rights, economic justice and aid to Central Americans and Colombians. We work to end U.S. policies, corporate actions and consumer behaviors that undermine these aspirations both here and abroad. Programs and campaigns include: Child/Sweatshop Labor, Jubilee/Debt Cancellation, Fair Trade, Colombia Immigrant Rights, Economic Globalization, School of the Americas, Rapid Response Network (RRN) on Human Rights and Youth and Young Adult Leadership Development.

We provide volunteers a supportive setting to learn about Central America/U.S. relations, peace and justice issues and local and national efforts for peaceful change.

Skills: Good communication skills and interest in Central American issues. No Spanish is required, but it wouldn't hurt.

Contact: Sarah Sommers, Administrative Coordinator

IRAQ VETERANS AGAINST THE WAR

630 Ninth Avenue, Suite 807 New York, NY 10036

(646) 723-0989
ivaw@ivaw.org
www.ivaw.org

Area: New York City and local chapters across the country

General Information: Iraq Veterans Against the War (IVAW) was founded by Iraq war veterans in July 2004 at the annual convention of Veterans for Peace (VFP) in Boston to give a voice to the large number of active duty service people and veterans who are against this war, but are under various pressures to remain silent.

Today, IVAW members are in 48 states, Washington, D.C., Canada, and on numerous bases overseas, including Iraq. IVAW members educate the public about the realities of the Iraq, and now Afghanistan, wars by speaking in communities and to the media about their experiences. Members also dialogue with youth in classrooms about the realities of military service. IVAW supports all those resisting the war, including Conscientious Objectors and others facing military prosecution for their refusal to fight. IVAW advocates for full funding for the Veterans Administration, and full quality health treatment (including mental health) and benefits for veterans when they return from duty.

The roles volunteers can fill vary by location, but in general we need help with outreach, fund-raising, event planning, media, graphic and web design. We also work closely with physical and mental health advocates, as well as artists, to provide direct services and therapy to veterans and their families. Full- and part-time volunteers are welcome to apply.

Skills: Knowledge of the military and/or veterans' issues is desirable but not required. Graphic design or web design skills are welcome. Experience with writing press releases, media outreach, and press conferences is a plus.

Contact: Find your local chapter on our website or call our national office

JACKSON AREA MINISTRIES

PO Box 603   (740) 286-1320
Jackson, OH 45640   (888) 237-3141

Area: Appalachian counties of southeast Ohio

General Information: Jackson Area Ministries (JAM) summer work camps offer adults and high school seniors the opportunity to give service to the Jackson area communities and churches. Volunteers have the opportunity to accomplish a specific project as a member of a work group and the chance to develop new relationships during the course of the service. Work camps are held in the summer from late June through August. Groups must make a request to work in February.

The work projects are designed to assist seniors and the poor, individuals and/or families in their home surroundings. We also do community projects for small churches. The projects vary according to the local host church assignment, the type of community and age of your group. Examples of past projects are: painting, building handicap ramps, minor building repairs, conducting Vacation Bible School, working in clothing banks, senior citizen centers, food pantries and gardening/yard work.

Skills: A variety of minimal skills are required. Most projects involve painting, carpentry and working cooperatively.

Contact: Rev. Robert E. Robinson

JAKE THOMAS LEARNING CENTRE

7575 Townline Road   (519) 445-0779
R.R. 1, Wilsonville   jtlc@worldchat.com
Ontario, Canada N0E 1Z0   www.jakethomaslearningcentre.ca

Area: On the Six Nations Reserve in Grand River Country; south of Toronto, Ontario and west of Buffalo, New York

General Information: The Jake Thomas Learning Centre is an independent experiential learning centre embracing the Iroquois peoples' lifeway. Founded in 1993 by the late hereditary Cayuga Chief Jake Thomas and his wife, Yvonne, the Centre's mission is to preserve and promote Iroquoian culture within the community and throughout the world. The Centre offers a series of language workshops in Cayuga, Mohawk and Onondaga; traditional teaching seminars on the Great Law, the Code of Handsome Lake, the Thanksgiving Address, the Creation Story, Healing Circles, Sweats, Medicine Walks, Traditional Counseling, and other traditional events, skills and indigenous onkwehonwe knowledge. The Library Resource Centre offers a full inventory of native specific library materials (audiovisual) language resources, all of which will be available on the Internet.

Skills: Experience welcome in: fund-raising, marketing, events organizing, speaking, research, secretarial, administrative/business management, program/curriculum developing are needed. Also needed are people with practical skills in Iroquois crafts, culinary, canning, carpentry, maintenance, auto mechanics, construction workers; gardening and farming, harvesting maple sap, graphic arts, printing, photography, writing, newsletter layout, indigenous sports/recreation. Educators, social workers, youth workers needed. Anyone able to help organize and digitize the Jake Thomas Archives.

Contact: Yvonne Thomas, Executive Director

JEWS FOR RACIAL AND ECONOMIC JUSTICE

135 West 29th Street, Suite 600   (212) 647-8966 Ext 13
New York, NY 10001   lane@jfrei.org
                              www.jfrei.org

Area: New York City

General Information: Jews for Racial and Economic Justice (JFREJ) is a membership organization founded in 1990 that pursues racial and economic justice in New York City by advancing systemic changes that result in concrete improvements in people's daily lives. JFREJ engages individual Jews, key Jewish institutions, and key Jewish community leaders in the fight for racial and economic justice in partnership with people of color, low-income people and immigrant communities in New York City. Through community organizing, political education and media advocacy, we educate ourselves and others.

Shalom Bayit: Justice for Domestic Workers is a campaign to involve Jews in the struggle for dignity, respect and better working conditions for domestic workers (nannies, house cleaners, and elder care providers). We organize in and with synagogues and by talking with employers about signing a standard employment contract; being present at rallies, actions and lobby days, and bringing the issues into Jewish synagogues and institutions. The Housing Justice campaign works in alliance with the Good Old Lower East Side (GOLES) to advocate for responsible development of the Seward Park Urban Renewal (SPURA) site and in alliance with Asian community organizations to ensure the community driven development of the East River Waterfront. We organize by knocking on doors to activate community members around our campaign and planning living room gatherings to further build commitment and educate these stakeholders.

Volunteers are integral to the planning of our community organizing campaigns; they learn how to facilitate conversations, do one-on-one meetings, strategize campaign goals, and represent JFREJ to ally organizations; they participate in actions, community building activities, and help plan alternative Jewish holiday celebrations.

Skills: No experience necessary, training provided.

Contact: Lane Levine, Community Organizer

JUBILEE PARTNERS

PO Box 68   (706) 783-5131 Ext 104
Comer, GA 30629   Fax: (706) 783-5134

Area: Comer, Georgia (east of Atlanta)

General Information: Jubilee Partners is a Christian community committed to serving poor and oppressed people. Our work includes several areas of service: resettling refugees, peacemaking, working against the death penalty and assisting various Nicaraguan projects. Volunteers are involved in teaching ESL, child-care, maintenance, gardening and office work. Study sessions are bi-weekly. Minimum age 19. Sessions are January to May; June to August; September to

JUBILEE PARTNERS

Volunteers teach English and other skills to refugee children who have come to the U.S. with their parents from many places throughout the world, such as Afghanistan, Eritrea and Ethiopia.

Photo: Jubilee Partners

December. Room and board plus $10 per week provided. Current refugees are from various African countries, as well as Burma.

Skills: Willingness to work where needed and an interest in Christian community. Maintenance, construction, auto mechanics and gardening skills are always needed.

Contact: Robbie Buller, Volunteer Coordinator

KAIROS DWELLING

2945 Gull Road
Kalamazoo, MI 49048

(269) 381-3688
kairosdwelling@aol.com

Area: Kalamazoo, Michigan

General Information: Kairos Dwelling is an inter-faith project providing physical care, emotional support and spiritual sustenance for the terminally ill person and their loved ones in a loving and compassionate environment. When people are living with a terminal disease, it is important to have fewer distressing symptoms, the security of a caring environment and the assurance that they and their family will not be abandoned. With the support of hospice services and our core staff of volunteers we can offer room, meals and 24-hour care giving to up to four guests. Priority is given to those with the greatest needs. There is no charge for our guests. We do this because we believe in the intrinsic value and dignity of each person and family.

Volunteers are provided with a 12-hour training program, and following the training will make a year commitment of one shift a month (minimum). All live-in volunteers make a commitment of 40 hours minimum a week for two months to one year. In return they will be given room and board with no other stipend.

Skills: A background in health care is helpful but not necessary. Bring a loving and compassionate heart.

Contact: Sue Shaw

KANATSIOHAREKE MOHAWK COMMUNITY

4934 State Highway 5   (518) 673-5356
Fonda, NY 12068   www.mohawkcommunity.com

Area: Northern New York State

General Information: For over 200 years the traditional Mohawk people of the Iroquois Confederacy have held a dream in their hearts that someday they would return to the beautiful Mohawk Valley. The dream came true in 1993. Today we farm, cultivate and preserve this land with the hope others will follow in our steps to ensure the continuation of our people. Since 1997 the community has offered workshops, lectures on Iroquois culture and Mohawk language classes during the summer months. We invite you to discover our culture and traditions by looking at our website. Information is provided on our annual festival as well as all our fund-raising activities, including a craft store and a bed & breakfast. Also, please explore and find out how you can help us as we attempt to teach our children about their heritage.

Skills: Enthusiastic and hard-working volunteers, fund-raisers, proposal writers, farm hands, events organizers and people with experience in agricultural and renewable energy.

Contact: Elvera Sargent

KOINONIA PARTNERS

1324 Georgia Highway 49 South   (229) 924-0391
Americus, GA 31719   hospitality@koinoniapartners.org
                                  www.koinoniapartners.org

Area: On our 573-acre farm outside Americus, Georgia

General Information: Koinonia is an intentional Christian community open to people of all faiths. Our community mission is to offer opportunities for spiritual renewal and to work for social justice by serving our neighbors and participating in projects that foster peace and reconciliation throughout the world. Interested people may apply to come as Visitors or as Community Interns. Visitors stay for up to two weeks and may share in work, study, devotions and service, common meals and community events. There is a suggested donation for visiting but we do not exclude based on income. Community Internships range from one to four months; sessions begin in January, February, June, and September. Community Interns share in community life, living and working together, and may receive a small weekly stipend. Depending on the season, our work can include baking and shipping mail order products; farm, garden, and grounds work; office tasks; serving children and seniors at our community outreach center; and helping with the upkeep of our buildings and the homes of our neighbors.

Skills: Skilled tradespeople and land workers are especially needed, but you are welcome regardless of your skill level.

Contact: Hospitality Coordinators

LACASA, INC.

202 North Cottage Avenue (574) 533-4450
Goshen, IN 46528 www.lacasagoshen.org

Area: Northern Indiana

General Information: LaCasa, Inc. was organized by area churches and incorporated in 1970 to provide housing and other human services for the benefit of Goshen's low- to moderate-income households. Born out of concern for the living conditions of migrant farm workers, LaCasa has grown into a full-service community housing development corporation with a staff of twenty-five. LaCasa's wide range of programs assist low- to moderate-income families. Our programs include the Home Ownership Center which offers classes and one-to-one counseling for pre-purchase of a home, analysis of credit and how to improve credit scores, reviews for possible grant and other assistance, and help with loss mitigation or foreclosure prevention. LaCasa administers savings accounts with matching funds and offers mortgage and rehab loans; Community Building and Organizing which helps neighbors identify community issues and set goals for improvements, and work with city government, local businesses, churches, and other partners to achieve their goals; Immigration and Language Services which provide assistance with paperwork for immigrants from any country who qualify for an immigration benefit under the

LA CLÍNICA DEL PUEBLO

Photos: La Clínica del Pueblo

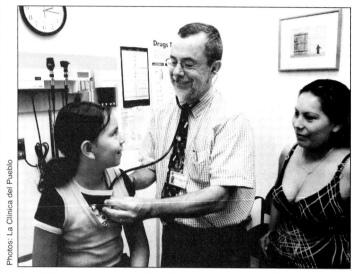

La Clínica provides culturally appropriate health services to over 7,500 people in the Latino community who otherwise could not afford it.

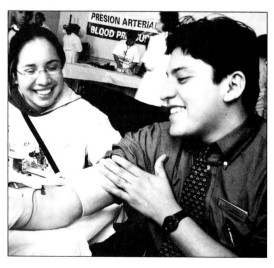

A volunteer draws blood at a weekend health fair held at a local church.

U.S. law; Housing Development which renovates housing through Help-A-House℠, which connects volunteers and donations with projects in Goshen that support safe and affordable housing. Volunteers repair the homes of low- to moderate-income homeowners and assist LaCasa in maintaining its affordable rental properties.

Skills: Volunteers are needed for assistance with housing renovations. Experience in painting, stripping woodwork, demolition, or landscaping is very helpful. A skilled LaCasa staff person works with volunteers.

Contact: Kate Irelan, Volunteer Coordinator

LA CLÍNICA DEL PUEBLO

2831 15th Street, NW
Washington, DC 20781

(202) 462-4788
volunteer@lcdp.org
www.lcdp.org

Area: Washington, DC metropolitan area

General Information: La Clínica del Pueblo was founded by volunteers in 1983 as a direct response to the linguistic and cultural barriers to health care for Latino immigrants in the District. Today it provides primary care, mental health care, social services, interpreter services, comprehensive HIV care, health education and advocacy for men, women and children throughout the Washington, DC metropolitan area. La Clínica's mission is to provide culturally appropriate health services to persons in the Latino community regardless of their ability to pay. La Clínica served over 7,500 individuals over the past year, providing more than 35,000 health services. Volunteers at La Clínica range from doctors to lay health educators and file clerks. Most jobs are long-term engagements, not one-time tasks. Volunteers must be in high school or older and be able to work independently.

Skills: Licensed medical professionals are always welcome, as are interested community members. Direct service volunteers must be able to speak Spanish.

Contact: Volunteer Coordinator

L'ARCHE MOBILE, INC.

151 South Ann Street
Mobile, AL 36604

(251) 438-2094
larchmob@hotmail.com
www.acan.net/~larchmob

Area: Mobile, Alabama

General Information: A Christian community where people with developmental disabilities live together as a family with non-handicapped persons. L'Arche Mobile has four homes and an activity centered program. We are looking for men and women 18 years of age and older who desire to create homes where faithful relationships based on forgiveness and celebration are nurtured. We honor the unique value and vocation of each person and view building relationships in community as a sign of hope and love. A one-year commitment is desirable.

Skills: Willingness to foster personal growth and share life in community with others. Must be 18 years of age or older with a minimum of a high school diploma or GED.

Contacts: Marty O'Malley, Director or Barbara Gaddy, Administrator

LEND-A-HAND CENTER, INC.

3234 Kentucky 718   (606) 542-4212
Walker, KY 40997   lahc8@juno.com

Area: In the Stinking Creek area, Knox County, Kentucky

General Information: Lend-A-Hand Center, Inc. is a private community service organization located on a farm in southeastern Kentucky, off the Cumberland Gap Parkway between the cities of Barbourville and Pineville. Irma Gall and Peggy Kemner, co-directors, began the work in 1958 in order to assist the people along Stinking Creek by utilizing good farming techniques, providing Sunday school and day camp programs, providing medical services (doctors, clinic sessions for people who do not have insurance or medical cards, transportation of medical patients and midwife services), and by setting an example of compassion, service and cooperation with one another.

Skills: A good attitude is the most important skill. A driver's license and a good driving record is required.

Contact: Irma Gall, Co-Director

LENOX HILL NEIGHBORHOOD HOUSE

331 East 70th Street   (212) 744-5022
New York, NY 10021   www.lenoxhill.org

Area: New York City

General Information: Founded in 1894, Lenox Hill Neighborhood House helps those in need on Manhattan's East Side. Each year, the House serves over 20,000 people of different generations, cultures, means and ethnic groups who live, work or attend school on Manhattan's East Side: children, teens, low-income families, unemployed people, older adults and homeless and former homeless people, among others. Volunteers enable Lenox House to respond effectively and personally to the needs of the community. They bring a variety of skills, knowledge and experience that enrich our programs and activities. Volunteers work with a team of professional educators, social workers and administrators. You will meet many new, interesting people while improving the community. Some volunteers serve on an ongoing basis while others help with short-term assignments or special events.

Skills: All skills are welcome.

Contact: Anthony Snowden, Volunteer Coordinator

LORETTO VOLUNTEERS

590 East Lockwood Avenue   (314) 962-8112
St. Louis, MO 63119   bmecker@lorettocommunity.org
                                                www.lorettovolunteers.org

Area: Denver, Colorado; rural Kentucky; St. Louis, Missouri; New York, New York; El Paso, Texas; Washington, DC

General Information: Our goal is to give volunteers an opportunity to share in the mission of the Loretto Community to work for justice and act for peace. Volunteer placements are determined on an individual basis. They have included a leadership program for low-income women, an empowerment program for women involved in the criminal justice system, a gardening/job development project for the homeless, a medical clinic for the homeless, a bilingual school, Catholic Charities' housing programs and emergency assistance centers, organic gardening, after-school/summer program for low-income children, ministry to gay and lesbian community, interfaith radio programming, and assisting Loretto's NGO representative at the UN.

Volunteers receive room and board, a stipend, health insurance and assistance with transportation as needed. Volunteers may be eligible for the AmeriCorps Education Award. Length of service: three months to one year.

Skills: Willingness to learn, gospel values, appropriate education/training for assignment, commitment to social justice, compassion and a sense of humor.

Contact: Barbara Mecker, Loretto Volunteer Coordinator

LOWER NINTH WARD HEALTH CLINIC

5228 St. Claude Avenue   (504) 309-0918
New Orleans, LA 70117

Area: New Orleans, Louisiana

General Information: The Lower Ninth Ward Health Clinic was created after Hurricane Katrina to provide community-based, culturally sensitive healthcare services to this New Orleans neighborhood. Already a medically under served area even before the storm, many healthcare professionals still have not returned and the Ninth Ward's Charity Hospital has not been reopened.

Co-founders, and local residents, Patricia Berryhill, RN, and Alice Craft-Kerney, RN, transformed Berryhill's home into the clinic. After overcoming enormous bureaucratic and financial hurdles, the clinic opened its doors in February 2007. It is currently the only full-time primary healthcare presence in the Lower Ninth Ward and does not refuse care to anyone. Patients from the greater New Orleans area, including St. Bernard, Jefferson, St. Tammany and St. James parishes, also seek health care services at the clinic. The Health Clinic offers the best healthcare possible in the most cost effective manner possible. Patients receive comprehensive medical checkups, disease management (Diabetes, Hypertension, Heart Disease, Asthma), HIV screenings and referrals to specialists. The clinic's holistic, personalized and patient-centered approach is designed to break barriers to quality health care and has resulted in a 98% client-satisfaction rating. Volunteers are needed for nursing, office work, advocacy and general clinic assistance, such as patient intake.

Skills: Medical personnel: call for specific requirements; Non-medical personnel: experience running an office and doing community outreach are helpful, but not required.

Contact: Alice Craft-Kerney, RN

LOWER PRICE HILL COMMUNITY SCHOOL

2104 St. Michael Street   (513) 244-2214
Cincinnati, OH 45204   jenw@lphcs.org
       www.lphcs.org

Area: Cincinnati, Ohio

General Information: The Lower Price Hill Community School removes barriers to education, provides instructional and guidance services, and assists individuals in meeting their educational and employment goals in a supportive and familiar environment.

Neighborhood residents, troubled by their children and grandchildren not graduating from high school, founded LPHCS in 1972. From modest beginnings in a window-less basement, Cincinnati's LPHCS has become a modern learning center occupying the entire top floor of a former elementary school in the heart of the neighborhood. Since 1978, LPHCS has provided tuition-free education to over 5,000 students and has awarded over 650 high school equivalency diplomas (GEDs). Many other students not enrolled as GED candidates have improved reading, math and composition skills at the community school. LPHCS also offers a college access program through Cincinnati State Technical and Community College as well as English for Speakers of Other Languages (ESOL) classes. Typical enrollment in all programs is close to 300 students. Over the years as many as 100 students have attained Associate or Baccalaureate degrees from area colleges because of the work of the community school.

Volunteers serve as GED tutors, English tutors, community outreach workers and computer skills training instructors. There is no minimum or maximum time period, or full- or part-time requirements. We ask that volunteers be over 18.

Skills: Ability to interact with a diverse population; tutoring experience, computer skills.

Contact: Jennifer Walters, Executive Director

LUTHERAN VOLUNTEER CORPS
1226 Vermont Avenue, NW (202) 387-3222
Washington, DC 20005 lvcrecruitment@lvchome.org
www.lvchome.org

Area: Oakland/Berkeley, California; Wilmington, Delaware; Chicago, Illinois; Baltimore, Maryland; Minneapolis/St. Paul, Minnesota; Seattle and Tacoma, Washington; Washington, DC; Milwaukee, Wisconsin

General Information: The Lutheran Volunteer Corps (LVC) is a one-year service program that works for social justice by placing volunteers in nonprofit agencies in urban areas. Lutheran Volunteers can serve with youth programs, homeless shelters, legal assistance centers, public policy organizations, environmental groups, AIDS/HIV services and more. Volunteers serve full-time while living in community with other volunteers and exploring a simplified lifestyle. LVC participants receive housing, health insurance, food expenses, transportation and a modest personal stipend. Volunteers must be 21 years or older; there is no upper age limit. Married couples are welcome to apply. People of all faith traditions and backgrounds are encouraged to apply.

Skills: An openness to challenge, flexibility and commitment.

Contact: Jen Moore, Recruitment Coordinator

MACON COUNTY CARENET

130 Bidwell Street   (828) 369-2642
Franklin, NC 28734   carenet@dnet.net
                                     www.maconcarenet.org

Area: Macon County, North Carolina

General Information: Macon County Care Network, also known as CareNet, is a faith-based, nonprofit, tax-exempt organization. It helps provide assistance when other agencies are either unavailable or insufficient to meet crisis needs. CareNet provides food and limited financial assistance to pay for things like prescriptions, utilities, fuel and rent on an emergency basis. Food boxes are also provided and a soup kitchen is open three days a week. Assistance is mainly provided for the working poor, the permanently dependent, children and the youth who live in poverty, and the potentially unemployed. No cash funds are distributed. Funds for the CareNet's mission come from churches and individuals and proceeds from our CareNet Thrift Store. CareNet serves residents of Macon County who have been assessed by our screening process. CareNet also offers a Women's Crisis Ministry and a Narcotics Anonymous program. We need volunteers to meet clients one-on-one to discuss their needs, maintain and update client information, cook and serve food in our soup kitchen, meet with the public and answer telephone inquiries with our office staff, stock the pantry, distribute food to clients, and do maintenance work.

Skills: All skills are welcome, no experience necessary.

Contact: Vanessa Bailey, Executive Director

MACON PROGRAM FOR PROGRESS

350 West Orchard View Drive   (828) 524-4471 Ext 243
PO Box 700   ewest@mppnhc.org
Franklin, NC 28734   www.mppnhc.org

Area: Macon County, in the mountains of western North Carolina, just west of Asheville, North Carolina

General Information: Macon Program for Progress is a nonprofit community action agency serving the low-income residents of Macon County. Macon Program for Progress participates in the Alternative Spring Breaks program and World Changers (a youth volunteer program of the North American Mission Board of the Baptist Church) each year in March and June respectively. Volunteers may participate in any of the following programs offered by the agency: Head Start, Early Start, Summer Day Care, Weatherization Program (energy related repairs) and Housing Rehabilitation. Meals, housing and travel arrangements are the responsibility of the volunteer. Group size is limited to 25 volunteers.

Skills: Knowledge of construction practices are required for the housing projects and bring your own tools if possible.

Contact: Chuck Sutton, Executive Director

MADRE

121 West 27th Street, Suite 301   (212) 627-0444
New York, NY 10001   volunteers@madre.org
                    www.madre.org

Area: New York City

General Information: MADRE is an international women's human rights organization that works in partnership with community-based groups worldwide to address issues of peace building, women's health, violence against women, and economic and environmental justice. Over the past 25 years, MADRE has built a network of community-based women's organizations worldwide. This network encompasses thousands of women and families—in Latin America, Africa, the Caribbean and more—who are on the front lines of our global crisis. As part of the MADRE network, they know that change is not only possible—it is already happening.

Helping Hands is a way to give women the resources they need to strengthen their communities and fortify organizations where women can fight for their rights. By providing humanitarian aid, such as medical supplies for local health centers, school supplies for classrooms and office supplies for community centers, Helping Hands directly helps women make concrete positive change in their lives.

We need help contacting donors for immediate relief supplies, organizing donations, setting up shipments of aid, advertising for the campaign and more. Internship positions are also available in the following

MADRE

Photos: MADRE

MADRE has built a network of community-based women's organizations who are on the front lines of the global crisis in Sudan, Iraq, Nicaragua, Cuba, Haiti, Guatemala, Kenya, Peru, Colombia, Panama, Palestine and elsewhere.

MADRE provides critical shipments of food, medicine, educational supplies, and other material aid to their sister organizations in Latin America, the Caribbean, Africa, Asia, and the Middle East.

departments: Helping Hands, communications, public education, development and human rights advocacy. Internships require a minimum time commitment of 15 hours a week for at least three months. There are many other ways you can volunteer right in your own community: Implement your own Helping Hands humanitarian aid campaign and collect everyday supplies for women and children, such as over-the-counter medication, children's school supplies, eyeglasses, and more. Invite MADRE to speak at your university, organization, community and religious center

Skills: In-office volunteer positions require proficiency with the English language, skills in research, and professional knowledge of Excel and Publisher. Spanish proficiency is a plus.

Contact: Meghan Beach, Volunteer Coordinator

MAGDALENE HOSPITALITY HOUSE

c/o Emmanuel Episcopal Parish   (301) 724-7111
16 Washington Street   (301) 777-3364
Cumberland, MD 21502   emmanuel@ang-md.org
                                        mlw@hereintown.net

Area: Cumberland, western Maryland, in the Appalachian Mountains

General Information: Magdalene Hospitality House (MHH) provides safe and secure housing for families visiting their loved ones incarcerated in FCI Cumberland, a medium security federal prison as well as a prison camp. Many families travel great distances and neither have the funds to rest at local hotels nor transportation to negotiate the distance between the city and the prison proper. Families stay one or two nights with previously confirmed reservations, and are served breakfast and dinner. Families are treated with respect and their privacy is preserved. MHH is entirely ecumenical with no religious proselytizing taking place. Donations of services, goods, and money are accepted to help defray expenses although in the spirit of Holy Hospitality donations are not required of guests. All work in providing services, from making beds to keeping schedules to fixing the furnace, is provided by volunteers.

We are seeking a full-time volunteer to live at the house as the caretaker. In addition to helping schedule guests' visits, this individual would be responsible for groundskeeping and general upkeep of the house. We also welcome workcamp groups, as we have several repairs that could be completed by a group in a week's time while staying at the house.

Skills: Listening skills, particularly for persons experiencing the collateral damage of the justice system, are crucial; skills also in public relations, house management and clerical work will be welcomed.

Contact: John and Donna Martin

MARIAN HOUSE

209 East Walnut Street   (814) 765-5646
Clearfield, PA 16830   marianhouse@pennswoods.net

Area: Clearfield County, Pennsylvania and local Appalachian area

General Information: Young People Who Care—Marian House is a Christian homeless shelter for women and children. Marian House provides a quiet and nurturing environment. Staff and volunteers work to empower each woman to make positive decisions for her future. The ministry includes: 24-hour shelter, meals, clothing, advocacy and assistance in obtaining needed services, educational workshops, supportive counseling and a safe and supportive environment. Volunteers, both full- and part-time, are needed to work directly with the guests who come to the shelter, assisting them with emotional support, being a mentor for life skills such as cooking, doing domestic tasks, transportation, assisting with children. Professional volunteers in social work and/or counseling may have the opportunity to use their skills. The minimum time period for volunteers to serve is one month and there is no maximum time limit. Age requirement: 20 years and up.

Skills: Social work experience, flexibility, organizing ability, common sense, non-judgmental desire to help others, life skills.

Contact: Sister Ruth Ann Madera, Director

MARY HOUSE OF HOSPITALITY

3579 County Road G   (608) 586-4447
Wisconsin Dells, WI 53965

Area: South Central Wisconsin

General Information: The federal prison at Oxford, Wisconsin which houses over 1,000 men is located in a rural farming area, and not accessible by public transportation, nor within walking distance of hotels. Twenty miles of rural roads lie between the visiting room at Oxford and the nearest Greyhound or Amtrak station. Many families have no money for restaurants or hotels and the remoteness means visits only once a year, or spending the night in the car at a truck stop. Visiting the prison with young children is particularly difficult. Since opening its doors in the fall of 1989, Mary House has served visiting families of inmates by providing transportation, meals, overnight lodging and perhaps most importantly, a family atmosphere of respect and fellowship. Mary House is based on a Catholic Worker model of voluntary service. It is staffed by live-in, and part-time volunteers who share a commitment to provide hospitality to those in need. Volunteer work includes driving guests, cooking, cleaning and yardwork. The site is rural and isolated so volunteers must be mature and emotionally healthy, and must have ownership of, or access to, a car. Mary House pays no stipend or insurance but offers a lovely rural hospitality experience.

Skills: Patience, driver's license, and ownership or access to a car. Willingness to live in a rural setting.

Contact: Cassandra Dixon, Volunteer Coordinator

MARYKNOLL AFFILIATES

PO Box 311   (877) 897-2386
Maryknoll, NY 10545   maryknoll.org

Area: Throughout the United States

General Information: Maryknoll Affiliates, begun in 1991, is a loosely knit organization of local Chapters sustained by four pillars: spirituality, global vision, community and action. Affiliates share in the mission and family spirit of Maryknoll Sisters, Brothers, Priests and Lay Missioners living lives of service in more than 30 countries. At present, there are over 900 Affiliates in more than 60 Chapters. Individuals interested may join an existing Chapter or form a new Chapter with a minimum of four people. Affiliates come together, most often on a monthly basis, to build small "mission communities." Activities of individual Chapters vary from place to place, some focusing on prayer and reflection and others involved in actions in their communities or with missions in other parts of the world. All Chapters are linked by a sense of commitment to the Maryknoll vision of a global community built on faith, peace and justice. We express the Maryknoll Spirit in the context of Chapters who gather for prayer, reflection and action. We challenge one another to go beyond borders, locally and globally, to work with the poor and excluded, and to strive for peace and justice for all of God's creation. We recognize that the Spirit who guides us on our journey moves without boundaries and that God's unconditional love is present in all cultures and peoples.

Skills: No particular skills are required.

Contact: Fred Goddard, Executive Coordinator

MARYKNOLL OFFICE FOR GLOBAL CONCERNS

PO Box 29132

415 Michigan Avenue NE

Washington, DC 20017

(202) 832-1780

ogc@maryknoll.org

www.maryknollogc.org

Area: New York City; Ossining, New York; Washington, DC

General Information: The Maryknoll Office for Global Concerns represents Maryknoll missioners and Catholic men and women who work around the world in impoverished communities. Our office follows issues of concern to the missioners, and the people they work with, such as debt, trade and investments, torture, HIV/AIDS, human security and ecology.

Volunteers help with research, attend coalition meetings, write newsletter articles and help with general office maintenance. Age requirements: 21 years plus. No maximum time; preferably a few days a week for several months, as a minimum.

Skills: Computer literacy, flexibility, interest in advocacy.

Contact: Judy Coode, Communication Manager

MENDENHALL MINISTRIES

PO Box 368

309 Center Street

Mendenhall, MS 39114

(601) 847-3421

volunteer@mbc-tmm.org

www.mbc-tmm.org

Area: South Central Mississippi

General Information: We are a Christian organization committed to seeking justice and improving the conditions of life in our community. Outreach programs designed to meet the needs of the community are a health clinic, nursery (age 3+) through high school, gymnasium with recreation program, farm, elderly housing and volunteer ministry.

Work groups: Any number of people from a church or organization can come and be housed in our one-hundred person Volunteer Center for one to three weeks to perform various tasks while learning of the ministry's work with the rural poor. Summer volunteer: eight-week program begins early June; options include: tutoring, farming, research, writing and other assigned duties.

Long-term volunteers: two-month to two-year commitments desired for service in any area of ministry. Volunteers are asked to raise funds to cover living expenses.

Skills: Required: Possess a servant's heart and a willingness to give of yourself and learn from others. Desired: Elementary through high school teachers, farmers, youth workers, carpenters, secretarial workers, nurses, writers, website managers, housing coordinator and researchers.

Contact: Ernestine Skiffer, Interim President

MERCI

676 Community Drive   (888) 440-9167
Goldsboro, NC 27530   merci@nccumc.org
                                       www.merciumc.org

Area: Eastern North Carolina including Columbus, Carteret, Duplin, Johnston and Wayne Counties

General Information: MERCI is an outgrowth of the North Carolina United Methodist Disaster Recovery Ministries in the aftermath of devastating floods caused by Hurricane Floyd's landfall in September 1999. Our volunteers helped repair or replace over 1,900 of the more than 17,000 homes rendered uninhabitable by this "five hundred year flood."

MERCI is now a permanent home repair/replacement and mission support ministry; teams of skilled and unskilled volunteers rebuild and repair homes for families who are victims of disaster or of the poverty that affects one of every five families in eastern North Carolina. Worldwide poverty and need fuel MERCI's mission support through humanitarian aid and medical supplies to Africa, Haiti, Latin America and Eastern Europe. In addition to packing these supplies, volunteers package kits: health and migrant kits, school kits, sewing kits, layettes for distribution in the U.S. and overseas as well as flood buckets for cleaning disaster-damaged homes.

MERCI provides housing for up to 50 volunteers at either the central center in Goldsboro or in Carteret County, site of response to Hurricane Ophelia of 2005. Volunteers cook their own meals in the kitchens provided and pay $20 per night per person to offset utilities expense and facility upkeep. MERCI has construction coordinators to supervise volunteers, provides all building materials and delivers these materials to the building site as needed.

Skills: MERCI welcomes volunteers with skills in construction, data entry and office management, warehousing and packing and are delighted to have volunteers who are willing to work.

Contact: Ann Huffman, Coordinator of Volunteer Assignment

MERCY CENTER

377 East 145th Street
Bronx, NY 10454

(718) 993-2789
jcf@mercycenterbronx.org
www.mercycenterbronx.org

Area: South Bronx, New York

General Information: Mercy Center is a neighborhood center for women and families in the Mott Haven section of the South Bronx. We provide educational, technical, human and supportive services to women, parents and other family members, empowering them to reach their full human potential and be agents of change in their families and communities. Widespread poverty and unemployment are rampant in the Mott Haven section of the South Bronx. Nearly half of all residents live below the poverty line. Violent crime, child abuse and domestic violence are constants in the environment. There are many people in the community working hard to raise their families. Most are women. Many are doing it alone, caught in a cycle of dependency, violence and poverty.

Volunteers contribute significantly to the mission of Mercy Center; a few are full-time, some give two days a week of their time and talents, dozens of others give 2–10 hours to the work we accomplish. We particularly need volunteers to accompany and advocate for Mercy Center participants dealing with housing, social service and immigration matters; tutor and homework assistance in the after-school program; tutor in the Saturday Reading Program; teach and assist in ESL classes and employment coaching. We also need professional volunteers with legal skills and counseling skills. All volunteers are welcome.

Skills: We particularly need volunteers with skills in tutoring, advocacy, running special events, grant writing and legal skills.

Contact: Judith Criado Fiuza, Program Manager

METROPOLITAN INTER-FAITH ASSOCIATION (MIFA)

910 Vance Avenue
Memphis, TN 38119

(901) 271-6432
www.mifa.org

Area: West Tennessee: Tipton, Lauderdale, Shelby and Fayette Counties

General Information: Since 1968, the Metropolitan Inter-Faith Association (MIFA) has been helping transform our community by helping change lives—from emptiness to fullness, from despair to hope, from darkness to light. Our community is the human family, that is, all of us: clients, volunteers, congregations, donors and staff. MIFA serves more than 60,000 people a year. Each of MIFA's nine programs is designed to make positive change in clients' lives.

Our programs touch infants as young as six weeks old to senior citizens older than 100. MIFA's many programs address specific needs such as transitional housing for homeless families; nutrition for approximately 2,300 seniors a day through the MIFA Meals program; job-readiness training for inner-city youth; emergency assistance with rent, utilities and food; job placement services; credit counseling; legal services and more.

Skills: Volunteer opportunities are available in many areas.

Contact: Charlie Nelson, Director of Volunteer Services

MID-SOUTH PEACE AND JUSTICE CENTER

1000 South Cooper   (901) 725-4990
Memphis, TN 38104   center@midsouthpeace.org
                                  www.midsouthpeace.org

Area: Memphis, Tennessee

General Information: Volunteers will work with programs, projects and campaigns on various issues related to local and global peace and justice issues. The Center's activities include: anti-war campaign seeking an immediate end to the occupation of Iraq and advocating an international presence acceptable to the Iraqi people and committed to human rights, including women's rights; cooperative organic community gardens in Orange Mound, a low-income African American neighborhood; Food Not Bombs, a community service program serving free vegetarian meals to those in need; Living Wage campaign demanding a fair wage for workers, in coalition with an array of faith, labor and community groups and Anti-Privatization campaign opposing the privatization of Shelby County's correctional facilities. Volunteers should be at least 15 years of age. Scheduling and term of service are flexible.

Skills: Strong work ethic and willingness to teach, learn and share ideas with, and from, the community. Desired: computer literacy; computer instruction and/or maintenance skills; community organizing; interest in organic gardening and/or cooking, art and performance; marketing, public relations and/or media experience; bookkeeping.

Contact: Jacob Flowers, Director

THE MINISTRIES

3680 Route 112   (631) 736-4800
Coram, NY 11727   www.theministriesonline.org

Area: Suffolk County, Long Island, New York

General Information: The Ministries has served the needs of Long Island adults, children and families since 1967. The volunteer program at The Ministries provides a solid volunteer corps for our many diverse programs such as Community Information and Referral Services, an emergency food program, and Seabury Barn, our short-term emergency shelter for runaway youth ages 12–17. Seabury Barn is a co-ed shelter providing short-term emergency services to boys and girls who are homeless, runaway, throwaway or abused. It depends a good deal on volunteer recreation aides who care enough to spend time with the youth at the Barn and at other recreational facilities.

Hunger is an ever-increasing reality of life in many Suffolk County households. When social systems fail to provide immediate relief for the hungry, we provide a three-day supply of nourishing food provided with dignity and confidentiality.

Volunteers are involved in all of these aspects of our work. Community Information and Referral Services volunteers are trained as community service workers. They are taught to use our extensive files on community resources and to give appropriate telephone referrals, particularly for families who are facing foreclosure, job loss and other financial hardships. Born of the ecumenical movement of the late 1960's, we continue our partnership in ministry with the Roman Catholic Diocese of Rockville Center, the Long Island Episcopal Diocese, Temple Isaiah, the Evangelical Lutheran Church in America, The United Methodist Church in America, The United Presbyterian Church in America, The New York Conference of the United Church of Christ and the Unitarian Universalists Association, plus many local individuals, families and other organizations to meet the human service needs of our community. The Ministries welcomes all Suffolk County residents without regard to race, religion, ethnicity, gender or sexual orientation.

Skills: Certified Social Work volunteers are welcome in our Youth, Family and Adult Counseling Programs which provide psychotherapy to uninsured and underinsured families, children and adults in need.

Contact: Ann Moran-Smith, MPS, Executive Director

MOTHER TERESA HOUSE

PO Box 13004   (517) 484-5494
Lansing, MI 48901   info@motherteresahouse.org

Area: Lansing, Michigan

General Information: Our mission at Mother Teresa House is to provide a home and care for terminally ill people who live alone or do not have the care they need in the last days of life. This is provided at no charge. The ministry, begun by Catholics, inspired by Mother Teresa and cherishing each person as a child of God, welcomes those of any faith to join us in serving.

Volunteers serve in our home in downtown Lansing doing whatever is needed, including personal care, cooking, cleaning, answering the phone, helping in the office and especially spending time with the guests in our care. Live-in volunteers serve 40 hours per week. Length of stay is usually 6–9 months. Shorter terms may also be available. Room, board and training are provided.

Skills: No special skills are needed. An ability to embrace the mission, commitment to working as part of a group, and openness to learn and to grow in selfless service are necessary.

Contact: Karen Bussey, Director

MUJER, INC. (MUJERES UNIDAS EN JUSTICIA, EDUCACIÓN Y REFORMA, INC.)

28905 South Dixie Highway   (305) 247-1388
Homestead, FL 33033   www.mujerfla.org

Area: South Florida

General Information: MUJER's mission is to promote healthy lifestyles, emotional wellness and stability through advocacy, violence prevention and community education to strengthen low-income Hispanic families. We provide family therapy, individual counseling for domestic violence and sexual assault, emergency shelter and relocation, women's support groups, emergency financial assistance, full case management, sexual assault hotline (24/7), on call victim advocacy, community education and outreach on rape, sexual assault, child abuse and HIV/AIDS. We also do family preservation through couples counseling, parenting programs and family violence prevention programs.

MUJER is looking for volunteers to help in fund-raising, as well as in marketing, public relations, investing, resource development and grants management. At least a three-month commitment for part-time volunteers is preferred.

Skills: Some experience or education in the area for which they are volunteering is preferred.

Contact: Susan Reyna, Executive Director

MULTIFAITH WORKS

115 16th Avenue   (206) 324-1520
Seattle, WA 98122   info@multifaith.org
                                                    www.multifaith.org

Area: Seattle, Washington and greater King County

General Information: Multifaith Works builds a community of compassion by mobilizing volunteers from many spiritual and cultural backgrounds to provide practical and emotional support and housing for people living with AIDS or other life-threatening illnesses. Our clients are referred by Case Managers in local organizations. Multifaith Works' programs work in unison to companion clients who frequently live in isolation. The Housing program operates five low-income houses for people living with HIV/AIDS and one for people living with MS. The Shanti Program offers one-to-one emotional support to people living with HIV/AIDS or other life-threatening illnesses through active listening and a comforting, sustaining relationship. Shanti volunteers go through an extensive training before matching with a client. Some volunteers support inmates in prisons and jails. The AIDS CareTeam program provides practical, emotional, and spiritual support for people or households affected by AIDS. Groups of 5–10 individuals (from a spiritual community, university or community at large) are trained to offer a compassionate presence. CareTeams do the things friends do: sharing a meal, providing transportation, listening.

Volunteer opportunities also exist for housing maintenance, office and fund-raising support, and client transportation. Multifaith Works accommodates volunteers over the age of 15, work groups, and both long-term and short-term volunteers. All volunteers receive support from professional staff.

Skills: All volunteers must go through training before placement. Shanti volunteers attend a four-day training; all other volunteers attend the one-day CareTeam training.

Contact: Dan Miller, Volunteer Program Manager

MY BROTHER'S TABLE

98 Willow Street
Lynn, MA 01901

(781) 595-3224
www.mybrotherstable.org

Area: Boston's North Shore

General Information: My Brother's Table (MBT) is a soup kitchen and more. We are dedicated to feeding the hungry in an atmosphere of dignity and respect. Lynn, a city north of Boston, is a former industrial city with a diverse population, high unemployment and high levels of poverty. MBT serves an average of over 200 meals every day. MBT believes that hunger is a community problem and must be addressed by the community. The Table receives no government funding and relies on private donations and the service of over 2,500 volunteers annually. All who come to MBT are served: mothers with children who can't make it through the month, people who live in one-room apartments with no cooking facilities, homeless individuals, people who have been broken through alcohol, drugs or a lack of love, the lonely and anyone in need. To address the causes of hunger, MBT also provides a wide range of advocacy services that include individual referrals, issue advocacy and special programs for the guests. A medical clinic operates once a week and includes a volunteer primary care physician, two volunteer nurses, an HIV/AIDS testing and counseling clinic, HIV/AIDS outreach workers and other outreach workers. All services are provided free of charge to guests.

Volunteers are needed for all aspects of the work at the Table including: help prepare and serve meals, work individually with guests, drive the van and truck, fund-raise and work in the office. Volunteers may participate in a wide range of activities depending on interest. Individuals and groups are invited to serve at the Table. Most volunteers work once or twice a month for a few hours. Full-time volunteer opportunities also exist.

Skills: All skills welcome, no particular skills required.

Contact: Executive Director

NATIONAL COALITION FOR THE HOMELESS

2201 P Street NW
Washington, DC 20037

(202) 462-4822 Ext 19
mstoops@nationalhomeless.org
www.nationalhomeless.org

Area: Placements in all 50 states

General Information: The National Coalition for the Homeless

(NCH) is an advocacy organization committed to the principles that affordable housing, access to healthcare, civil rights, and living wages are fundamental rights in a civilized society. We want to end homelessness/poverty in this country and the world. We need your help to do so. Our goal is to go out of business by solving this important social problem/issue. The work of the NCH centers on expanding and enforcing the rights of homeless people through public education, community organizing, litigation, lobbying, technical assistance and research.

Volunteer/interns assist with research and writing, local/state/federal legislation, public education projects, and grassroots organizing. Work schedules are flexible to meet the needs of volunteers/interns and the ongoing work of NCH. Because we are a grassroots organization, interns get a lot of responsibility. We provide training and supervision to interns willing to take on all kinds of tasks.

Skills: Written and verbal communications skills, ability to organize one's work in an efficient and professional setting preferred.

Contact: Michael Stoops, Acting Executive Director

THE NATIONAL FAMILY FARM COALITION

110 Maryland Avenue NE, Suite 307   (202) 543-5675
Washington, DC 20002   www.nffc.net

Area: Offices in Washington, DC; and Stoughton, WI

General Information: The National Family Farm Coalition aims to empower family farmers by reducing the corporate control of agriculture and promoting a more socially just farm and food policy. Founded in 1986, the NFFC represents family farm and rural groups in roughly 30 states. Our members face farm loss and deepening recession in rural communities. This is caused primarily by instability in farm prices and increasing corporate control of farm pricing, farming practices and markets in farm inputs and products. Our mission is to unite and strengthen the voices and actions of NFFC's diverse grassroots members to demand viable livelihoods for family farmers, safe and healthy food for everyone, and economically and environmentally sound rural communities. The Coalition's leaders have identified opportunities for effective policy reform, particularly in relation to agribusiness concentration and the demise of family farmers and their rural communities. NFFC sees increasing openness to our analysis by the media, labor and environmental constituencies, social-justice organizations and policy makers. Capacity-building resources are needed for members to organize their fellow farmers and allies to change the policies that support the present, unsustainable food system.

We have enjoyed working with interns over the years and would welcome volunteers in several capacities including updating our website as needed on an ongoing basis; researching and updating our press and media list; recording oral histories of our farmers and leaders (could be long-term/several years); constructing a timeline of significant family farmer and NFFC events (1–2 weeks); grant writing (ongoing); editing videos of NFFC events. College age and above welcome.

Skills: Concern for family farmers and sustainable rural development vital; writing, typing and literacy in Microsoft software and online research useful; experience with Dreamweaver or other website management; audio and video editing; flexibility and creativity sought.

Contact: Katherine Ozer, Executive Director

NATIONAL FEDERATION OF COMMUNITY DEVELOPMENT CREDIT UNIONS

116 John Street, 33rd Floor
New York, NY 10038

(212) 809-1850 Ext 215
powens@cdcu.coop
www.cdcu.coop

Area: Office in New York City and credit unions in 45 of the 50 states

General Information: The National Federation of Community Development Credit Unions (the Federation) is dedicated to strengthening credit unions and increasing access to capital and financial services for the residents and businesses of low-income and minority communities. Founded in 1974, our mission is to help low- and moderate-income people and communities achieve financial independence through community development credit unions (CDCUs). The Federation provides capital, professional education, technical assistance, and targeted research and training to our member credit unions. The Federation's network of 225 CDCUs serve more than one million low-wealth individuals with more than $4 billion in community-owned assets. For almost a century, credit unions have offered hardworking Americans an affordable alternative to banks. More than 70 years ago, a small number of credit unions began to emerge with the specific mission of serving low-income and minority communities beyond the reach of banks and mainstream credit unions. CDCUs specialize

NATIONAL FEDERATION OF COMMUNITY DEVELOPMENT CREDIT UNIONS

Volunteers from the community work with credit union staff, aided by volunteers who serve on the various boards and committees. Staff members at the Bethex Federal Credit Union are from the Bronx community that they serve.

Photo: Susan Angus

Photo: NFCDCU

A volunteer at the Santa Cruz Community Credit Union works at the volunteer income tax assistance (VITA) site.

in serving populations generally considered the hardest to serve, including low-income wage earners, recent immigrants and people with disabilities. CDCUs are nonprofit, tax-exempt (but not charities) and cooperatively owned and governed—one member, one vote. These community-based (including many that are faith-based) and government-regulated, fully insured financial institutions offer an economic lifeline to low-income communities that have been abandoned by commercial banks and targeted by high-priced check cashers and predatory lenders. CDCUs retain capital and income within communities by providing residents of these communities with fairly priced loans, including to members with imperfect, limited or no credit history. CDCUs also offer personal financial counseling and consumer education at little or no cost.

Volunteers have been critical to the success of both the Federation and the credit unions. The Federation works with volunteers who offer support on new product development. CDCUs have volunteer board officials who serve as the policy makers. Volunteers also serve on various credit union committees including supervisory, credit, marketing and financial education. We are looking for dedicated volunteers who are interested in long- or short-term assignments.

Skills: Background in finance, accounting, technology, marketing, fund-raising or anyone with a strong commitment to community economic development.

Contact: Pamela Owens

NATIONAL HOSPICE AND PALLIATIVE CARE ORGANIZATION

1700 Diagonal Road, Suite 625   (800) 658-8898
Alexandria, VA 22314   info@caringinfo.org
                                               www.nhpco.org

Area: Over 3,200 hospice providers across the United States

General Information: National Hospice and Palliative Care Organization is the oldest and largest nonprofit membership organization representing hospice and palliative care programs and professionals in the U.S. The organization is committed to improving end-of-life care and expanding access to hospice care with the goal of profoundly enhancing quality of life for dying Americans and their loved ones. The contributions of volunteers are a core component of the hospice philosophy of care that maximizes quality of life and provides compassionate care to the dying. Hospices provide volunteers with a wide range of opportunities that vary depending on the specific hospice provider and community. Volunteer activities can include assisting patients and families, fund-raising, administrative work, support for bereavement activities and more. Hospices will screen all volunteer applicants and provide volunteer training programs.

Skills: Hospice providers need volunteers with a variety of skills and experience. Volunteers must be willing to work as team members whose goal is to provide comfort and compassion to those at the end of life and their loved ones.

Contact: NHPCO Hospice Helpline

THE NATIVE AMERICAN CULTURAL FOUNDATION
PO Box 30804   (440) 884-9652
Cleveland, OH 44130

Area: Northeast Ohio

General Information: The Native American Cultural Foundation (NACF) serves the Native American Community of greater Cleveland and northeast Ohio, who are primarily the people of many different indigenous nations from all states in the U.S. as well as Canada, Mexico and South America. NACF is a nonprofit Cultural and Environmental Foundation. Its members consist of many different indigenous Nations that rely on the good will of community volunteers to aid them in advancing their mission to preserve and promote Native American Culture and preserve our natural resources.

NACF is expanding programs and needs volunteers to aid in environmental issues, social events and family activities as well as raising financial support for scholarships for Native American high school and college students. Our goal is to unite the Native American Community by promoting and understanding spiritual values and traditional ceremonies that increase cultural and spiritual awareness with native and non-native communities to inspire pride in our diversities.

Skills: Familiarity with Native American culture and lineage is desirable, and we are particularly looking for volunteers who are of Native American heritage, but all who want to support our goals and help carry out our mission are welcome to contact us about what they can do.

Contact: Ken Demsey

NEIGHBORHOOD COALITION FOR SHELTER (NCS)

157 East 86th Street   (212) 537-5150
New York, NY 10028   mcavanaugh@ncsinc.org
                                  www.ncsinc.org

Area: New York City

General Information: The Neighborhood Coalition for Shelter (NCS) serves people who are chronically homeless, formerly homeless, or at risk of becoming homeless. Established in 1982 by religious and community leaders on Manhattan's Upper East Side, NCS was founded on the premise that homelessness is the responsibility of the entire community. The collaboration that became NCS has provided more than 20,000 people with food and clothing, counseling and treatment, shelter and employment and, in many cases, homes to call their own. With its partners in the community, NCS's board, staff and volunteers powerfully demonstrate what neighbors can do to reduce, prevent and ultimately end homelessness. Short- and long-term projects and one-time commitments are available at four locations. Volunteers can help pick up donations, serve meals, lead practice interview sessions, provide recreation including karaoke, musical entertainment and educational games, and volunteer in the shelter.

Skills: Flexibility and desire to help.

Contact: Millicent Cavanaugh, Director of Volunteer Services

NEIGHBORHOOD HOUSE

179 Robie Street East   (651) 789-2500
St. Paul, MN 55107   info@neighbor.org
                                  www.neighb.org

Area: St. Paul, Minnesota

General Information: Neighborhood House is a multicultural, multilingual center, open to all, and committed to the success of refugees and new immigrants. It was founded in 1897 by the women of Mount Zion Temple, in order to help Russian and other Eastern European Jewish families settle in the St. Paul area. Neighborhood House is a first-stop agency offering essential programs that help people put down roots in their new home, learn important life skills, strengthen their families, and contribute to building a diverse and thriving community. Neighborhood House has been privileged to work with people from more than fifty ethnic populations as they build and sustain

NEIGHBORHOOD HOUSE

Photos: Neighborhood House

Neighborhood House's food shelf has food from many different cultures, and volunteers from all over the world.

English Language Learning is one of Neighborhood House's largest programs, with over 80,000 teaching hours in the past year. Immigrants whose first languages include Spanish, Hmong, Somali, Ethiopian, and Russian learn valuable language skills that will help them in their daily lives.

productive new lives. From Mexico to Laos, Bosnia to Somalia, events half a world away often determine who comes to Minnesota as immigrants and refugees. Once in America, they find that world events continue to influence their lives in the form of federal and local policies that regulate immigration, documentation, and mobility.

Signature programs include a culturally appropriate food shelf that stocks food familiar to participants from Africa, Latin America and Asia; English Language Learning programs that are filled to capacity every term; and a unique approach that works with entire families, not just individuals. Located on the west side of St. Paul in an area with deep immigrant roots, Neighborhood House is a key local cultural institution deeply involved in the neighborhood and the city. Housed in a new building dedicated to the community building efforts of the late Senator Paul and Sheila Wellstone, Neighborhood House has expanded programming and is seeing a dramatically higher number of participants.

Primary volunteer opportunities include teaching English Language Learning and General Education development classes; helping in our culturally appropriate food shelf; and working with young people in our Youth Program. Clerical and event help is also needed.

Skills: Fluency in Spanish, Hmong, Somali, Ethiopian and/or Russian is welcome, not required.

Contact: Volunteer Manager

THE NEW AGRARIAN CENTER

MPO Box 357   (440) 774-3627
Oberlin, OH 44074   evbryant1@yahoo.com
                               www.gotthenac.org

Area: Volunteers will work in Lorain County Ohio (Oberlin, Elyria and Lorain) and in Cuyahoga County (Cleveland and possibly some suburbs of Cleveland)

General Information: The New Agrarian Center (NAC) is located at the George Jones farm 30 miles west of Cleveland, Ohio. The NAC seeks to develop, support and educate people about local food systems. The farm is a 70-acre working organic farm and is part of a network of local farmers that supply food for NAC's City Fresh program in Cuyahoga and Lorain Counties. The organization began City Fresh in Cleveland in 2005 to establish fresh food

THE NEW AGRARIAN CENTER

Volunteers help to convert land donated by a local hospital into a growing space for the community, with the goal of improving access to healthy food in urban neighborhoods.

markets in the inner-city where there are none. The program serves low-income residents who lack access to healthy fresh food and includes support for the development of urban gardens, nutrition education and an urban market gardener training program.

Much of the volunteer work is at the George Jones Farm in Oberlin. Volunteers will assist the growers in all aspects of organic farming including field work and produce preparation for our various markets. In addition, there are other opportunities to help with City Fresh. Produce is packed into share bags, and there are City Fresh markets where produce is distributed. There is also a network of urban growers who have opportunities for volunteers.

Volunteers can work for any length of time, but at this time we have no housing available except a tent and campsite in our woods. They can work full- or part-time, but need to be physically able to handle farm labor, and we require a minimum age of 18 years old.

Skills: Any volunteer help is welcome. The labor is unskilled, but prior farm and/or garden experience would certainly be an asset.

Contact: Evelyn Bryant, Educator, Operations Manager

NEW HOPE HOUSE

PO Box 1213   (770) 358-1148
Griffin, GA 30224   newhopehouse@netzero.com

Area: Rural Georgia

General Information: New Hope House provides housing and emotional support to families who travel long distances to visit with their incarcerated loved ones facing death sentences. In Georgia there are death penalty trials every day—sometimes as many as five trials going on at the same time. Our presence at these trials not only benefits the families, but also attorneys new to the process.

Volunteers can visit with these family members in their homes and at New Hope's guest house, and they have the option of attending capital appeals, trials and retrials, as well as working with "Georgians For The Alternative to the Death Penalty" to change the current death penalty rules in Georgia. Volunteers are also needed for gardening, maintenance and hospitality services (cleaning and cooking) at New Hope House. Minimum age 20. No minimum time commitment, but at least a week is preferable, and longer. Year-round availability appreciated. No health insurance, but local medical help available. Room and board and $15 a week.

Skills: Flexibility and being a good listener.

Contact: Ed Weir

NICARAGUA NETWORK

1247 E Street SE   (202) 544-9355
Washington, DC 20003   nicanet@afgj.org
                               www.nicanet.org

Area: Washington, DC, or in special cases, Nicaragua

General Information: The Nicaragua Network is a 30-year-old network of community groups throughout the U.S. that works in solidarity with the people of Nicaragua. The Network was founded in 1979 to support the popular struggle to overthrow the 45-year U.S.-supported Somoza family dictatorship. Following the victory, the Network has supported the efforts of the Sandinista Revolution to provide a better life for the nation's people. Thus, for three decades, the Network has been a leading organization in the United States committed to social and economic justice for Nicaragua, Latin America and the World, based on respect for sovereignty and self-determination. The Network advocates for sound U.S. foreign policies that respect human rights and international law. The Nicaragua Network provides information and organizing tools to a network of 200 solidarity, sister city, and peace and justice committees across the U.S.

The national office in Washington, DC facilitates the activism of local groups by providing weekly and monthly publications including the *Nicaragua Network Hotline*, the *Nicaragua News Service*, the *Nicaragua Monitor*, and occasional monographs. We arrange speaking tours of Nicaraguans in the U.S. and political/economic study tours to Nicaragua. We work in collaboration with other groups to promote fair (instead of "free") trade and Third World debt cancellation, and to oppose policies of the IMF and World Bank. Additional priority issues are trade, opposition to water privatization, and support for the environment and human rights. When specific needs arise, the Nicaragua Network raises money for humanitarian relief.

Skills: In the Washington, DC office, computer literacy and writing skills are necessary. For Nicaragua, knowledge of Spanish is required.

Contact: Chuck Kaufman, National Co-Coordinator

NORTHERN CAMBRIA COMMUNITY DEVELOPMENT CORPORATION (NCCDC)

4200 Crawford Avenue
Northern Cambria, PA 15714

(814) 948-4444
norcam@charterpa.net
www.norcam.org

Area: West central Pennsylvania

General Information: Northern Cambria Community Development Corporation's goal is to ensure safe, affordable and accessible housing for all members of the community. We work with low-income, first-time home buyers to acquire substandard housing stock in Cambria County and rehabilitate it with the help of volunteers. Such housing usually comes at a reasonable price because of the extensive work involved. The home buyer goes through a process that assesses their income and repayment ability. After qualifying, the prospective home buyer is then eligible for a determined loan amount and can purchase a home with these funds. The loan is repayable over a 30-year period at a 1% interest rate. We hope to build two new houses each summer. We provide a work-camp experience for groups as large as 30 people. For a one-week stay, we ask for a donation of $125 per participant.

Skills: We accept individuals of all skills levels; we know whoever has the motivation and willingness to learn can contribute immeasurably.

Contact: Jerry Brant, President

OLD FIRST REFORMED UNITED CHURCH OF CHRIST

151 North 4th Street   (215) 922-4566
Philadelphia, PA 19106   Fax: (215) 922-6366

Area: Philadelphia, Pennsylvania

General Information: Old First Reformed United Church of Christ is a historic church in downtown Philadelphia with an extensive outreach ministry, which includes a winter shelter for the homeless that serves approximately 30 men, and a weekly food and clothing cupboard that serves approximately 50 men and women. There are several opportunities for volunteering with our variety of programs.

Volunteers are needed for Service Internship opportunities. The full year volunteer coordinates the winter shelter for the homeless, recruits and trains volunteers for our weekly food and clothing cupboard, seeks and maintains donations, and schedules and hosts urban work camps for youth and adults. We also need eight to nine summer Urban Service Interns to staff a multiracial, multi-class, literacy based day camp, which serves approximately 40 children between the ages of 5–11. Volunteers must be 18 years or older and are provided with housing and a stipend. Full year position starts in August or September; summer intern term is June–August.

Skills: Maturity, organizational skills, willingness and desire to work with all ages and a diverse community, and enthusiasm for hard work.

Contact: Rosemary Polo, Church Secretary

OPEN DOOR COMMUNITY

910 Ponce de Leon Avenue, NE   (404) 874-9652
Atlanta, GA 30306   (770) 246-7627
                     odcvolunteer@bellsouth.net
                     www.opendoorcommunity.org

Area: Atlanta and the state of Georgia

General Information: Open Door is a residential Christian Community working among the hungry and homeless in Atlanta and prisoners throughout Georgia, particularly those on Death Row. The Open Door

OPEN DOOR COMMUNITY

Volunteers and members of the community march outside of Grady Hospital, the primary source of medical care for the poor in Atlanta, protesting the city's plan to charge low-income people for their prescriptions beyond their means.

provides breakfast, a soup kitchen, a clothes closet, showers, a free medical and foot care clinic, and engages in community action for justice, including anti-death penalty advocacy. We also publish a monthly newspaper, *Hospitality*, and sponsor the Hardwick Prison Trip, providing transportation for families and friends to visit loved ones at the largest Georgia state prison complex. Resident Volunteers stay for six months or more and live in a community of racial and gender diversity. The Community provides everything you need, plus a stipend of $11.50 per week.

In Atlanta, the city government's "Blueprint to End Homelessness" estimated that only 2,000 people in the city are "chronically homeless," but many service providers believe there are more than 10,000. The city's "solution" is a converted jail with 270 beds and referrals to other programs and resources. The Atlanta Housing Authority has destroyed thousands of public housing units, replacing them with mixed-use developments by private, for-profit developers, with a fraction of the units allocated for below-market rents. The Open Door Community partners with other organizations in Atlanta to advocate on behalf of affordable housing, adequate healthcare, and jobs with a living wage for all people. In our daily life together, we struggle to live the Matthew 25 mandate: feed, clothe, visit and serve people whom the American System judges to be "the least of these."

Skills: Willingness to live and work sacrificially, and an attitude of openness to learning from your experiences in the community.

Contact: Chuck Harris, Volunteer Coordinator

PARK SLOPE CHRISTIAN HELP, INC. (CHIPS)

200 Fourth Avenue   (718) 237-2962
Brooklyn, NY 11217   www.chipsonline.org

Area: Park Slope neighborhood of Brooklyn, New York

General Information: CHIPS, a non-sectarian, voluntary, community-based organization, serves the needs of the poor and homeless in the Park Slope neighborhood of Brooklyn, New York. Our goal is to work together with church communities, the civic community, local merchants, local business people, volunteers, neighbors and guests to improve our lives. Our specific objectives are to provide healthy and tasty meals for those who are hungry in a safe, home-like, Christian environment, that is free from drugs, alcohol and the violence of the streets. CHIPS is managed by the Franciscan Sisters of the Poor and a Board of Directors. Service is provided by volunteers, senior aides, youth groups, special education providers and a few staff members. Volunteers are needed daily from 8 am to 3 pm.

Skills: No previous experience necessary.

Contact: Sr. Mary A. Maloney, Director

PART OF THE SOLUTION (P.O.T.S.)

2763 Webster Avenue   (718) 220-4892 Ext 12
Bronx, NY 10458   serve@potsbronx.org
         www.potsbronx.org

Area: Bronx, New York

General Information: Founded in 1982, Part of the Solution (P.O.T.S.) has grown from a storefront soup kitchen to an extensive community-based organization, offering multiple services to homeless and low-income people of New York. P.O.T.S.' mission challenges us to be a loving community in the Bronx that nourishes the basic needs and hungers of all who come to our door. Community Service is not just an opportunity to "give back" but also an opportunity to share in the lives of people. P.O.T.S. recognizes that volunteers have a basic need and hunger, too. We will respond. Our Community Dining Room is a restaurant style serving space. Volunteers are the wait staff, bus staff, maître d' and plate expediters. We believe the real service, though, is sitting down at one of the tables of four and sharing in the meal. A conversation at the table is the first step to building a greater community.

Skills: No specific skills required, any skill will be put to use.

Contact: Taina Rodriguez, Kitchen and Volunteer Coordinator

PEACE AND JUSTICE CENTER

21 Church Street   (802) 863-2345 Ext 3
Burlington, VT 05401   www.pjcvt.org

Area: Burlington, Vermont

General Information: The Peace and Justice Center's mission is to create a just and peaceful world. To this end, we work on the interconnected issues of economic and racial justice, peace, and human rights through education, advocacy, training and nonviolent activism, and community organizing. Our program focuses on racial and economic justice, peace and human rights. Volunteers work with staff on specific projects and must be at least age 18. No minimum/maximum in terms of time commitment. Need to be based in Vermont, preferably Burlington.

Skills: Computer competence, organizing experience desired.

Contact: Wendy Coe or Andrea Arratoon

PEASLEE NEIGHBORHOOD CENTER

215 East 14th Street   (513) 621-5514
Cincinnati, OH 45202   www.peasleecenter.org

Area: Cincinnati, Ohio in the neighborhood of Over-the-Rhine

General Information: Peaslee Neighborhood Center, located in downtown Cincinnati, was created 25 years ago through the hard work of neighborhood mothers who wanted an educational resource for their children in their community. Peaslee serves the Over-the-Rhine and neighboring communities as a center for community-based education initiatives, a forum to address social justice issues, and a fully licensed child development center. The center is a place where families and children can access and participate in educational programs that foster creative expression, self-determination and social change. Peaslee seeks to empower people and provides programming that focuses on education, arts and music. The Child Development Center, our largest program, serves infants, toddlers and pre-schoolers. Peaslee Schoolyard uses gardening to enhance children's learning through nature. In addition to the center, Peaslee has collaborated with many neighborhood groups organizing around issues including schools, adequate recreation space, affordable housing and welfare reform.

High school and college students can arrange visits to the center for an orientation to learn about our neighborhood. These groups are involved in "urban plunges" and participate in service-learning projects. Volunteer opportunities include assisting teachers in the child-care center, working in the Edible Garden, assisting with art and music events, receptionist duties, maintenance and building needs and computer technical assistance.

Skills: Ability to work well with a wide variety of people; desire to work with children and youth; interest in gardening/nature; information technology skills; building maintenance skills; publications and marketing skills

Contact: Annaliese Newmeyer, Child Development Center Director

PHILIPPINES WORKERS SUPPORT COMMITTEE

2252 Puna Street   (808) 595-7362
Honolulu, HI 96817   witeck@hawaii.edu

Area: Honolulu, Hawaii

General Information: The Philippines Workers Support Committee was founded in 1983. It is an international labor solidarity network based among trade unionists and labor supporters in the U.S., which distributes information and analysis from the Kilusang Mayo Uno (May 1st Labor Center) in the Philippines. Membership dues: $15/year ($25 for unions, organizations). Speakers and videos available for rental/showing. We sponsor tours to the Philippines and the U.S. (for Philippine trade unionists) and work on educational issues of international labor.

Skills: Experience in organizing forums or fund-raising is helpful.

Contact: John Witeck, Coordinator

PROJECT PLASE, INC.

Photo: Project PLASE, Inc.

The staff and volunteers of Project PLASE assist clients with advocacy, counseling and finding long-term or permanent housing.

PROJECT PLASE, INC.

1814 Maryland Avenue
Baltimore, MD 21201

(410) 837-1400
info@projectplase.org
www.projectplase.org

Area: Baltimore, Maryland

General Information: Fifty-four percent of Maryland's homeless citizens reside in Baltimore City. Baltimore now has more new AIDS cases than San Francisco, with over 50,000 people who are substance abusers, and more than 40,000 people infected with AIDS/HIV. The homeless population is diverse, but has a high percent of black, young poor and people who have become addicted to drugs. They need housing and a myriad of supportive services. PLASE, which stands for People Lack Adequate Shelter and Employment, has dedicated itself to aiding homeless persons in Baltimore since 1974 through our Transitional and Permanent Housing Programs. We operate four transitional housing shelters (62 beds total) where individuals may stay while we help them get stabilized and access the resources they need. We then assist them in finding long-term/permanent housing.

Once individuals find permanent housing, we continue to work with them to ensure their success, prevent the recurrence of homelessness and provide supportive services for as long as they need them.

These services include case management, addiction recovery services, and life skills training, among other things. We also work to connect our clients with outside agencies, e.g. to get substance abuse treatment, financial assistance and medical care.

Other than Project PLASE, there is no housing program for the medically fragile, homeless person in the Baltimore Metropolitan Area, despite an outcry from medical institutions and social workers for such a program. With the changes in medical insurance practices in recent years, this population is pushed out of institutions ever more quickly. PLASE's waiting list includes nearly 1,000 homeless persons with medical, mental health, addiction and psychiatric illnesses.

Project PLASE volunteers gain an increased understanding and knowledge of homelessness and a deeper feeling of connection to and concern for the Baltimore community. Volunteers can work full- or part-time and range in age from late teens to 60-plus. They are able to work directly with PLASE clients, work on improving our shelters or provide administrative assistance to the organization.

Skills: Any experience working with the homeless population is welcome but not required.

Contact: Andy Dubosky, Communications and Development

PROTESTANT COMMUNITY CENTERS, INC.

25 James Street   (973) 621-2273
Newark, NJ 07102   amadsen@cacofnj.com
                                                   www.cacofnj.com

Area: Newark, New Jersey

General Information: The Protestant Community Centers (PCCI) is a multi-service agency which serves the needs of children and residents in and around the city. Volunteers are needed for commitments of six months to a year (in some instances, stipends can be made available) to work with children, youth and adults in Newark. Volunteers can also apply for short-term specialized projects such as research, public relations, technology, grant writing, building repairs, outreach, etc. Summer volunteers and workcamp groups also welcome.

PCCI, with affiliated Community Agencies Corp. of New Jersey, is always in need of individuals to assist with the literacy, after-school and summer programs consisting of: educational support (tutoring and mentoring) and music, arts, crafts and drama; trips; community service; scouting; leadership; recreation and sports. St. Timothy's Home is a group home for 10 boys placed there by the courts for various reasons—such as neglect, abuse, minor incidents with the law. We are seeking full-time child-care workers and full-time house parents to supplement and strengthen this program.

Skills: Some experience is required in the more technical aspects of our agency. However, we provide intensive and ongoing training to continually motivate and educate volunteers. Having a driver's license and a clean driving record is a big plus.

Contact: William Madsen, Deputy Director

PROVIDENCE HOUSE

703 Lexington Avenue
Brooklyn, NY 11221

(718) 455-0197 Ext 32
info@providencehouse.org
www.providencehouse.org

Area: Brooklyn, Queens and New Rochelle, New York

General Information: Providence House (PH) began in 1979 when four Sisters of St. Joseph offered hospitality and a place to stay to a mother who was coming out of prison and reuniting with her young child. Many more mothers and children have followed over the past 25 years; over 7,000 women and 4,000 children have lived at Providence House. From the beginning, we focused on providing shelter and a supportive environment to homeless, formerly incarcerated women and their children. Guided by values of hospitality, nonviolence, compassion and community, our goal has been to help women become self-sufficient and recreate lives of stability for themselves and their children.

Volunteers complement our staff and support our mission by participating in a wide variety of tasks. Our volunteer program is flexible. Short-term volunteer opportunities include assisting in the Child Care Center; participating in Household repairs; providing tutoring/GED assistance; organizing drives for the women and children (school supplies, books, personal hygiene, household and childcare items, etc.); coordinating an arts and crafts project.

Providence House also welcomes long-term volunteers to serve as a member of the core community in a capacity similar to how the Sisters/core communities function now. This can be women in their 20's, 30's +, who could be graduating college or attending graduate school; they could also be professional women working in the local area. Their "job description" is to be a live-in presence for the women at the house, participating in the life and activities of the Providence House that they would be residing in, particularized to the unique ways that each PH community defines itself (shared prayer, shopping/household responsibilities, etc.) The candidate would be expected to make a financial contribution to cover lodging, food, household expense— which we would work out with each candidate, being respectful of their specific situation. Individuals must be at least 18 years old.

Skills: Female volunteers only, for those who request room and board and would live in PH. Must be able to live and work with a diverse group of people in an urban area and willing to support our mission and values. A volunteer's skills are defined by what that specific volunteer can do. Since there is no standard volunteer profile, each volunteer brings different abilities and capabilities.

Contact: Paula Migliore, Director of Mission Effectiveness

QUEST FOR PEACE/QUIXOTE CENTER

PO Box 5206   (301) 699-0042
Hyattsville, MD 20782   www.quest.quixote.org

Area: Washington, DC metropolitan area

General Information: The Quest for Peace, over the last 20 years, has gathered and shipped more than $160 million in donated humanitarian aid and development funds to the rural poor of Nicaragua. In Nicaragua, the Institute of John XXIII coordinates the Quest. The Quest's policy of "liberating development" fosters grassroots economic development. We assist rural people with projects of their choice that provide jobs and internal markets. Our aid supports small producers, assists people to get the homes, jobs, health care and education that they need and desire. In the U.S. we work to enact policies that are just toward the people of Nicaragua. Time periods for service are negotiable. Interns/volunteers should be college age or above.

Skills: Good writing and verbal skills. Spanish is a plus. Ability to work in a team dynamic on a variety of projects.

Contact: Carol Ries, Co-Director

RACHEL CARSON COUNCIL, INC.

PO Box 10779   (301) 593-7507
Silver Spring, MD 20914   rccouncil@aol.com
                                               www.rachelcarson.org

Area: Washington, DC area

General Information: RCC is a library and clearinghouse for information on pesticides and alternatives to their use. It maintains extensive files: including data on toxicity, effects on human and domestic-animal health and on how pesticides affect non-domestic animals and plants. The Council also has information on less toxic means of pest control. It produces educational materials on these topics and distributes this information to the public. Each day the Council responds to many requests for information from individuals, businesses, schools and agencies. Although progress has been made in the area of erecting institutional and legislative frameworks for the protection of the environment, and a gradual improvement in public awareness has occurred, we still face a future as perilous as before.

While it may seem that we are now better equipped to deal with environmental problems, the problems of today are often more complex and threatening than those we faced in the past. Thus the need for the Council's services remains strong. RCC is not a lobbying or activist organization. The physical library is open to the public by appointment. The Council is also a repository for historical information about Rachel Carson, the author of Silent Spring, the book that, in 1962, launched the environmental movement. Volunteers must be adults and must commit to serving a minimum of four hours a week.

Skills: Researchers and writers with background in chemistry, biology; librarians; persons skilled in MS Access.

Contact: Diana Post, President

RAINFOREST ACTION NETWORK

221 Pine Street, Suite 500   (415) 398-4404
San Francisco, CA 94104   rainforest@ran.org
                                               www.ran.org/get_involved/

Area: San Francisco Bay Area, California

General Information: Rainforest Action Network (RAN) works to protect the earth's rainforests, their inhabitants, and the natural systems that sustain life through education, grassroots organizing and nonviolent direct action. Begun in 1985, RAN works internationally in cooperation with other environmental and human rights organizations on major campaigns to protect rainforests, defend Indigenous rights, and prevent climate chaos. Methods include negotiation to resolve problems; public pressure; direct action, such as letter writing campaigns, boycotts, consumer action campaigns, demonstrations and selective bans; grassroots organizing in the U.S.; building coalitions and collaborating with other environmental, scientific and grassroots groups; organizing conferences and seminars; conducting research; supporting economic alternatives; facilitating communications between U.S. and Third World organizations; spear-heading public education and media outreach projects; making small grants to front-line communities working to defend their forest homes.

Skills: Research, grassroots organizing, data entry and mailings.

Contact: Nancy Johnson, Volunteer/Intern Program Director

REAL CHANGE HOMELESS EMPOWERMENT PROJECT

2129 Second Avenue
Seattle, WA 98121

(206) 441-3247 Ext 212
volunteer@realchangenews.org
www.realchangenews.org

Area: Seattle, Washington

General Information: Real Change provides income opportunity to poor and homeless people in Seattle through publication and street sales of a weekly urban-issues newspaper. Our mission is to create opportunity and a voice for low-income people while taking action to end homelessness and poverty. Real Change offers the opportunity to make an immediate difference in a homeless person's life and extends an invitation to further action through various programs we offer. We are always looking for volunteer journalists, photographers, editors, event planners, graphic designers and people to act as receptionist in our small office. Volunteers can also become active in the Real Change Organizing Project (RCOP). RCOP is a program of Real Change that works to build power and take action on issues of housing affordability, growing inequality and human and civil rights.

Skills: Patience, strong communication skills, organizational skills, familiarity with computers and the ability to work well independently are required. We are looking for responsible, committed people to help us fulfill our mission of organizing, educating and building alliances to create solutions to homelessness and poverty.

Contact: Polly Jirkovsky, Volunteer Coordinator

RECORDING FOR THE BLIND AND DYSLEXIC

Photos: Recording for the Blind and Dyslexic

RFB&D has over 7,000 trained volunteers working in 29 studios nationwide recording textbooks for students who would otherwise have no to access to the material due to their learning disabilities.

Students and professionals who are unable to read standard print effectively due to a disability are able to listen to and learn from the one-of-a-kind collection of educational audiobooks.

RECORDING FOR THE BLIND & DYSLEXIC

National Headquarters (866) 732-RFBD
20 Roszel Road www.rfbd.org
Princeton, NJ 08540

Area: Throughout the United States

General Information: Recording for the Blind & Dyslexic (RFB&D) is the nation's educational library of recorded textbooks for students with print or physical disabilities that make reading standard print or handling a book difficult or impossible. Originally founded more than 60 years ago to help blinded veterans of World War II, RFB&D now serves students and professionals with print disabilities with its one-of-a-kind collection of educational audio books. Students rely on RFB&D's unique accommodation to access the printed page and to achieve educational success. All of RFB&D's accessible titles are recorded by volunteers. There are currently more than 7,000 volunteers working in 29 RFB&D studios nationwide as readers, recording directors, outreach representatives, fund-raisers and office assistants. RFB&D especially needs readers with background in math and science. Training is provided for all volunteers.

Skills: Volunteers with educational background in specialty and technical subject areas are especially needed, but not required.

Contact: Lori Alvarez, Unit Administration

RISING HOPE, INC.

PO Box 906 (914) 276-7848
Croton Falls, NY 10519 risinghopeinc@optonline.net
www.risinghope.org

Area: Ossining, Stormville, Staten Island, Warwick, Fishkill and Woodbourne in New York state

General Information: Rising Hope, Inc. provides college-level educational programs for men in prison in order to awaken them to their innate potential to learn and grow intellectually, psychologically, spiritually, morally, socially, and vocationally, and to equip them to work effectively for the benefit of themselves, their families and others wherever their lives may take them. Our programs have been developed and succeeded with a focus on Christian theology, however, we treat this subject matter academically, without proselytizing, with respect for other religions, and invite each person to assess the material in light of his or her own perspective and faith orientation. We welcome, without regard to religious affiliation or belief, participation at all levels—as students, teachers, volunteers, board members—of all whom join our effort. We seek to apply principles of faith to our endeavor, asking and trusting in God, each according to our own faith for inspiration, guidance, and providence. We are committed to integrity, openness, honesty, and sincerity in all our actions. We choose to remain an all-volunteer organization in order to focus our energy on running our program rather than fund-raising, and to maximize our cost-effectiveness. We thus avoid the expenses and fund-raising burden that having paid employees requires.

Skills: For mentors and coordinators, no special qualifications. For instructors, at least a masters degree.

Contact: Deborah Moore or Bob Lukey

RIVINGTON HOUSE

45 Rivington Street
New York, NY 10002

(212) 539-6219
gerryl@vcny.org
www.vcny.org

Area: New York City

General Information: Rivington House—The Nicholas A. Rango Health Care Facility is a 206-bed AIDS-specific residential health care facility. Rivington House also provides an AIDS day treatment program. The focus of care is to engage each individual in the process of healing the body, mind and spirit by accepting people as they are, meeting them where they are and nurturing growth and change when possible.

Volunteers visit our residents and day treatment program participants one-on-one or during social and other group activities. They operate the library and new gift shop. Other volunteers instruct our residents and clients in computer/Internet use, reading and ESL. Staff, residents and clients are also helped by volunteers who operate the coffee and book carts and assist in the administrative, recreational therapy and nutritional services areas. We are open to new ways that volunteers can help improve the quality of life for our residents and clients.

Volunteers must be 16 and older. Some opportunities require some experience; training and education are provided for most activities.

Skills: Desire to help, positive outlook and good listening skills.

Contact: Gerry Logan, Director of Volunteer Services

ROSWELL PARK CANCER INSTITUTE

Elm & Carlton Streets　　　　　　　　　(716) 845-5708
Buffalo, NY 14263　　　　　　　susan.siegel@roswellpark.org

Area: Buffalo, New York

General Information: Roswell Park Cancer Institute (RPCI) was founded in 1898 by Dr. Roswell Park. RPCI was the first full-service cancer center in the world. Leading the battle against cancer for over a century, RPCI is the only upstate New York facility to hold both the National Cancer Institute designation of "comprehensive cancer center" and membership in the National Comprehensive Cancer Network. To be comprehensive means that a cancer center maintains an exemplary leadership role in setting national standards for cancer care, research, prevention and education. RPCI has over 21,000 active patients. Over 80% of those patients are from the western New York region. We have an extensive summer youth volunteer program. Volunteers must be at least 15 years old. All year-round training provided. All placements are individualized according to the skills of the volunteer and the needs of the Institute.

Skills: Patient care: compassionate, outgoing, good listener, able to relate to persons with serious illness. Research: knows library literature searches, computer skills, able to devote substantial blocks of time. Education: knows prevention strategies, public speaking, commitment to public health issues. Administrative: management, finance, clerical, fund-raising, customer service, communications.

Contact: Susan Siegel, Director of Volunteer Services

RURAL ADVANCEMENT FOUNDATION INTERNATIONAL-USA (RAFI-USA)

PO Box 640　　　　　　　　　　　(919) 542-1396 Ext 201
Pittsboro, NC 27312　　　　　　　　　　regina@rafiusa.org
　　　　　　　　　　　　　　　　　　www.rafiusa.org

Area: Pittsboro, North Carolina; Anywhere via Internet

General Information: The Rural Advancement Foundation International-USA (RAFI-USA) cultivates markets, policies and communities that support thriving, socially just and environmentally sound family farms. While focusing on North Carolina and the southeastern United States, we also work nationally and internationally. RAFI is creating a movement among farm, environmental and consumer groups to ensure that: family farmers have the power to earn a fair and dependable income; everyone who labors in agriculture is respected, protected and valued by society; air, water and soil are preserved for future generations; the land yields healthy and abundant food and fiber that is accessible to all members of society; the full diversity of seeds and breeds, the building blocks of agriculture, are reinvigorated and publicly protected.

RAFI's Farm Sustainability program serves small and mid-scale family farmers by assisting them in transitioning to more sustainable farming operations and increasing their chances for success. We assist individual farmers who are facing financial crisis, provide training and publications for farmers and advocates on significant agricultural issues, and advocate for policies that encourage and support the transition to sustainable farming operations.

The Just Foods program promotes a systems-based approach to a more sustainable food and fiber system. We promote meaningful standards for organic agriculture, comprehensive labels for products grown in environmentally sound and socially just ways, and improved certification programs. Through research, analysis, education, advocacy and coalition-building, we educate farmers and consumers about diversity's importance in agriculture, emphasize how GE foods could jeopardize long-term food security and farmers' livelihoods, evaluate new technology based on economic viability, environmental soundness, and social justice, and create new and expanded production, marketing and research opportunities for sustainable and organic farmers.

Skills: Computer, phone, library, graphics, typing, data entry, research. Agriculture experience not necessary but will help in some areas.

Contact: Regina Bridgman, Office and Communications Manager

RURAL COALITION

1012 14th Street NW, Suite 1100   (202) 628-7160
Washington, DC 20005   lpicciano@ruralco.org
                              www.ruralco.org

Area: Nationwide

General Information: The Rural Coalition/Coalición Rural is an alliance of regionally and culturally diverse organizations working to build a more just and sustainable food system which brings fair return to minority and other small farmers and rural communities; ensures just and fair working conditions for farmworkers; protects the environment and delivers safe and healthy food to consumers. We advocate for national policies which support these goals, along with economic development initiatives that bridge the digital divide and help our diverse members market their products from their farms.

We are constantly reaching out to younger generations to train to carry on our advocacy work with members of Congress and the Administration. We accept volunteer college/university interns, fellows and others, year-round without regard to age, sex, race or ethnicity. The length of service is negotiable, anywhere from a semester to one year. Because we take such care and measure in analyzing and implementing our policy strategies, we encourage our volunteers to be knowledgeable of food and foreign policies, conservation issues, Congress and the legislative process, and communication strategies.

Skills: Some college required.

Contact: Lorette Picciano, Executive Director

ST. FRANCIS XAVIER MISSION

55 West 15th Street (212) 627-2100
New York, NY 10011 Fax: (212) 675-6997

Area: Chelsea neighborhood of New York City

General Information: The St. Francis Xavier Mission encompasses five programs: the Welcome Table soup kitchen, Food Pantry, Education Program (EOP), Xavier Men's Shelter and All Saints Clothing Room. The Welcome Table aims to be more than just another "soup kitchen"—we strive to impart a sense of dignity and hope to those shown little respect in society. Since 1983 nearly one million meals have been served by our volunteers. Each Sunday we serve an average of 840 meals to our guests. The same ideals of dignity and respect guide us in our work at the monthly client-choice Food Pantry, which allows guests to choose the foods they want. The All Saints Clothing Room operates on Sunday morning to provide approximately 60 guests per week, who are going through the interview process, with toiletries, undergarments, casual outfits, and business attire. The Xavier Shelter welcomes up to 15 men, 365 nights a year. Our volunteers stay with the guests each night and provide them with an evening snack and breakfast. We take one further step in serving homeless and formerly homeless through the EOP, a life skills training and mentoring program. EOP meets for 24 sessions and there are two semesters per year.

Skills: Just enthusiasm, patience, cheerfulness.

Contact: Cassandra Agredo

SAMARITAN HOUSE OF ATLANTA, INC./CAFÉ 458

PO Box 89125   (404) 523-1239/(404) 446-4680
Atlanta, GA 30312   adsmith@samhouse.org
                                              www.samhouse.org

Area: Atlanta, Georgia

General Information: Samaritan House of Atlanta/Café 458 helps homeless men and women achieve self-sufficiency through personalized employment readiness and life stabilization programs. Our life stabilization program, Café 458, provides noon-time meals, case management and support services to chronically homeless men and women, many of whom struggle with addiction issues, mental health concerns and severe physical disabilities. Our comprehensive Employment Readiness Program's services help our guests develop skills to become gainfully employed (a post office address, resume development, mock-interview workshops, job boards and goal-setting sessions). Additional services include meals, counseling, clothing closet, storage space, laundry facilities, toiletry items, shower facilities, community Voice Mail, telephone access, mailing address and referrals to address specific issues.

Skills: Interpersonal skills, administrative and management skills, counseling, meal preparation and a valid driver's license.

Contact: Alison Smith, Volunteer and Outreach Coordinator

SAN ANTONIO CHILDREN'S MUSEUM

305 East Houston Street   (210) 212-4453 Ext 1314
San Antonio, TX 78205   volunteer@sakids.org
                                              www.sakids.org

Area: San Antonio, Texas

General Information: The San Antonio Children's Museum is dedicated to providing engaging hands-on experiences where "Kids Play to Learn and Adults Learn to Play." The museum, a nonprofit organization, was founded by a group of dedicated volunteers committed to building a community space for early childhood development. Since our opening in 1995, more than two million visitors have explored three floors of hands-on exhibits that spark children's imagination and help them discover a world of knowledge. The museum's exhibits and programs, geared for children ages newborn to ten years, focus on early childhood learning, especially in the creative arts and sciences. We are dedicated to reaching a broader audience and bringing opportunities to children outside of the museum. A new outreach program

SAN ANTONIO CHILDREN'S MUSEUM

A volunteer guides children in a lesson in the museum's weekly FETCH! Science Lab Program.

called Museum To Go! takes arts and science programming to school groups, church groups, scout troops, and clubs.

Volunteers are an essential part of the museum's team and help us deliver valuable and memorable experiences to our guests and the community. We need volunteers to assist with exhibits, art and science activities, outreach events, special events and more. Volunteers of all ages are needed, minimum age is 14. Volunteers age 18 and older must consent to a background check and attend a volunteer orientation. Individual volunteers and groups are needed year-round during the week, weekend and occasional evenings.

Skills: Must be friendly and enthusiastic, reliable and flexible.

Contact: Lynne Lee, Volunteer Coordinator

THE SERVICE CENTER OF CATHOLIC SOCIAL SERVICES

555 Dauphin Street
Mobile, AL 36602

(251) 434-1500
sbruder@mobilecss.org
www.servicecentermob.org

Area: Mobile, Alabama

General Information: The Service Center provides limited emergency assistance to families and individuals in the form of food, used clothing, furniture or appliances and, when possible, financial assistance with utilities, rent or medicine. In keeping with the Gospel mandate to feed the hungry and shelter the homeless, the Service Center is a part of the social ministry of the Archdiocese of Mobile. The people we serve range from the homeless and chronically poor to middle income folks experiencing a crisis due to illness, job loss, or disaster such as an accident, house fire or hurricane. We have a limited budget and keep our paid staff to a minimum. We need volunteers to manage and coordinate food, clothing and furniture donations, enter data into the computer or answer telephones as well as advocate with the power company and other agencies on behalf of our clients. We are open Monday through Friday and see between 50 and 70 people a day. Every fall season we organize Christmas activities and gifts for those in need, matching donors with recipients. Volunteers are urgently needed; we try to match their talents with our need and work out schedules on an individual basis. Minimum age 18. Winters in Mobile are mild; this is an ideal location for retired persons wanting to escape a harsher climate while at the same time making a contribution and helping the less fortunate.

Skills: A compassionate heart that is non-judgmental.

Contact: Sister Beth Marie Ruder

S.H.A.P.E. COMMUNITY CENTER, INC.

3903 Almeda
Houston, TX 77004

(713) 521-0629
shape@shape.org
www.shape.org

Area: Houston, Texas

General Information: S.H.A.P.E. Community Center (Self Help for African People Through Education) is a leading community organization in the Greater Houston area that has led the way in fighting for justice, equal opportunity, human rights since 1969. S.H.A.P.E.'s ongoing programs include after school and summer youth enrichment activities and leadership programs, free computer classes and math tutoring, parenting support groups and family counseling. Its family center has a Vegan Café, hosts a monthly holistic food workshop, and various health initiatives such as pediatric eye screening and exercise clinics for the aged. The center also has an annual Freedom Tour that retraces the Civil Rights Movement, Pan African Festival and Kwanzaa Celebrations. S.H.A.P.E. also has a strong non-partisan Get Out The Vote initiative, registering and transporting people to the polls to vote. For over 40 years, S.H.A.P.E. has survived the ebbs and flows of the civil rights movement, serving people in the community. The center, which originally had a staff of two, now supports 12 full- and part-time staff and hundreds of volunteers, who are a key component to S.H.A.P.E.'s success.

Skills: Volunteers are especially needed with general administrative and office skills. We also need IT specialists and computer education instructors, graphic artists, academic tutors, organizers and grant writers.

Contact: Deloyd Parker, Jr., Executive Director; Jacqueline Mitchell, Executive Assistant

SIOUX YMCA

PO Box 218 B Street   (605) 365-5232
Cheyenne River Reservation   crandall@siouxymca.org
Dupree, SD 57623   www.siouxymca.org

Area: Cheyenne River Reservation, South Dakota

General Information: Since 1879, Sioux YMCA's mission has been to develop and strengthen the children and families in the reservation communities so they can fulfill their greatest individual and collective spiritual, mental and physical potentials. We provide a variety of issue-based programs, special events, educational trips/camping experiences and support services for youth and families living in small villages on the Cheyenne River Reservation. Our programs serve mostly youth and teens by targeting poverty reduction through leadership and entrepreneurship, as well as educational support and wellness.

We are based in a log cabin in Dupree and hold outreach programs and community camps for several villages throughout the reservation. While the reservation is economically one of the poorest in the United States, the culture is rich in relationships, traditions and the desire to make a better life. We work closely with Tribal organizations, local schools and churches, Tribal Ventures, community health representatives and community center organizations and their leaders.

Volunteers work with Sioux YMCA staff on many projects and programs. Volunteers must be able to travel long distances over gravel roads to serve the communities outside of Dupree. Candidates need to serve for a minimum of 6 to 8 weeks, preferably longer; be at least 19 years old, with a preference to those over 21 or older; be a U.S. citizen able to lift 35 lbs. unassisted; have a valid driver's license, a good driving record and commit to an alcohol-, tobacco- and drug-free lifestyle while serving with the Sioux YMCA. We need volunteers and interns September through May. Special summer positions for individuals are available. College Alternative Spring Break trips may be arranged. Housing is provided; most meals are generally at a volunteer's own expense.

Individuals sometimes arrive with inaccurate, preconceived notions of Native Americans and Reservation life, which stem from common media stereotypes, false assumptions and agendas of media. We encourage volunteers to visit and/or volunteer at cultural events, such as a Pow Wow, keeping in mind that many ceremonies are deeply personal to the participants. The Sioux YMCA is here to serve and work towards the best interests of the youth and their families.

Skills: Experience in recreation, working with children, ability to live and work in another culture, flexibility and creativity are helpful skills.

Contact: Claudia Wieland-Randall

THE SOLDIERS PROJECT

c/o LAISPS   (818) 761-7438
12011 San Vicente Boulevard, #310   or (877) 576-5343
Los Angeles, CA 90049   info@thesoldiersproject.org
                                 www.thesoldiersproject.org

Area: Sacramento and Southern California; Chicago, Illinois; New Jersey; Long Island, New York; Seattle, Washington

General Information: The Soldiers Project provides free, unlimited, confidential psychological treatment to all military services members and their extended families. All therapists are licensed and have special training in the treatment of war-related psychological problems, including family issues related to deployments and homecoming. All therapists are volunteers. Volunteers with expertise in grant writing, publicity, administration are especially needed.

Skills: For therapists, professional license and malpractice insurance is required. For others, comfort with public relations and the web.

Contact: Judith Broder, MD

SOUTH WEST NETWORK FOR ENVIRONMENTAL & ECONOMIC JUSTICE

804 Park Avenue SW   (505) 242-0416 Ext 10
Albuquerque, NM 87102   rosa@sneej.org

Area: Albuquerque, New Mexico and throughout the Southwest

General Information: The South West Network for Environmental &

Economic Justice (SW Network) brings together activists and grass-roots organizations from across the Southwest, West and border states of Mexico. Our purpose is to develop and broaden collective regional strategies and perspectives on environmental degradation and other social, racial, generational, economic and gender injustices. The SW Network recognizes the direct link between economic and environmental issues. As indigenous people and people of color, we recognize that the demand for a safe, clean environment and workplace can only be achieved by building a multiracial, multicultural, multigenerational and international movement with gender equality that promotes environmental and economic justice. Furthermore, sustainable economic development alternatives must be defined by the communities most impacted by these policies. The SW Network supports the struggle for sovereignty of indigenous people and tribes.

Skills: We need volunteers to help with research in environmental issues related to both sides of the U.S./Mexico border; data entry and website entry, update and upkeep.

Contact: Rosa Cruz-Samudio

SOUTH WEST ORGANIZING PROJECT (SWOP)

211 10th Street SW
Albuquerque, NM 87102

(505) 247-8832
swop@swop.net
www.swop.net

Area: Albuquerque, New Mexico

General Information: Our mission is to empower our communities in the Southwest to realize racial and gender equality and social and economic justice. SWOP is a multiracial, multi-issue, community-based organization founded in 1980. We work for the self-determination of all people, social and economic justice at home and abroad, and live by the principle that as community and working people we have the right to control our own lives and resources.

Development in New Mexico is heavily influenced by economic interests outside the state. Since the 1840s, extraction type industries—mining, cattle ranching, timber, nuclear weapons development and now "high tech" electronics—have exploited our natural, labor and economic resources. This is one of the poorest states, and people of color are the majority. SWOP works to promote sustainable development and to assure that businesses and industries that promise jobs for New Mexicans follow through with their commitments. Volunteers help bring the talents, resources and skills of people in the community together and help us reach our objectives by educating, organizing and developing leadership in our communities.

Contact: Roberto Roibal, Field Operations

SOUTHERN APPALACHIAN LABOR SCHOOL

PO Box 127   (304) 779-2772
Kincaid, WV 25119   www.sals.info

Area: Southern coalfield counties of West Virginia

General Information: The mission of the Southern Appalachian Labor School (SALS) is to provide education, research and linkages for working class and disenfranchised people in order to promote understanding, empowerment and change. SALS is committed to developing a real comprehension of the social, economic and legal structures which affect the lives of Appalachian people. SALS operates a Community Center in Beards Fork that provides educational services and resources to a dozen coal camp communities along Loup Creek and adjacent areas.

The center also provides housing for work camp participants who come to assist the SALS housing projects, such as rehabilitation of dilapidated and energy-inefficient homes, construction of new homes, as well as education and support in financing homes. In addition, SALS concentrates on health care, political, environmental and economic reform within the communities. Through the Worker Education Program we weave together a "union" of communities and broaden the definition of union to include children, families and seniors as well as workers, all joined together to make a difference and to take back control over their lives.

Skills: Volunteers of all ages willing to learn on-the-job.

Contact: John David, Director

SOUTHERN MUTUAL HELP ASSOCIATION

3602 Old Jeanerette Road   (337) 367-3277
New Iberia, LA 70563   www.smha.org

Area: Iberia Parish, Louisiana

General Information: Southern Mutual Help Association (SMHA) is a grassroots community development corporation that focuses on human development as well as rural housing. Responsive to the needs of many people and groups in a large low-wealth area of South Louisiana, SMHA offers an affordable housing program that includes comprehensive education in family development and adjustment to transitioning economies for the farming and fishing communities of rural Louisiana; leadership skills programs for new community groups; and advice for small businesses. SMHA has a history of over three decades of community work. Volunteers should be mature people who are able to make a long-term commitment. A minimum commitment of an entire summer or a year is desired.

Volunteers need to be self-sufficient, willing to accept very basic accommodations. Volunteers will be welcomed at local centers providing meals. The work of recovery and reconstruction in these areas will continue for two to five years. Commitments of at least one week or more are required for this recovery and reconstruction work.

Skills: Mature attitude and experience with people; carpentry, electrical and plumbing skills are especially needed. Able-bodied volunteers willing to help with the physical labor are needed and welcome.

Contact: Helen Vinton

SPROUT

893 Amsterdam Avenue   (212) 222-9575
New York, NY 10025   leadership@gosprout.org
    www.gosprout.org

Area: New York City

General Information: SPROUT is a nonprofit organization dedicated to helping people with developmental disabilities and mental retardation grow through challenging and safe travel experiences. Every year we serve 1,800 adults with developmental disabilities through our overnight vacation program. We also offer the NYC activity program that organizes afternoon and evening recreational activities. We hope to enhance the mobility, self-confidence and socialization of our participants. SPROUT strives to break down some of the barriers that exist between participants and the general public.

SPROUT works exclusively with volunteers, called leaders. Leaders are responsible for the overall safety and enjoyment of their group, 24 hours a day during SPROUT trips. Duties include safety monitoring, providing physical and emotional support, activity planning, budgeting and enhancing fun. The work is hard yet immensely rewarding as you get to work with a wonderful population, develop leadership skills and gain insight into your own abilities. While leading trips—which go to about 50 different destinations, from the East Coast to California or Las Vegas—all your trip-related expenses (accommodation, activities, transportation and meals) will be paid by SPROUT. Minimum age is 21 years old. Volunteers must be able to travel, to or stay in, New York for the duration of their volunteer commitment.

Skills: Potential leaders are caring, responsible and fun-loving people, who like working with people with special needs and traveling. A driver's license is strongly preferred.

Contact: Michelle Ramos, Director of Leadership

THE STEWPOT

408 Park Avenue
Dallas, TX 75201

(214) 746-2785 Ext 238
bruceb@thestewpot.org
www.thestewpot.org

Area: Dallas, Texas

General Information: The Stewpot is a comprehensive resource center for homeless and at-risk individuals of Dallas. The Stewpot also offers comprehensive children and youth programs. We provide programming offering the neediest members of our community a foundation on which to rebuild their lives. The children and youth program is a sequential program for at-risk children in grades 1–12 with the idea of stopping the cycle of poverty before it can begin. Regular volunteers, no age requirement, help with serving lunch, mail service, the medical clinic, and Saturday School and Venturing Crew programs.

During the summer, churches and schools from all over the country bring teen volunteers to participate in the summer visiting youth program for a week. These volunteers are immersed in urban ministry by serving lunch at The Stewpot, acting as junior counselors for the inner city children's day camp and visiting various other agencies in the Dallas area. They live at First Presbyterian Church for the week they are serving, and have breakfast and lunch provided. The age requirement for this program is 14 and older.

Skills: Willingness to serve and learn.

Contact: Suzanne Dwight, Director of Children and Youth

TEACHING FOR CHANGE

PO Box 73038
Washington, DC 20056

(800) 763-9131
info@teachingforchange.org
www.teachingforchange.org

Area: Washington, DC

General Information: Teaching for Change (TfC) is a nonprofit organization of K–12 teachers and parents. TfC works with school communities to develop and promote pedagogy, resources and cross-cultural understanding for social and economic justice in the Americas. These projects reflect our goal of promoting peace, justice and human rights through critical, anti-racist, multicultural education. Nationally, the TfC catalogue reaches over 60,000 educators a year, greatly increasing access to and use of progressive teaching resources. The catalogue is now available online. Teaching for Change is also active in local school reform efforts in the DC area. Our Teaching for Equity Project works with the DC public schools on an equity approach to multicultural education. Our Tellin' Stories Project has developed a ground-breaking approach to strengthening the role of parents in urban schools. We are an active partner in a collaborative effort to strengthen the public's voice in public education called DC Voice.

Various jobs are available for interns/volunteers, including information specialist, marketing consultant and various positions related to publications and outreach.

Skills: Marketing, computer desktop publishing, curriculum development and website development are all helpful.

Contact: Deborah Menkart, Director

TEN THOUSAND VILLAGES

704 Main Street
Akron, PA 17501

(717) 859-8100
kim.vandonk@tenthousandvillages.com
www. tenthousandvillages.com

Area: Akron, Pennsylvania and throughout the U.S. and Canada

General Information: Ten Thousand Villages is a nonprofit, fair trade retail organization which provides vital and fair income to Third World people by marketing their handicrafts and telling their stories in North America. Ten Thousand Villages works with purchases from artisans who would otherwise be unemployed or underemployed. This income helps pay for food, education, health care and housing.

Thousands of volunteers in Canada and the U.S. work with Ten Thousand Villages in their home communities. Ten Thousand Villages is a nonprofit program of the Mennonite Central Committee, a relief service and peace agency of the North American Mennonite and Brethren in Christ churches, and has been working with people around the world since 1946. We need adult volunteers from all age and gender groups. Individuals, couples and groups are encouraged to volunteer. Work assignments can last from one day to two years and nearly anything in between. Positions are available at the Ten Thousand Villages Pennsylvania warehouse, as well as retail store locations throughout the U.S. and Canada.

Contact: Kim van Donk, Human Resources Placement Coordinator (for warehouse opportunities). For in-store opportunities, contact the store manager directly using info on our website under "Stores and Festivals."

TRINITY CENTER

462 West 18th Street   (814) 453-2468
Erie, PA 16502   Fax: (814) 455-8861

Area: Erie, Pennsylvania

General Information: We are a drug and alcohol prevention agency working with inner city, at-risk youth and their families. We ask that our volunteers be at least 18 years old and be positive role models. The youth in our After School Program are K–8th graders and our Youth Group is made up of 6–12th graders. Trinity Center needs volunteers to work one-on-one with youth reading, playing games, doing puzzles and working on computers. We also have a boxing gym and are looking for volunteers interested in boxing, or who have a background in either boxing or other martial arts.

Skills: Willingness to teach and learn from experiences.

Contact: Karen Naricevicz, Director

UNITED MINISTRIES

606 Pendleton Street   (864) 232-6463
Greenville, SC 29601   info@united-ministries.org
                                             www.united-ministries.org

Area: Greenville County, South Carolina

General Information: United Ministries addresses the immediate needs of the poor in Greenville; we also help them build better lives for themselves and their families. We provide opportunities for people in Greenville County who lack education or employment skills, who are in financial crisis, or who are homeless. We provide a measure of stability to families in financial stress by assisting with basic needs such as rent, utilities, food, heat, and prescriptions. We remove barriers for individuals who are motivated to improve their employment situation through training and case management. We provide a middle-school and GED program for adults. Volunteers are essential to all our ministries. Volunteers teach and tutor in our Adult Education program. Volunteers interview participants, work in the food pantry, help with clerical work, distribute supplies at the day shelter for homeless people, work on committees of various sorts, among other things. Part-time volunteers work out schedules with the Volunteer Coordinator. A potential volunteer can also inquire about establishing a full-time internship schedule and assignment.

Contact: Keith Traut, Executive Director

UNITED STATES FUND FOR UNICEF

125 Maiden Lane   (800) 4-UNICEF
New York, NY 10038   www.unicefusa.org/volunteer

Area: Anywhere in the United States

General Information: For over 60 years, UNICEF, the United Nations Children's Fund, has been the world's leader for children, helping them to survive and thrive, from early childhood through adolescence and into healthy adulthood, currently working in 155 countries and territories. As the world's largest provider of vaccines for developing countries, UNICEF supports health and nutrition programs, quality basic education for all boys and girls, access to clean water and sanitation, and the protection of children from violence, exploitation and HIV/AIDS. In the U.S., the U.S. Fund for UNICEF raises funds to support life-saving programs around the world. Through educational advocacy and fund-raising activities, volunteers increase public awareness about the issues facing children around the world. Volunteers help neighborhood schools with the Trick-or-Treat for UNICEF program, conduct community awareness activities and organize various fund-raising activities on behalf of UNICEF.

Contact: Register through our website or call the 800 number.

URBAN ECOLOGY CENTER

1500 East Park Place
Milwaukee, WI 53211

(414) 964-8505
uec@urbanecologycenter.org
www.urbanecologycenter.org

Area: Milwaukee, Wisconsin

General Information: The Urban Ecology Center (UEC) began in 1991 as a group of volunteers seeking to revitalize Riverside Park, an abandoned and crime-ridden urban park in Milwaukee. The organization now has two neighborhood environmental community centers that host over 65,000 visits annually by people of all ages. UEC educates and inspires people to understand and value nature as motivation for positive change, neighborhood by neighborhood. We provide outdoor science education for urban youth; protect and use public natural areas making them safe, accessible and vibrant; preserve and enhance these natural areas and their surrounding waters; and promote community by offering resources that support learning, recreation, stewardship and camaraderie.

The UEC's Neighborhood Environmental Education Project connects the teachers and students of urban schools to the natural world in their own community through hands-on science and recreational opportunities. Eighty-five percent of these students are part of the federal free and reduced lunch program. The UEC revitalizes county parks once abandoned and overgrown; they are now safe sites for recreational use, native habitat restoration and urban field research. As the Center has grown, involving more and more people in positive behaviors outside, crime in our county parks has significantly decreased.

Each year, hundreds of teen and adult volunteers serve individually or in groups to help further the mission of the UEC. Long-term individual volunteers giving 2–4 hours weekly serve as teaching assistants, research assistants, land stewards, receptionists, and park rangers. One-time service groups are welcome April–October to work on restoration projects in both of the parks that we serve. Unpaid research and environmental education internships are available during the school year.

Skills: A wide range of skills and interests are needed, though volunteers who have experience teaching and/or working with children of all ages or who have knowledge of the natural world and current environmental issues are particularly helpful.

Contact: Susan Winans, Volunteer Coordinator

URBAN SERVANT CORPS

1660 Ogden Street
Denver, CO 80218

(303) 894-0076
servantcorps@earthlink.net
www.servantcorps.org

Area: Denver, Colorado

General Information: Urban Servant Corps (USC) is a Lutheran volunteer program involved in ministries serving inner-city Denver. USC provides up to 18–24 full-time volunteer staff members to community service agencies each year. These agencies provide stability to the most vulnerable people in the neighborhood, such as people who are homeless, women and children living in poverty, and kids living in "at-risk" environments. USC volunteers provide valuable staff to community service agencies at a fraction of what it would cost to hire salaried staff. The overall goal of the USC is to minister to the needs of people in the inner city of Denver as an expression of God's love for the world. USC carries out its faith commitments by: living in a Christian community house in central Denver, promoting our mutual growth in faith and ministry; working in cooperation with other organizations and churches that provide immediate assistance to the disadvantaged; seeking an understanding of the issues that arise in the neighborhood and addressing and responding to these issues; hosting foreign exchanges to broaden our range of issues to include global perspectives; and sharing experiences with others and encouraging those persons to pursue their own education through experience and involvement.

Volunteers begin their one-year term of service in September of each year and finish service in mid-August. USC encourages prospective volunteers 21 years or older to apply and prefers those with college degrees.

Skills: College education or equivalent experience

Contact: Laura Folkwein, Executive Director

VENEZUELA SOLIDARITY NETWORK

1247 E Street SE
Washington, DC 20003

(202) 544-9355
vsn@afgj.org
www.vensolidarity.org

Area: Washington, DC

General Information: Venezuela Solidarity Network mobilizes grassroots activism throughout the U.S. to expose and oppose U.S. government interference in Venezuela's sovereign affairs and to support the gains that the majority poor in Venezuela have gained through the Bolivarian process. The Emergency Response Network mobilizes subscribers to respond to disinformation in the U.S. corporate media and U.S. government provocations against Venezuela. We also organize and promote study tours to Venezuela and speaking tours and conferences in the U.S. Our Respect for Democracy campaign seeks to educate and mobilize people in the U.S. to support participatory democracy and to oppose U.S. interference in other countries' elections.

Skills: Organizing experience, research and writing skills required. Computer, web and video proficiency, Spanish language skills desired.

Contact: National Coordinator

VERMONT COMMITTEE ON SOUTHERN AFRICA

288 Flynn Avenue, #20   (802) 862-4418
Burlington, VT 05401   rtkemp@aol.com

Area: Burlington, Vermont

General Information: Eight years ago in solidarity with the people of South Africa, and in recognition of the greatly needed support from the international community that fought to end apartheid in order to help end poverty, the Vermont Committee on Southern Africa began collecting new and used hard science textbooks. We make the books available to schools and library systems throughout southern Africa, including Zimbabwe, Rwanda, Uganda, Kenya, Sierra Leone, South Africa, Namibia, Botswana and Ivory Coast. Chemistry, biology, medicine and nursing books are among those needed.

Anyone may help from wherever they are, and especially if they are traveling to and from South Africa. Local volunteers compile a catalogue of the book inventory as books are received, and the schools and libraries in southern Africa choose what they need. Volunteers raise funds locally to pay for the shipping costs.

Contact: Richard T. Kemp

VOICE OF CALVARY MINISTRIES

1065 Pecan Park Circle   (601) 353-1635
Jackson, MS 39209   willbrewer@vocm.org
                                 www.vocm.org

Area: Urban Jackson, Mississippi

General Information: Voice of Calvary Ministries is an inter-denominational Christian community development organization. Founded in

Mendenhall, Mississippi by Dr. John M. Perkins in 1960, our mission is to rebuild people to rebuild communities through the gospel. We serve as a resource in Christian community development by providing holistic programs that build strong individuals, families, churches and communities to enable them to reach their full potential, physically, spiritually, economically and socially. All of the ministries are committed to cultivating partnerships among residents so that we can take responsibility for rebuilding our own neighborhood in West Jackson.

We invite you to join us as we work together for change. Programs include new home construction, housing renovation, low-income home ownership opportunities, adult learning programs (GED, financial literacy), youth leadership development and tutoring.

Short- and long-term volunteers are accepted. Short-term volunteers serve for one week. Long-term volunteers must raise their own support for the first year of service, and have completed one year of college or be 19 years of age. We also offer an eight-week summer internship program for young adults beginning in June.

Skills: Experience in the following fields is helpful: construction (carpentry, landscaping), electrical, plumbing, clerical, graphic design, elementary education

Contact: Will Brewer, Volunteer Coordinator

WAR RESISTERS LEAGUE
339 Lafayette Street   (212) 228-0450
New York, NY 10012   www.warresisters.org

Area: New York City

General Information: Believing war to be a crime against humanity, the War Resisters League (WRL), founded in 1923, advocates Gandhian nonviolence as the method for creating a democratic society free of war, racism, sexism and human exploitation. Current programs include the Anti-Militarism Program which focuses on stopping the companies that promote war and profit from the bloodshed, such as Halliburton, Bechtel, Alliant Technologies, and Lockheed-Martin. The WRL's Youth and Counter Militarism Program, based in New York City, provides youth with the resources and training necessary to agitate against military recruitment in their schools and communities. Its long-term goal is to bring youth organizers and young veterans together to help build a unified, national anti-war movement. The program produces materials, offers training and works in a number of national coalitions.

The Nonviolent Activist, the War Resisters League's 24-page bi-monthly magazine, features news and analysis of violence and wars around the globe and resistance to them. Interns and volunteers are welcome any time of the year for any length of time; the Freeman internship provides a small stipend and requires a minimum of 20 hours/week for three months or longer.

Skills: Computer, graphics, writing skills help but are not required.

Contact: Judith Atiri, Coordinator of the National Office

WESTERN SERVICE WORKERS ASSOCIATION (WSWA)

5040 Perry Avenue   (916) 456-1771
Sacramento, CA 95820

Area: Sacramento Valley, California

General Information: Western Service Workers Association (WSWA) is a grassroots organizing drive, working to permanently improve working and living conditions for the Sacramento Valley's lowest-income workers, many of whom have service jobs at minimum wage. Over 10 percent of Sacramento County's workforce is unemployed due to federal military base closures and subsequent related business shut-downs. The bases were major employers in the region and have now been converted by state law into zones for private business enterprises which receive up to $2.25 million in government subsidies, taxpayer-guaranteed loans and other extraordinary waivers of safety and other regulations.

WSWA volunteers and organizers have uncovered up to 80 percent unemployment in the lowest income areas of Sacramento and 8,000 individuals are documented as homeless as a result of these governmental policies. WSWA offers its members an 11-point self-help benefit plan that includes emergency food, clothing, non-emergency dental care, preventive medical care, legal assistance, child care, and job referral. The association brings together diverse groupings from the community to fight corporate welfare programs and policies that further exacerbate poverty conditions.

Skills: No experience is required. All skills are helpful and will be put to use. On-the-job training is provided in benefit advocacy, public speaking, desktop publishing, community organizing, door-to-door canvassing and much more.

Contact: Bill Jennett, Operations Manager

WOMEN AGAINST MILITARY MADNESS (WAMM)

310 East 38th Street, Suite 222   (612) 827-5364
Minneapolis, MN 55409   wamm@mtn.org
www.worldwidewamm.org

Area: Minnesota

General Information: Women Against Military Madness (WAMM) is an action-oriented peace and justice organization formed in 1982. *Worldwide WAMM,* our newsletter which is published 10 times per year, provides information and discussion on topics related to the militarization of our culture, human and other costs, arms control, U.S. military intervention, military recruiting and corporate globalization. WAMM is a volunteer-driven organization with a small staff. Volunteers help the staff perform office duties, serve on committees crucial to WAMM's mission, maintain our newsletter and help conduct outreach. Volunteers can serve on one of our committees concerning the following topics: Middle East, Iraq, Newsletter, fund-raising, Tackling Torture at the Top, New Member, East Africa, Counter Recruitment, Third Monday Movies, American Empire, St. Joan of Arc/WAMM Peacemakers and the Book Club. WAMM also offers internships throughout the year.

Contact: Volunteer Coordinator

THE WOMEN'S CONNECTION

4042 Glenway Avenue   (513) 471-4673
Cincinnati, OH 45205   twc@thewomensconnection.org
www.thewomensconnection.org

Area: Cincinnati, Ohio

General Information: The Women's Connection is a welcoming neighborhood center where women can find support as well as educational and social events. The Women's Connection supports women by listening, providing them with information and resources, and connecting them to these resources. Founded by Sisters of Charity in 1997 in Price Hill, a very low-income neighborhood of Cincinnati, Women's Connection is constantly striving to develop programs that meet needs not otherwise being addressed. Current programs include women's enrichment workshops, employment connections and job readiness training for women, a domestic violence support group, an AA group for women, adult literacy testing, parenting classes, tutoring for children, life-skills programs for girls ages 8–18 and children's summer camps. We also offer parallel programs in Spanish for women's enrichment, information and referrals. Volunteers help in every capacity: mentoring and tutoring children, answering phones, interpreting, greeting, helping with administrative projects and serving on committees. Full-time and part-time volunteer opportunities are available. The minimum commitment for part-time volunteer work is two months. Full-time volunteer placements are a minimum commitment of six months.

Contact: Volunteer Coordinator

WOMEN'S INTERNATIONAL LEAGUE FOR PEACE AND FREEDOM (WILPF)

777 UN Plaza, 6th floor
New York, NY 10017

(212) 682-1265
wilpfun@igc.org
www.wilpf.int.ch

Area: Geneva, Switzerland and New York City; and chapters in 37 other countries

General Information: The Women's International League for Peace and Freedom (WILPF), established in 1915, is committed to the achievement of peace and justice and the full enjoyment of human rights. WILPF brings together women from all over the world who are opposed to war, violence, exploitation and all forms of discrimination and oppression, and who wish to unite in establishing peace based on economic and social justice for all.

The PeaceWomen Project of WILPF monitors and works toward rapid and full implementation of United Nations Security Council Resolution 1325 on women, peace and security. WILPF is an international NGO with a United Nations office in New York and national sections on all continents, which are all coordinated by the International Secretariat in Geneva. WILPF is involved in peace, human rights and disarmament work at the local, national and international levels. Our expertise is based on our practical work and intervention in a multicultural, international framework, on research and analysis, and on our participation in ongoing international debates for over 85 years. WILPF has consultative status with the United Nations Economic and Social Council.

Skills: Experience in political activism is an advantage, good writing and speaking skills needed.

Contact: Director

WOMEN'S LUNCH PLACE

67 Newbury Street   (617) 267-1722
Boston, MA 02116   lisa@womenslunchplace.org
                          www.womenslunchplace.org

Area: Boston, Massachusetts

General Information: Women's Lunch Place is a daytime shelter where homeless and poor women and their children find support, friendship, and a nutritious home-cooked meal and a safe haven from the streets. It provides a place for women who have suffered unbearable losses of family, friends and home to regain a sense of dignity and self-esteem. Each day we serve a well-balanced breakfast and lunch to approximately 120 women and provide our guests with clothing, toiletries, and the opportunity to take a hot shower and do their laundry. A doctor or nurse is available five days a week to provide free medical care to women who otherwise would not be able to afford it at all. Our shelter also has a "nap room" where women who sleep on the street have a safe and quiet place to rest, and a resource center with several computers where women can search for jobs or apartments. Two full-time advocates help our guests with their complicated legal, social, financial and medical issues. We strive to create a community by inviting guests to participate in our yoga classes, art therapy groups, open art studio sessions, and knitting and quilting groups.

Volunteers play a crucial role, helping staff prepare meals, meet guests' emergency needs, assist with housing or apartment searches, and help with administrative tasks. We ask volunteers to make at least a three month commitment with at least eight hours of service per month so that we can continue to provide a stable community for our guests.

Skills: No particular skills needed, just a desire to work as a team toward a common goal.

Contact: Lisa Schottenfeld, Volunteer Coordinator

WORKERS INTERFAITH NETWORK FOR ECONOMIC JUSTICE

3035 Directors Row   (901) 332-3570
Building B, Suite 1207   msinterfaith@yahoo.com
Memphis, TN 38131   www.midsouthinterfaith.org

Area: Memphis, Tennessee

General Information: The Workers Interfaith Network for Economic

Justice educates and organizes people of faith on campaigns that will improve wages, benefits and working conditions for Mid-South workers, especially those who earn low wages. Campaigns of the organization include the Memphis Living Wage Campaign (a coalition of 40 faith, community, and labor organizations working to pass a local living wage law), and specific worker rights campaigns that ensure that low-wage workers' right to organize is respected. Full- and part-time internship and volunteer opportunities on living wage and worker rights campaigns include organizing members on phone, letter writing and direct actions such as rallies and prayer vigils; speaking to congregations, community organizations, unions and student groups about current campaigns; conducting background research for campaigns; writing for membership publications; and clerical and office tasks including data entry and mailings. Volunteers should be at least 16 years of age. Internships are available for either semester or year-long periods. Periods of volunteer assignments are flexible.

Skills: Required: Passion for social and economic justice; ability to work with limited supervision; comfortable working with Christians, Jews and Muslims. Desired skills or experience: computer literacy; community organizing; strong verbal and written communication skills; fund-raising; and experience working with faith communities.

Contact: Rebekah Jordan, Executive Director

WORLD FELLOWSHIP CENTER
PO Box 2280   (603) 447-2280
Conway, NH 03818   office@worldfellowship.org
                                                  www.worldfellowship.org

Area: White Mountains of New Hampshire

General Information: World Fellowship's mission is to promote peace and social justice through education and dialogue inspired by nature. We host retreats, conferences, groups and individuals, couples and families in five guest houses on our 455 mostly-wooded acres. Our dining room features organic produce we grow, as well as organic bread made with flour milled on site. Volunteers are incorporated in a variety of ways. Potential duties include, but are not limited to, housekeeping, dining room service, growing or preparing food, skilled carpentry and arts and crafts. Volunteers under 18 may serve with a parent on site.

Skills: Flexibility, pride in work well done.

Contact: Andy Davis, Co-Director

YOUNG PEOPLE WHO CARE, INC.

PO Box 129   (814) 263-4177
Frenchville, PA 16836   Fax: (814) 263-7106
bethanyyouth@pennswoods.net

Area: Clearfield County, Pennsylvania (Appalachia)

General Information: Founded in 1976 by a group of Catholic young people who were inspired by a Pastoral Letter about the injustice of the disparity in the Appalachian region and decided to organize a program to address the poverty there with the guidance of Sister Therese Dush. Clearfield County is Pennsylvania's second poorest county. Young People Who Care is now a year-round, full-time program, run by the Sisters of the Anawim, that organizes volunteers to assist struggling people in Clearfield County with services that are not otherwise being provided. Volunteers provide services such as yard work, home repairs, tutoring, visitations/errands for homebound individuals and the elderly, emergency housing assistance, managing a used clothing store and outreach to pregnant women.

Volunteer activities take place at Mercy Mission (clothing and household item store), the Bethany Retreat Center (spiritual and service center for adult and youth groups), Marian House (a shelter for women and children—see separate listing on page 134), other local institutions and the homes of community members. Volunteers of any duration are welcome, but there is a greater need for longer-term commitments, including summer-long. Individuals as well as groups, such as Alternative Break, clubs or youth groups, are encouraged to serve. Room and board are provided. A stipend and health insurance is offered after three months. Volunteers are encouraged to expand their interests and talents while sharing a life of simplicity and hospitality within the community. In keeping with community sustainability, long-term volunteers will have the opportunity to take on leadership roles.

Skills: All skills are encouraged; an interest in learning and serving is most important. Training is provided as needed. Carpentry, farming, maintenance, office work and counseling are valuable.

Contact: Sister Suzanne Thibault

UNITED WORLD
COLLEGES

The United World College (UWC) schools, located in 12 countries around the world, are committed to the ideals of peace, justice, international understanding and service to needy communities. U.S. citizens apply to the UWCs either in the 10th or 11th grade for this two-year, pre-university program of International Baccalaureate studies and community service. All 50 U.S. students admitted to the UWCs each year are awarded full scholarships covering tuition, room and board from the two-year program. Information about admission can be found on the admission section of **www.uwc-usa.org,** and the application deadline is early in January for fall admission.

Part 4

INTERNATIONAL VOLUNTEER PLACEMENTS

These non-government organizations provide volunteer opportunities outside the United States. Most charge at least nominal fees to cover costs, and do not include the travel involved. Many will offer you assistance in ways to raise the money needed to participate.

ACTION RECONCILIATION SERVICE FOR PEACE/ AKTION SUEHNEZEICHEN FRIEDENSDIENSTE

1501 Cherry Street   (215) 241-7249
Philadelphia, PA 19102   info@actionreconciliation.org
                            www.actionreconciliation.org

Area: Germany

General Information: Action Reconciliation Service for Peace (ASF) is a German peace and volunteer organization founded in the aftermath of World War II to confront the legacy of the Nazi regime. It is our mission to learn from history, take a stand today and help create a positive future. Every year ASF sends approximately 200 volunteers to 13 countries for one year of service. Most are Germans working in Eastern and Western Europe, Israel and the USA. We also have an international program for volunteers from our partner countries and welcome young Americans into our German projects. Americans have been volunteering with ASF in Germany since the late 1960s.

Volunteers work on a wide range of projects. Our work with Holocaust survivors is core to our mission. ASF provides peace and Holocaust education, takes an active stance against racism and anti-Semitism and is engaged in peace work. We have various projects in Jewish communities in cities such as Berlin, and at memorial and educational sites of former concentration camps. We also work with contemporary marginalized groups including the homeless, people with disabilities, people with AIDS, refugees, and the LGBT community. Furthermore, ASF is involved in community organizing and strives to empower children, youth and women.

ASF provides volunteers with orientation/evaluation seminars, international volunteer conferences, room and board, pocket money and health, accident and civil liability insurance. Year-long service begins in September of each year. Application deadline for Americans to volunteer in Germany is January 31.

Skills: Volunteers must be open to intercultural dialogue, be enthusiastic about their projects and have an interest in diversity issues. The basis for our work is awareness of our personal history in the context of larger historical events, especially the history of National Socialism and the Holocaust. Basic knowledge of the German language is necessary.

Contact: Magdalena Scharf, Director, U.S. Program

AFS INTERCULTURAL PROGRAMS, INC.

71 West 23rd Street, 17th Floor (212) 807-8686
New York, NY 10010 info@afs.org
www.afs.org

Area: United States and Worldwide

General Information: AFS is one of the world's largest nonprofit volunteer-based organizations providing intercultural learning opportunities to help people develop the knowledge, skills and understanding needed to create a more just and peaceful world. AFS offers international exchange programs for high school students, young adults and teachers. AFS has a presence in over 50 countries where AFS Partner organizations, each with a network of volunteers and a professionally staffed office, oversee the intercultural exchange experience of our participants. Volunteer/Internship opportunities are also available in our New York office. We welcome applicants who have made previous housing arrangements in the area, have excellent organization and communication skills and are dependable and prompt.

Skills: Experience in graphic design, survey analysis, grant writing, press release writing, video editing, market research, historical projects, translations, legal work, finance and human resources.

Contact: Tim Murray, Director of Finance and Administration

AFS INTERCULTURAL PROGRAMS/USA

1 Whitehall Street, 2nd Floor (800) 876-2377
New York, NY 10004 volunteer@afs.org
www.afsusa.org

Area: United States and Worldwide

General Information: AFS Intercultural Programs/USA (AFS-USA)

annually sends more than 1,500 high school students for semester, year-long and summer programs abroad to more than 40 countries. AFS's mission is to work towards a more just and peaceful world by providing international and intercultural learning experiences to individuals, families, schools, and communities through a global volunteer partnership. AFS welcomes more than 2,800 high school students from countries around the world to live with U.S. families and attend local high schools. AFS also has a program for young adults 18 years of age and older, and the AFS Visiting Teacher program that welcomes teachers from other countries into U.S. schools. Students who study abroad with AFS can focus on special areas such as community service, environmental conservation, cultural heritage preservation, language study, and volunteering to assist others. AFS volunteers work in communities throughout the U.S. with high school students and their families, make presentations in schools, meet with community organizations, plan special events, and help young people from other countries to feel at home in the community.

AFS was founded in 1947 by volunteer ambulance drivers from World Wars I and II who believed the way to insure future peace among nations was to educate a generation of enlightened world leaders through international student exchange.

Skills: Strong interest in learning and sharing in a new culture.

Contact: AFS Regional Service Centers

AMAZON-AFRICA AID ORGANIZATION

PO Box 7776
Ann Arbor, MI 48107

(734) 426-1300
info@amazonafrica.org
www.amazonafrica.org

Area: Santarem, Para, Brazil

General Information: The Amazon-Africa Aid Organization supports a health clinic run by the Fundacao Esperanca, a nonprofit Brazilian health and education organization, which has been providing health care along the Brazilian Amazon for over 35 years. We need volunteer dentists to work in our fully modern clinic. Volunteers usually stay for a minimum of two weeks and can stay longer if they wish. Room and board is provided, but volunteers must provide their own flight arrangements, as well as visa costs. We accept volunteers year-round. In late 2005, the states of Para and Amazonas were declared federal disaster areas due to the worst drought in the region in 60 years. Over 900 towns and villages were facing shortages of food and water and there were outbreaks of diarrhea and malaria. As a result, more of the surrounding population has migrated to Santarem and created more of a burden on an already taxed infrastructure. Volunteers are urgently needed to play a great part in sustaining the operation of the dental clinic. Hygienists and assistants are welcome if they accompany a dentist.

Skills: Dentist (DDS)

Contact: Rachel Chapa, Executive Director

AMIGOS DE LAS AMÉRICAS

5618 Star Lane
Houston, TX 77057

(800) 231-7796
info@amigoslink.org
www.amigoslink.org

Area: Dominican Republic, Honduras, Mexico, Nicaragua, Panama and Paraguay

General Information: Amigos de las Américas (AMIGOS) is an international, volunteer-based nonprofit that builds partnerships to empower young leaders, advance community development and strengthen multicultural understanding in the Americas. Since 1965, AMIGOS has given high school and college volunteers the opportunity to experience hands-on cross-cultural understanding and leadership by living with host families in rural communities and volunteering as public health and community development workers. Volunteers are empowered to take leadership roles in planning programs and facilitating community involvement while exemplifying confidence and cultural sensitivity. AMIGOS volunteers typically partner in teams of two or three and spend six to eight weeks in June, July and August living and working in one of six Latin American countries. AMIGOS programs include: community-based initiatives; community nutrition; family nutrition; environmental education; technology education; health education; physical education and home improvement.

Skills: AMIGOS volunteers must complete a training program, must be 16 years old and have completed their sophomore year of high school before departure to Latin America. Volunteers must have studied at least two years of high school Spanish (or the equivalent) before departure.

Contact: Glenn Bayron, Director of Volunteer Programs

AMIZADE GLOBAL SERVICE-LEARNING & VOLUNTEER PROGRAMS

PO Box 6894   (304) 293-6049
343 Stansbury Hall   volunteer@amizade.org
Morgantown, WV 26506   www.amizade.org

Area: Amizade has partnerships abroad in Cochabamba, Bolivia; Santarém, Brazil; Quito, Ecuador; Cape Coast, Ghana; Petersfield, Jamaica; Puerto Morelos, Mexico; Auschwitz, Poland; Belfast, Northern Ireland; Karagwe, Tanzania. Within the United States, Amizade has partnerships in the Navajo Nation (Tuba City, Arizona and Crown Point, New Mexico); Selma, Alabama; Greater Yellowstone, Montana; Pittsburgh, Pennsylvania; and Washington, DC.

General Information: Amizade ("friendship" in Portuguese) is an international nonprofit organization that offers volunteer and service-learning programs in communities around the world. Our programs focus on global education, community-driven service, intercultural exchange and recreational activities. Since 1995, we have provided unique opportunities for thousands of students and volunteers to fully experience a new culture by staying within a community and serving alongside local residents who are working to improve people's lives. Amizade collaborates with service organizations around the world to identify and develop sustainable projects that are both beneficial to the local communities and rewarding for volunteers. Amizade offers short-term and long-term volunteer placements, customized group programs for six or more, and service-learning courses for college credit. Volunteers pay program fees which cover a donation to the community service project, room and board, on-site transportation, cultural and recreational activities, and administrative costs. We welcome volunteers from all backgrounds and nationalities. Individuals 12–17 years of age must be accompanied by an adult.

Skills: Enthusiasm about a new culture and a willingness to help. On many of our programs, a basic knowledge of Spanish and/or Portuguese is particularly helpful, but not required. While many programs involve masonry and other light construction activities, construction experience is not required because Amizade cooperates with local experts at volunteer sites to facilitate all projects.

Contact: Rebekah Harlan, Program Coordinator or Eric Hartman, Executive Director

ASSOCIATION OF ANDEAN ARTISANS (AAA)

Pasaje Catedral s/n   (591) 4-4508367
Cochabamba, Bolivia   artesanosandinos@hotmail.com
                             www.artesanosandinos.com

Area: Cochabamba, Bolivia

General Information: The Association of Andean Artisans (AAA) represents 230 weavers from four weaving centers in the rural area outside the city of Cochabamba, Bolivia. The AAA is entirely run by its weavers and is at a critical point in becoming a fully-sustainable entity, and an exciting development success story. The Association supports the revival of traditional weaving techniques in these Quechua and Aymara communities who use all-natural-dyed sheep wool. The AAA has a small store off the plaza in the city of Cochabamba which sells a variety of weavings, and serves as its base of operation for the centralized wool-dyeing process as well as meetings and marketing efforts.

Volunteer opportunities in 2009–2011 include the following: sales and/or marketing work at the store for expanding domestic and international contacts and points of sale; research and organization for museum-quality display of antique and contemporary weavings adjoining the store; assistance in development and/or implementation of eco/weaving-tourism projects in the rural villages; production and design work based at the store and/or in the partner villages; internet and website design and/or support by on-location or distance volunteers; sales and/or marketing work for international contacts/partners also available for distance volunteers.

Skills: For on-site volunteers, strong Spanish skills required.

Contact: Please email basic personal information and area of volunteer interest.

BUILDING GOODNESS FOUNDATION

PO Box 4325   (434) 973-0993
Charlottesville, VA 22905   volunteer@buildinggoodness.org
                             www.buildinggoodness.org

Area: San Mateo, Guatemala; L'Acul, Thomassin, Haiti; Wum, Camaroon; Villa Soleada, Honduras; Gulf Coast Mississippi, Central Virginia, and Mattaponi Indian Reservation (near Richmond, Virginia)

General Information: Building Goodness Foundation (BGF) is a non-profit organization powered by skilled volunteers from the construction

BUILDING GOODNESS FOUNDATION

A volunteer works with local residents on the construction of a water delivery system in Villa Soleada, Honduras.

Photos: Building Goodness Foundation

Volunteers prepare to hoist an end truss into place for a Haitian Kay (which means house in Creole). Crew camping quarters are in the background.

The volunteer crew stands in front of a completed Haitian home with the proud owner, who also participated in a re-forestation program.

trades and surrounding communities. Bringing together volunteers from every part of the construction industry and using donations of time, money, materials, and expertise, BGF builds clinics, schools, shelters, community centers, specialized housing, and other structures for communities in need. We build for our local community in Charlottesville, Virginia, for impoverished and disaster-stricken areas such as the Gulf Coast, in developing countries like Haiti and Guatemala and in other communities around the world. Instead of focusing solely on individuals in need or residential projects, BGF seeks out ambitious projects with the greatest potential to nurture the connections between people and help them produce prosperity and peace for the entire community.

Individuals or groups may join one of our trips, which are led by qualified Team Leaders who undergo a five day training program where they acquire the various skills needed to run the BGF trips. Requirements for volunteers participating in BGF trips include two Pre-Departure Orientation Meetings, where team members become acquainted with each other and set the goals and expectations of the trip.

Non-construction volunteers are also a critical part of our team. You don't have to be a carpenter, mason or designer to make a difference. Other ways to volunteer at BGF include working on a committee, preparing mailings, event support and representing BGF in outreach activities. Beyond the bricks and mortar of a new structure, BGF volunteers build lasting relationships with the people they are helping that profoundly improve the lives of all involved.

Skills: Building, design and construction volunteers are the most needed. However, anyone willing and interested in participating in construction projects is welcome. While we do not require that volunteers have construction skills, a cooperative, positive attitude and willingness to contribute to the goals of the team is a must!

Contact: Ethan Tate, Program Coordinator

CANADIAN CROSSROADS INTERNATIONAL

317 Adelaide Street West, Suite 500   (416) 967-1611 Ext 221
Toronto, ON   laurier@cciorg.ca
Canada M5V 1P9   www.cciorg.ca

Area: Bolivia, Burkina Faso, Ghana, Guatemala, India, Ivory Coast, Kenya, Mali, Niger, St. Vincent, Senegal, Suriname, Swaziland, Togo and Zimbabwe

General Information: Canadian Crossroads International (CCI) is a nonprofit organization dedicated to helping build and support the capacity of civil society in the Global South. Key sectors are HIV/AIDS and health ; education and literacy; human rights; good governance and democratization; and agriculture and local economic development. CCI aims to facilitate the sharing of resources and skills by supporting partnerships between organizations in the North and the South working on similar issues. These partnerships are driven by the needs expressed by the Southern partners, and are consolidated through exchanges of skilled personnel, continual dialogue and the gradual building of solidarity and trust between partner organizations.

Contact: Laurier Brown, National Communications Officer

CAPE CARES: CENTRAL AMERICAN RELIEF EFFORTS

PO Box 1049   (508) 631-4848
East Orleans, MA 02643   admin@capecares.org
                                     www.capecares.org

Area: Honduras

General Information: Cape Cares, a group of medical doctors, dentists, optometrists, chiropractors, pharmacists, nurses, dental hygienists, paramedics, translators and numerous support personnel has formed an independent organization of caring individuals to provide ongoing health care services to the needy people of Honduras. Founded in 1988, Cape Cares sends teams of 10 to 16 people several times a year to treat various medical, dental, optometric and chiropractic problems. A minimum time commitment of one week is required. A team remains at one of Cape Cares' three sites for one week and, typically, treats approximately 500 people within that week. With only 900 physicians in Honduras, and only one dentist per 26,000 people, the services provided by Cape Cares are desperately needed and greatly appreciated by the Honduran people. With a population of 4.5 million people, the average worker makes five lempera per day (approximately $1.25), and $600 per capita per year. The cost of beans or one pound of rice is also five lempera, requiring a full day of work just to feed the family.

Skills: Doctors, dentists, nurses, hygienists, paramedics and other medical professionals, as well as translators, are always needed. Non-medical professionals are also needed to help with support work necessary to make the team projects possible. Spanish speaking ability is not a necessity, but it is a great asset.

Contact: Lisa M. Scapellati, Administrator

CAPE CARES: CENTRAL AMERICAN RELIEF EFFORTS

Photos: Cape Cares

A volunteer doctor with a young patient and her mother, at Cape Cares' Los Encitos, Honduras site.

Townspeople wait in line at one of its three sites. Cape Cares volunteer doctors and dentists see up to 700 patients in a week.

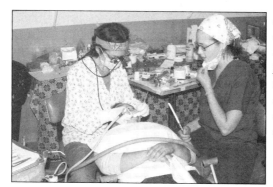

A volunteer dentist, one of a team of medical professionals, concentrates on her work while a volunteer aide assists.

CHILD FAMILY HEALTH INTERNATIONAL

995 Market Street, Suite 1104   (415) 957-9000
San Francisco, CA 94103   info@cfhi.org
        www.cfhi.org

Area: Bolivia, Ecuador, India, Mexico, South Africa; San Francisco, California

General Information: Child Family Health International (CFHI) is a global family of committed professionals and students who work at the grassroots level to promote the health of the world community by: fostering learning and service that sparks transformational personal change for all involved; working towards sustainable solutions in healthcare services and disease prevention; emphasizing respect and understanding across cultures; facilitating the sharing of medical resources, knowledge and experience, giving priority to underserved communities. CFHI's program provides future medical professionals global health experiences through service-learning clinical electives in Bolivia, Ecuador, India, Mexico and South Africa. Participants study and work with local medical professionals at each site. Programs run year-round, four to eight weeks each. Medical Spanish courses are available. Scholarships, fellowships and other funding ideas are also available. Volunteers must be 21 years or older. CFHI works with over 190 partner physicians throughout the world. These partners receive income, grants for health projects and medical supplies in return for hosting CFHI students.

Local San Francisco volunteers are also needed in our San Francisco office. These individuals, however, will not be involved in direct healthcare service or work with children.

Skills: Medical students and professionals only for the international health care program.

Contact: Nick Penco, Program Coordinator

CROSS-CULTURAL SOLUTIONS

2 Clinton Place   (914) 632-0022
New Rochelle, NY 10801   info@crossculturalsolutions.org
        www.crossculturalsolutions.org

Area: Brazil, China, Costa Rica, Ghana, Guatemala, India, Peru, Russia, Tanzania, Thailand

General Information: Cross-Cultural Solutions is a nonprofit organization founded in 1995 with 250 staff members worldwide. To date, we have brought approximately 10,000 participants to ten countries around the world. Cross-Cultural Solutions' mission is to operate volunteer programs around the world in partnership with sustainable community initiatives, bringing people together to work side-by-side while sharing perspectives and fostering cultural understanding. We are an international organization with no political or religious affiliations.

Cross-Cultural Solutions offers Volunteer Abroad, Intern Abroad and Insight Abroad. Volunteer Abroad and Intern Abroad Programs operate year-round and range from 2 to 12 weeks. Insight Abroad is one week and is available in Brazil and Costa Rica, with special holiday dates in Peru and Guatemala. Volunteer placements allow participants to make a real difference in the community. Placements include programs with children, young adults, adults, the elderly, HIV/AIDS prevention, as well as health care, education and community development.

Cross-Cultural Solutions has Special Consultative Status with the United Nations and is in partnership with CARE, one of the world's largest international humanitarian organizations.

Skills: Desire to serve others and interest in cultural exchange.

Contact: Kristen Sager, Communications Manager

CUSO-VSO

44 Eccles Street, Suite 200   (613) 829-7445
Ottawa, ON   (888) 434-2876
Canada K1R 6S4   www.cuso-vso.org

Area: Africa, Asia, the Pacific, Latin America and the Caribbean

General Information: CUSO-VSO is one of North America's largest nonprofit volunteer-based development organizations. We are a member of the VSO International Federation. Each year, we send hundreds of global citizens to work on collaborative development projects in more than 40 countries in Africa, Asia, the Pacific, Latin America, the Caribbean and Eastern Europe.

CUSO-VSO volunteers work at the crossroads between hope and hardship. We place volunteers of all ages who have the professional skills and sensitivity needed to help people in some of the world's most disadvantaged countries help themselves.

Skills: Sound expertise in focus areas such as education, HIV/AIDS, disability, health and social well-being, secure livelihoods, participation and governance, environment and natural resource management.

Contact: Through our website above or by telephone

EL PORVENIR

Photos: El Porvenir

Eighty percent of rural Nicaraguans do not have access to clean drinking water, due to deforestation and limited government intervention. El Porvenir's volunteers work with communities to create tree nurseries around existing village wells.

Volunteers build latrines to provide rural Nicaraguans with sanitary facilities. Other water and sanitation projects include building village wells and communal washing facilities.

EL PORVENIR

1420 Ogden Street, #204   (303) 520-0093
Denver, CO 80218   info@elporvenir.org

Area: Nicaragua

General Information: El Porvenir sponsors sustainable self-help water and sanitation projects in rural communities in Nicaragua and partners with local communities who initiate all projects. Eighty percent of rural Nicaraguans do not have access to clean water or sanitation facilities and the government does little to alleviate this problem. For 15 years, we have worked with over 45,000 people to build 450 water and sanitation projects. Due to deforestation, the water table on which the water projects depend is dropping, and this is why we work with villages to create community tree nurseries from which they can reforest around their wells and on their own land. We hear from many villagers that they have asked for help from mayors and other NGOs but they were turned away. El Porvenir has responded to their requests, helping them to help themselves meet their basic needs. One- or two-week work groups join local families in building projects several times a year. Participants stay in simple hotels in small towns, commuting to the village daily. Recreational and educational activities are included; groups may travel to a beach or volcano as well as meet with representatives of a health clinic or a historian. Costs range from $800-$1,050 for trips (airfare not included). Cost includes lodging, food, in-country transportation, activity fees, two bilingual guides, as well as the tools and materials for the project.

Skills: Construction skills and Spanish are not required but welcomed.

Contact: Elisabeth Santana, Director of U.S. Operations

FRONTIERS FOUNDATION

419 Coxwell Avenue   (416) 690-3930
Toronto, Ontario   frontiersfoundation@on.aibn.com
Canada M4L 3B9   www.frontiersfoundation.ca

Area: Northern Canada

General Information: Frontiers Foundation's mission is to implement enduring relief of human poverty throughout Canada and abroad in tangible advancement projects. Our projects promote development through a partnership with community members who know and understand their own needs, without aspiring to change their way of life. Volunteers and members of the host communities exchange and share cross-cultural information and experiences, learning from each other and fostering an understanding between aboriginal peoples and volunteers from around the world. We need skilled volunteers from around the world and Canada to join groups of international volunteers on housing construction and renovation projects in low-income, rural communities across northern Canada. Volunteers are needed for at least 12 weeks, must be at least 18 years old and in good physical condition. Transportation, food and lodging are provided.

We also have volunteers working in various positions within the schools in the Northwest Territory, Nunavut and the Yukon in our Northern Education Project. These volunteers need to have specific skills in any one of the different areas: tutoring; assisting in libraries; teaching music and drama or basic technical skills such as woodworking or carpentry; or assistance in student residences. This program requires a commitment of either September through the end of January or February through the end of June.

Skills: Carpentry, general building or residential renovation, bricklaying, plumbing or electrical work experience are preferred, but anyone with a strong desire to learn may apply.

Contact: Marco A. Guzman, Executive Director

GLOBAL CITIZENS NETWORK

11000 West 78th Street, Suite 303   (800) 644-9292
Minneapolis, MN 55344   info@globalcitizens.org
                                         www.globalcitizens.org

Area: Ecuador, Guatemala, Kenya, Mexico, Nepal, Peru, Tanzania, Thailand; Native American communities in Arizona, New Mexico and Washington

General Information: In 1992, Global Citizens Network (GCN) was founded by a group of volunteers that strove to provide individuals with cost-effective opportunities to interact locally and internationally with people of diverse cultures who share common global values. GCN is currently making an impact by sending teams of 6 to 12 people to rural communities both locally as well as around the world. The teams, led by a trained team leader, spend one to three weeks in their chosen community and become immersed in the daily life of the local culture. Volunteers stay in local homes or as a group in a community center. Community projects are initiated by the local people and may

GLOBAL CITIZENS NETWORK

Photos: Global Citizens Network

Volunteers help the community in Tumbatu, Chota Valley, Ecuador to rebuild their community plaza.

African high school students work with GCN volunteers in Odienya, Kenya to build a health clinic.

range from building wells, roads or greenhouses to helping at a village clinic or school. GCN is a mission-driven adventure travel nonprofit agency. The tax-deductible fee ranges from $750–$2,050 (airfare is additional). GCN maintains a small staff and a handful of focused programs each year.

Skills: No specific skills are required. For Spanish-speaking sites (Mexico and Guatemala), knowledge of some basic Spanish phrases is extremely helpful.

Contact: Eden Rock, Director

GLOBAL VOLUNTEERS

375 East Little Canada Road
St. Paul, MN 55117

(651) 407-6100
(800) 487-1074
email@globalvolunteers.org
www.globalvolunteers.org

Area: Africa, Americas, Asia, Europe and South Pacific

General Information: Global Volunteers is a nonprofit, nonsectarian international organization that strives to wage peace and promote justice through mutual understanding. Since 1984, Global Volunteers has engaged teams of volunteers to work with, and under the direction of, community members in developing communities worldwide, including the U.S. Work projects are determined by the host communities, directed by local leaders, and generally focus on children. There are four principal projects: caring for at-risk children; teaching conversational English; building, painting and renovating community buildings; and providing health care. Projects last one to three weeks and are offered throughout the year. All ages and backgrounds are welcome, including students, groups, seniors and families. Volunteers pay a tax-deductible service program fee that ranges from $995 (domestic) to $3,295 (international) to cover food, lodging, transportation (at the site), project materials and the services of an experienced team leader. Student, companion and former volunteer discounts are available.

Skills: No special skills are necessary to join most Global Volunteers service programs—only a curiosity about the world, a desire to be of service, and a high degree of flexibility. Volunteers who wish to participate on health care and business teams must provide a current resume and applicable license information for acceptance. Volunteers must be willing to take direction from local leaders, to work as part of a team, and be respectful of diverse cultures. Native English speakers sought for English teaching projects. Otherwise, volunteers should have a working knowledge of English to communicate with other team members and team leaders.

Contact: Volunteer Coordinator

GOOD SHEPHERD VOLUNTEERS

337 East 17th Street   (888) 668-6GSV Ext 718
New York, NY 10003   www.gsvolunteers.org
     gsv@goodshepherds.org

Area: Mexico, Paraguay, Peru

General Information: Good Shepherd Volunteers (GSV) is a service association of women and men which strives to embody the gospel values of the Good Shepherd in today's world. The Sisters of the Good Shepherd and the volunteers share the same work and values in this collaborative project. The basic elements of the GSV philosophy are value of the individual, simplicity, social justice, community and spirituality. GSV requires one-year commitments for domestic placements and two years for international. Applicants of all races, ethnic backgrounds and orientations are encouraged to apply. Though the GSV program is affiliated with the Roman Catholic Church, applicants from all Christian traditions are welcome. Must be at least 21 years or older, be a high school graduate and have some college education or work experience.

Skills: International placements have a language requirement of conversational Spanish.

Contact: John Alvarez, Program Coordinator

GUATEMALA ACUPUNCTURE AND MEDICAL AID PROJECT (GUAMAP)

PO Box 85371   (520) 623-6620
Tucson, AZ 85754   lamidbar@gmail.com
     www.guamap.org

Area: The Peten, Guatemala; Tucson, Arizona

General Information: GUAMAP, in association with the non-governmental health organization ASECSA (Asociación de Servicios Comunitarios de Salud), delivers acupuncture treatment and education to the northern villages of Guatemala, an area which lacks trained healthcare providers as a result of decades of civil war, displacement and poverty. GUAMAP offers Spanish-speaking, licensed acupuncturists the opportunity to participate in two- and three-week programs designed to spread acupuncture information and education to local clinics. Volunteers are equipped with appropriate supplies and teaching tools to conduct training courses at the local level. Volunteers must be 21 years of age, board certified with a current license and must have completed one year of postgraduate, supervised experience with a public clinic.

Volunteers are also needed to teach the more advanced promoters; five years of practice and demonstrated experience in teaching acupuncture are required. Rural Guatemalans earn less than $2 a day. Living in areas too remote to be reached by government-sponsored health services, many of these poor villages have no access to adequate medical care other than acupuncture and acupuncture has made a significant positive difference. Many war- and storm-induced health problems are successfully treated by acupuncture. The setting, while rural and remote, is a training center with prepared meals, beds, washing facilities and electricity. Trainee health promoters are literate to a sixth grade level; visuals and experiential hands-on teaching are critical.

Skills: We need licensed acupuncturists with five years practice experience, current certification in Traditional Chinese Medicine, speaking knowledge of Spanish, some knowledge of Guatemala, and experience teaching acupuncture. We also need local volunteer organizers to help raise funds and awareness.

Contact: Laurie Melrood, Volunteer Coordinator

INSTITUTE FOR INTERNATIONAL COOPERATION AND DEVELOPMENT (IICD)

PO Box 520
1117 Hancock Road
Williamstown, MA 01267

(413) 441-5126
info@iicd-volunteer.org
www.iicd-volunteer.org

Area: Africa, Bolivia and Brazil

General Information: Institute for International Cooperation and Development (IICD) trains and sends volunteers to work in community development projects in Africa and Latin America. These projects are in the areas of education, healthcare, HIV education and agriculture. For example, you may be part of the TCE Program (Total Control of Epidemic) and work with HIV/AIDS education in southern Africa, lead a tree planting campaign in Angola, develop a new curriculum for

INSTITUTE FOR INTERNATIONAL COOPERATION AND DEVELOPMENT (IICD)

Photos: IICD

A volunteer gives computer training to community members. IICD's volunteers serve developing communities in Africa and Latin America and focus on projects in education, agriculture, and health care.

A volunteer works with families in Mozambique to cultivate a vegetable garden to help people affected by the HIV/AIDS epidemic.

a vocational school in Mozambique or work with street kids in Brazil. All programs include a preparation and follow-up period in the U.S. Preparation entails language and regional studies, practical training and fund-raising. The follow-up period includes giving presentations and making educational materials. Program fees range from $3,300-$3,800 which covers training, room and board, international insurance and airfare. Fund-raising ideas and some financial aid are available. The program is open to anyone 18 years or older.

Contact: Else Marie Pederson, Promotion Director

INTERNATIONAL YMCA

5 West 63rd Street, 2nd Floor   (212) 727-8800
New York, NY 10023   chiu@ymcanyc.org
     www.internationalymca.org

Area: Australia, Brazil, Chile, China, Colombia, Dominican Republic, Ecuador, England, Gambia, Ghana, Guatemala, Hong Kong, Jamaica, Kenya, South Korea, Malta, Mexico, Peru, South Africa, Thailand, Venezuela

General Information: The International YMCA is a branch of the YMCA of Greater New York, the largest YMCA association in the U.S., serving more than 8,000 people annually through international exchange programs since 1911. Our programs strive to create bridges of tolerance and understanding across geographic, cultural and ethnic divides.

Programs include: International Camp Counselor Program (ICCP), Summer Work and Travel, International Training and Internship, Global Teens, and Go Global. Opportunities exist to volunteer abroad with YMCAs and other NGOs around the world in fields such as youth development, English instruction, capacity building and more.

Skills: Foreign language skills may be required in some cases.

Contact: Chad Nico Hiu, Program Director

MARYKNOLL CHINA VOLUNTEER TEACHERS PROGRAM

29 Cadence Court   (973) 889-1557
Morristown, NJ 07960   mckenna@chinaserve.org

Area: Northern and Southern Provinces of the People's Republic of China

General Information: To carry out our commitment to facilitate service work in the People's Republic of China, we seek to place active and committed Christians in universities where their dedication and example will be of service to the young Chinese people. Learning English from native speakers is a priority for Chinese students, as emphasized by the government of the People's Republic of China throughout the entire education system. We hope that as a result of language interchange, volunteer teachers will understand more about China and the Chinese will understand more about the West.

Long-term placements for ESL teachers are one year. Short-term placements are four-week intensive summer programs. A 10-day orientation in Hong Kong is provided for the long-term program and a three-day orientation for the short-term program. Volunteers receive round trip transportation from Hong Kong to the teaching site in mainland China, emergency medical insurance, accommodations at both the teaching site and in Hong Kong and a monthly living stipend. Volunteers live in community with other volunteers on the Chinese college campus. Deadline for applications is March.

Skills: College degree is required, in any major. Teaching experience, educational credits and courses in teaching ESL are especially valuable but not a requirement.

Contact: Maretta McKenna, Assistant Coordinator

OPERATION CROSSROADS AFRICA, INC.

34 Mount Morris Park (212) 289-1949
New York, NY 10027 oca@igc.org
www.operationcrossroadsafrica.org

Area: Africa

General Information: Operation Crossroads Africa (OCA) sponsors summer programs in Africa for anyone 18 and older. The five major types of programs are community construction, agriculture/reforestation, community health/medical outreach, education/training and women in development. Participants can earn academic credit by using their participation as part of an independent study project.

Programs will be conducted in East, West and Southern Africa. Participation fee is $3,800, which covers round-trip airfare to Africa, living and travel costs in Africa and pre-program orientation in the U.S.

Skills: No special skills are required.

Contact: Willis Logan, Director of Program Services

PEACE BRIGADES INTERNATIONAL-USA (PBI-USA)

1326 9th Street NW
Washington, DC 20001

(202) 232-0142
www.pbiusa.org
info@pbiusa.org

Area: Washington, DC; Colombia, Guatemala, Indonesia, Mexico, Nepal

General Information: Peace Brigades International (PBI) is an international nonprofit organization, inspired by nonviolent philosophies such as those of Gandhi and Martin Luther King, Jr. PBI has been promoting nonviolent activism and defending human rights since 1981. We envision a world in which people address conflicts nonviolently, where human rights are universally upheld, and social justice and intercultural respect have become a reality. We believe that lasting solutions to conflict cannot be imposed from the outside, but must be based on the capacity and desires of local people.

PBI operates independently and in a nonpartisan manner, sending teams of highly qualified field volunteers to accompany human rights defenders and communities and to document conflict. Protective accompaniment is a technique pioneered by PBI for protecting human rights defenders. With this strategy, we have protected the lives of hundreds of threatened activists, many of whom have faced death threats and all of whom have faced severe harassment from military, paramilitary or other violent groups due to the nature of their work. Groups we accompany include indigenous communities, environmental organizations, lawyers, women's organizations, trade unions and relatives of the disappeared.

PBI currently operates field projects in Colombia, Guatemala, Indonesia, Mexico and Nepal. PBI-USA is one of 16 country groups which focus on supporting the field projects through volunteer recruitment, fund-raising, political support networks, domestic peace, nonviolent education and outreach activities.

Contact: Katherine Hughes-Fraitekh, Executive Director

PEACETREES VIETNAM

2200 Alaskan Way, Suite 435
Seattle, WA 98121

(206) 441-6136
info@peacetreesvietnam.org
www.peacetreesvietnam.org

Area: Quang Tri Province, Vietnam

General Information: PeaceTrees Vietnam's mission is to work

POR UN MEJOR HOY (FOR A BETTER TODAY)

Photo: Por un Mejor HOY (For a Better Today)

A volunteer plays a game with local children in a Mexican community. HOY's "participatory trips" promote peace, cross-cultural understanding and cooperation.

alongside the Vietnamese people to build the capacity for a safe and healthy future for the children of Quang Tri Province. What began in 1995 as a small grassroots effort to remove land mines and unexploded ordnance so trees could be planted and friendships could grow has since blossomed into a full-fledged partnership with the people of Quang Tri Province to promote peace, friendship and renewal. PeaceTrees sponsors the removal of deadly explosives, teaches children about the dangers of unexploded mines and bombs, conducts environmental and community restoration projects, assists UXO victims and their families, and brings together international volunteers and residents of Quang Tri to work alongside one another and open a new chapter in our relationship. Our citizen diplomacy trips are aimed at bringing American and Vietnamese volunteers together to plant trees and participate in other community restoration projects in Quang Tri Province. Contact us directly for tuition and expense information.

Skills: Knowledge of Vietnamese is helpful, but not a requirement.

Contact: Fred Gregory, Executive Director

POR UN MEJOR HOY (FOR A BETTER TODAY)

c/o Rebecca Barnhart   (213) 703-8205
682 Irolo Street, #702   hoycommunity@gmail.com
Los Angeles, CA 90005   www.hoycommunity.org

Area: Mexico (urban and rural settings)

General Information: By linking the socially-aware traveler as a volunteer with local programs, Por un Mejor HOY contributes to community growth and provides personally enriching experiences while promoting cross-cultural travels, an exchange of knowledge and skills, multiculturalism, cooperation and peace.

In 2004, HOY launched its nonprofit program of low-cost "participatory trips" to Mexico. Travelers (over 18) contribute their enthusiasm and abilities to assorted community organizations in the capital and rural settings. Mutually enriching contact between a community and a visitor may be accomplished through a wide variety of activities: searching out and talking with street kids; working with mentally- and physically-challenged children and adults; making adobe bricks, maintaining paths in an eco-park; or building a playground. Most trips last two weeks, with volunteer work carried out Monday–Friday. HOY is run entirely by volunteers and needs volunteers for events, as well as for office tasks and nonprofit development.

Skills: No special skills required.

Contact: Katy Barnhart, Co-founder

SCI-INTERNATIONAL VOLUNTARY SERVICE

5505 Walnut Level Road   (206) 350-6585
Crozet, VA 22932   information@sci-ivs.org
                                      www.sci-ivs.org

Area: 73 countries around the world

General Information: SCI-International Voluntary Service (SCI-IVS) is the U.S. branch of Service Civil International, the world's second oldest international voluntary service organization. SCI recruits and provides volunteers to hundreds of grassroots, non-governmental service organizations worldwide, in many different areas of service. It also organizes various educational and training seminars in the philosophy and conduct of volunteer work.

The U.S. branch of SCI supports UNESCO's *Manifesto 2000 for a Culture of Peace and Non-violence* as our statement of purpose.

UNITARIAN UNIVERSALIST SERVICE COMMITTEE

Photo: Unitarian Universalist Service Committee

UUSC volunteers on a field trip learn about food sovereignty through the farmer-to-farmer program.

Through its nonprofit partner organizations worldwide and through the SCI network of international and regional offices, SCI-IVS USA participates in the exchange of over 18,000 volunteers each year in short-term international group workcamps and in long-term volunteer postings in 73 countries.

SCI-IVS USA accepts volunteers as young as 16 for camps in North America. For overseas camps the minimum age is 18, and for camps in Asia (except Japan and Korea), Africa and Latin America the minimum age is 21. There is no maximum age except for certain partners that have age limits. The fee for SCI overseas camps is $175, and for domestic camps $65. Some partner organizations may charge an additional fee. Placements for couples, families and the disabled are available in some camps.

Skills: No particular skills are required. For African, Asian and Latin American placements, some previous workcamp experience is desired. African and Latin American camps may require foreign language skills.

Contact: Please call or email us for more information

UNITARIAN UNIVERSALIST SERVICE COMMITTEE

689 Massachusetts Avenue   (617) 868-6600
Cambridge, MA 02139   www.uusc.org

Area: Throughout the United States and internationally

General Information: The Unitarian Universalist Service Committee (UUSC) envisions a world free from oppression and injustice, where all can realize their full human rights. UUSC partners with grassroots organizations, standing with these communities as they confront unjust power structures, and mobilizes supporters to challenge oppressive policies,with four major program focuses: Economic Justice, Civil Liberties, Environmental Justice, and Rights in Humanitarian Crises. In each program area, we focus on issues of race, class and gender and their roles in perpetuating injustice and human rights abuses.

JustWorks camps are week-long projects that help volunteers examine the causes and damaging effects of injustice while donating their time and skills. Participants may help Katrina survivors repair a home, tutor a child, help a small-scale farmer in Guatemala to produce coffee, or they may work alongside Native Americans in Clinton, Oklahoma to repatriate burial remains improperly removed from a community. Participants work alongside activists and other concerned individuals to reach positive solutions.

Contact: Please call our office for more information

UNITED NATIONS VOLUNTEERS PROGRAMME (UNV)

Postfach 260 111   (49-228) 815-2000
D-53153 Bonn, Germany   www.unv.org

Area: Worldwide

General Information: The United Nations Volunteers (UNV) was created by the UN General Assembly in 1970 to serve as an operational arm in development cooperation at the request of UN member states. It is unique in the UN family and as an international volunteer undertaking.

It is administered by the UN Development Programme (UNDP) and serves the entire UN system.

More than 7,300 qualified and experienced women and men of over 166 nationalities served in the developing world in 2004 as UN Volunteer specialists and field workers. Currently, 70 percent of UNVs come from developing countries and 30 percent from the industrialized world. UNVs work in technical, economic and social fields, under four main headings: in technical cooperation with governments that are short of skills; with community-based initiatives for self-reliance; in humanitarian relief and rehabilitation; and in support of human rights, electoral and peace-building processes. They are professionals who work on a peer basis. They listen and discuss; teach and train; encourage and facilitate. Volunteers also share and exchange ideas, skills and experience.

UNVs have served in over 140 countries. Today 30 percent are at work in Africa, 25 percent in Asia and the Pacific; the remainder are in the Arab States, the Caribbean, Central and South America, and with newer programs in Central and Eastern Europe. Thirty percent serve in the world's poorest nations. UNV works in partnership with governments, UN agencies, development banks and non-governmental and community-based organizations.

Contact: Please visit the website for more information.

U.S.-CHINA ENGLISH TEACHING PROJECT

Xinyu City, Jiangxi Province   (646) 486-2446
People's Republic of China   or (877) 867-6150
                                                            leejugen@yahoo.com.cn

Area: Xinyu, Jiangxi Province, People's Republic of China

General Information: Native English-speaking conversation teachers for primary and middle school Chinese students (age 7-17) are needed in the public schools of Xinyu, a city in south central China. This project was started by Andrew Lee Jugen, a young teacher and native of Xinyu, in coordination with Commission on Voluntary Service & Action, to expand the ability for Chinese children to improve their spoken English skills. This is a great opportunity to build international friendship, teach children spoken English and learn about China today. Teachers receive a monthly living stipend from the Xinyu school, as well as comfortable housing and meals.

Xinyu is a "small" city (for China) of 1.3 million people, with a steel factory in the southern end of the city supplying a large percentage of local jobs and income. The city is surrounded by rural agricultural villages and countryside. Many of the students are from the countryside; others are the children of factory workers, engineers, doctors, farmers, shopkeepers and a wide cross-section of the community. China is developing rapidly, with a national focus on improving the education and economic conditions in rural and less developed areas.

All students in primary and middle schools in China study English, but the Chinese teachers who teach reading and writing English do not have the oral English skills to teach the spoken language well. Students, parents and teachers in Xinyu welcome foreign teachers and are wonderful hosts.

Native English-speaking people with college degrees who can devote five or ten months are welcome to apply. Schedule of school terms: the fall term is late August to mid-January; the spring term is early February to early July. For a full term or full school year commitment, the host school will reimburse your round trip airfare.

Skills: Anyone with a college degree and some experience in teaching or working with people as a leader or instructor, and with ESL experience, can apply through CVSA. The most important credential is respect for China, love for children, and an interest in friendship between the people of China and the U.S.

Contact: Susan Angus at CVSA

THE VILLAGE EXPERIENCE

623 Northview Avenue

Indianapolis, IN 46220

(917) 862-9236

info@experiencethevillage.com

www.experiencethevillage.com

Area: Kenya, Ethiopia, South Africa, India, Thailand, Jordan, Guatemala, Jamaica

General Information: The Village Experience is a socially pro-active business dedicated to uplifting impoverished communities in the developing world through efforts in international trade and tourism. We create a market for fair trade projects in the developed world; consult on product development, marketing, and packaging; and fundraise to start new handicraft initiatives in the villages we support.

We operate humanitarian service trips to the developing world that

VISIONS IN ACTION

A volunteer teaches English in Moshi, Tanzania. Visions in Action volunteers contribute to—and learn from—the developing world by working as part of a community committed to social justice.

focus on three elements: volunteer work with charities in the community, cultural education and adventure. We only use locally owned and operated hotels, ground operators, tour companies and guides to help boost the local economy in each of the destinations we travel to. Volunteers can sign up to join us on a trip to Kenya, Ethiopia, South Africa, India, Thailand, Jordan, Guatemala, Jamaica, or others. Our trips range in length from one week to three weeks. Volunteers under the age of 16 need to be accompanied by a parent. Individuals, couples, and families are all encouraged to sign up. Contact us for information on fees and transportation costs. Among the community development projects is a school for the developmentally disabled; women's weaving cooperative; interfaith projects; women's fair trade projects; health, nutrition, and education projects; orphanage work site; girls' place of safety project.

Skills: No special skills needed, just an open mind and a willingness to learn. Those with art, sewing, or craft skills are encouraged to sign up to help with the handicraft projects. We are always looking for talented people to send to our villages to train the locals in making new products.

Contact: Kelly Campbell, Founder and Partner

VISIONS IN ACTION

2710 Ontario Road NW
Washington, DC 20009

(202) 625-7402
visions@visionsinaction.org
www.visionsinaction.org

Area: Africa and Latin America

General Information: Visions in Action (VIA) is committed to achieving social and economic justice in the developing world through grassroots programs and communities of self-reliant volunteers.

Supported Volunteers work directly on VIA's relief and development programs in Africa, such as VIA's education and food security programs in Liberia and an HIV/AIDS counseling and testing program for internally displaced persons in Uganda. Supported Volunteers with particular skills help to run these programs effectively. Available Supported Volunteer positions are detailed on the VIA website in the Employment Opportunities section.

Classic Volunteers support the work of local NGOs in a wide variety of sectors. We offer 6- and 12-month fee-based Classic Volunteer programs in Mexico, South Africa, Tanzania and Uganda.The programs feature an orientation, including intensive language study, followed by a 5- or 11-month volunteer placement. VIA volunteers work in a variety of International Development fields including, but not limited to, health care, HIV/AIDS, education, children, human rights, community development, law, women, environment, agriculture, and refugee relief. Volunteers are provided with: housing in co-ed group houses, health insurance, visa, staff support and program administration. Nationals of any country may apply and ages 20 and up are eligible. Short-term (3-5 weeks long) summer programs are also available in Mexico and Tanzania for applicants age 18 and older.

Skills: For long-term volunteers, at least two years of college or equivalent experience. Volunteer placements are arranged based on volunteer experience and interest. Basic Spanish required for positions in Mexico.

Contact: Volunteer Coordinator

VOLUNTEER BOLIVIA

Volunteer Bolivia incorporates volunteers of all ages and provides a language immersion program for the volunteers while they are in service to the community.

VOLUNTEER BOLIVIA

Calle Ecuador 342
Cochabamba, Bolivia

(594) 452-6028
info@volunteerbolivia.org
www.volunteerbolivia.org

Area: Cochabamba, Bolivia

General Information: Founded in 2001, and located in Cochabamba, Volunteer Bolivia is an international volunteer organization that combines a volunteer service learning experience with a language immersion program for an unforgettable intercultural experience. The city of Cochabamba is an excellent place to spend your volunteer time as it is centrally located and known for its superb weather, regional cuisine and mix of cultures. Volunteer Bolivia offers both short- and long-term volunteer experiences. Short-term volunteers fulfill the needs of a variety of children's centers around Cochabamba and our volunteers work alongside Bolivian educators by: assisting tutoring and enrichment programs; designing arts and crafts projects for all ages; and developing extracurricular activities such as sports programs.

Long-term volunteers stay with us for more than five months, speak intermediate Spanish and have an expertise that matches our Bolivian colleagues' needs. These volunteers contribute in areas such as: translating and interpreting; office and computer work; graphic and web design; and research, writing, and editing. In the past, specialized volunteers have also contributed as healthcare workers, physical therapists, graphic designers or in the area of project development.

We have a variety of types of volunteers from gap year to retired folks and even the occasional family.

Skills: No specific skills necessary; but knowledge of Spanish is helpful.

Contact: Lee Cridland

WATER FOR PEOPLE

6666 West Quincy Avenue
Denver, CO 80235

(720) 488-4597
abritton@waterforpeople.org
www.waterforpeople.org

Area: Volunteers work throughout the United States and Canada and in our program countries of Bolivia, Guatemala, Honduras, India and Malawi.

General Information: Water For People helps people in developing countries improve their quality of life by supporting the development of locally sustainable drinking water resources, sanitation facilities and hygiene education programs. Launched in 2006, Water For People's World Water Corps volunteer program puts the passion, skills and talents of many supporters to use in strategically supporting the Water For People vision abroad.

World Water: Corps volunteers travel overseas and carry out specific tasks that support our water, sanitation, and hygiene education programs. Volunteers are not involved with the actual design or construction of systems, but engage in activities such as scoping studies, mapping initiatives, and program monitoring that help Water For People's in-country staff plan and evaluate their work, and assist partner organizations grow their capacity.

Skills: Spanish language skills greatly desired. A history of rigorous travel and experience in the developing world is helpful.

Contact: Andrew Britton

WATER FOR PEOPLE

Photo: Kate Fogelberg

A World Water Corps volunteer discusses the functionality of Water For People projects installed last year in their community in Ajoya in East Meninpur, West Bengal, India.

Photos: John Niewoehner

Community members in Cotzol, Guatemala (above) pitch in to dig a five-mile water pipeline; and volunteers provide education to families (right) about water, sanitation, and hygiene.

WINANT AND CLAYTON VOLUNTEERS, INC.

1393 York Avenue   (212) 737-2720 Ext 31
New York, NY 10021   www.winantclaytonvolunteer.org

Area: United Kingdom

General Information: Winant and Clayton Volunteers, Inc. is a summer volunteer exchange program with the United Kingdom. Americans began the Winant volunteer adventure crossing the Atlantic by ship in 1948, working that initial summer literally with their hands to rebuild blitz-torn London. To date, 2,000 volunteers have spent nine weeks in the summer contributing their energies in social service programs. This caring, cross-generational teamwork between the U.S. and Great Britain grew from the post-World War II dreams of two extraordinary men, John G. Winant, U.S. Ambassador to Great Britain, and Reverend Philip "Tubby" Clayton, private Chaplain to Her Majesty, the Queen Mother.

Volunteers work with trained social workers on projects dealing with people of all ages and a variety of needs. Most are placed in central London, specifically the East End, in programs such as: a community center for Somali and Bangladeshi immigrants, a physical rehabilitation program, a preschool program, a program for homeless alcoholics, a community drug program and a drop-in service center for persons with HIV/AIDS. Volunteers live in the communities where they work, in housing provided by their placements: with families, in flats or dormitory rooms. Volunteers are responsible for airfare, which is arranged as a group. The Winant volunteers are Americans of all ages who have exported their skills and enthusiasms since the inception of the program. Since 1959, British volunteers, the Claytons, have traveled to the U.S. to provide similar services and enjoy the "inside" experience in reverse. Minimum age is 18.

Skills: Energy, maturity, flexibility, humor and strong interpersonal skills.

Contact: Dinushka De Silva, U.S. Coordinator

WITNESS FOR PEACE

3628 12th Street NE   (202) 547-6112
Washington, DC 20017   witness@witnessforpeace.org
                                  www.witnessforpeace.org

Area: Colombia, Mexico, Nicaragua, Venezuela; Washington, DC

General Information: Witness For Peace (WFP) is a politically independent, grassroots organization, committed to nonviolence, led by faith and conscience, with a mission to support peace, justice and sustainable economies in the Americas. International Team Volunteers (ITVs) make a renewable two-year commitment to work and live in community in one of our four offices throughout Latin America. ITVs take on many responsibilities, including documenting human rights abuses; studying the effects of U.S. policy and corporate practices and the policies of international financial institutions; providing socio-political analysis of local affairs; and facilitating delegations of U.S. citizens who gather information necessary to work to change U.S. foreign and economic policies. Volunteers must be U.S. citizens, 21 years or older.

Skills: Must be fluent in English and Spanish, with a Bachelor's degree or a substantial commensurate experience.

Contact: Sharon Hostetler, International Programs Director

WORLDTEACH

c/o Center for International Development
Harvard University
79 John F. Kennedy Street
Cambridge, MA 02138

(800) 483-2240
Fax: (617) 495-1599
info@worldteach.org
www.worldteach.org

Area: China, Chile, Costa Rica, Ecuador, Guyana, Marshall Islands, Namibia, Poland, South Africa

General Information: WorldTeach places volunteers in the above countries to teach for one year or one summer (two months). One-year assignments are open to college graduates, some require native English fluency. U.S. citizenship is not required. Volunteers teach English or other subjects where assistance is requested. Placements are in public schools, colleges or community organizations. Summer programs (June-August) are open to all individuals, 18 years of age or older with an interest in teaching and global service. Long-term volunteers (not summer) receive a small monthly living allowance from the host institution. Housing is provided by host schools or with a local host family. Program costs include round-trip international airfare from a U.S. departure city, health insurance, visa/work permit, pre-departure materials, orientation training and in-country staff support. Program costs range from $1,000 U.S. to $5,990 U.S., depending on the destination and duration of the program (some programs are funded or subsidized by host country institutions).

Skills: No prior teaching or foreign language experience is required.

WORLDTEACH

Photo: WorldTeach

A volunteer teaches English to a class of young students. Prior teaching experience is not required, and WorldTeach provides training including language classes and cultural orientation.

WorldTeach provides an intensive in-country orientation which includes ESL teaching methods and practice, language classes and cross-cultural training.

Contact: Amy Moran, Recruiting Coordinator

YOUTH CHALLENGE INTERNATIONAL

305-20 Maud Street   (416) 504-3370
Toronto, ON   generalinfo@yci.org
Canada M5V 2M5   www.yci.org

Area: Costa Rica, Ghana, Guatemala, Guyana, Kenya, Nicaragua, Tanzania and Vanuatu

YOUTH CHALLENGE INTERNATIONAL

Photo: Youth Challenge International

YCI mobilizes youth in Canada and in local communities to be involved on community projects together.

General Information: Youth Challenge International (YCI) builds the skills, experience and confidence of young people by involving them in substantive overseas development projects in partnership with local organizations that serve youth. YCI has active programs impacting youth in Canada, Africa, Central and South America, the Caribbean and the South Pacific. Over 2,500 volunteers have had life-changing experiences with YCI since 1989. YCI involves volunteers in hands-on projects in developing countries to address local development issues. For ages 18 to 30. Programs are from 5 to 12 weeks long. YCI believes that young people should play a central role in addressing youth issues. A key component of our work is combining the energy and skills of volunteers with those of local youth. Your skills and interests will mobilize local youth to become involved and provide great reach and results.

Contact: Erin Nesbitt

Part 5

ADDITIONAL AGENCY RESOURCES

These agencies are sources of information, resources or assistance for people or organizations involved in service to others or organizing in their community. Some also involve volunteers in their activities.

ADAPTIVE DESIGN ASSOCIATION

313 West 36th Street   (212) 904-1200
New York, NY 10018   www.adaptivedesign.org

General Information: The mission of the Adaptive Design Association (ADA) is to ensure that children with disabilities get the customized equipment they need to participate fully in home, school, and community life. The central elements of our mission are to design and build individualized equipment for children, to engage the community in the process of creating that equipment, and to promote the widespread establishment of adaptive design services and education. The equipment is designed and made by specialists at ADA who have had years of education and experience in the field of adaptive equipment. Input from parents, therapists, teachers, and social workers is critical to assure the greatest potential of the equipment.

ADA offers classes in the basics of cardboard carpentry and adaptive design to therapists, teachers, and parents. Through hands-on training, ADA teaches participants how to turn their ideas into functional pieces. Many students express reservations about their creative potential or mechanical aptitude, but by the end of their first project, most are delighted to discover skills they never realized they had. ADA also promotes the expansion of adaptive design services through collaboration with schools, universities, hospitals, parent groups, and area businesses.

Contact: Alex Truesdell, Executive Director

ARTHUR MORGAN INSTITUTE FOR COMMUNITY SOLUTIONS (A program of Community Service, Inc.)

PO Box 243   (937) 767-2161
Yellow Springs, OH 45387   (866) 767-2161
                                    info@communitysolution.org
                                    www.communitysolution.org

General Information: The Arthur Morgan Institute For Community

Solutions (founded in 1940 as Community Service, Inc), a nonprofit organization, has been a leader in the growing peak oil awareness movement for nearly five years, where we have been active in public education, original research and publication, and solutions design.

AMIFCS organized and put on the First, Second, Third and Fourth U.S. Conferences on Peak Oil and Community Solutions with over 1000 attendees combined, produced the award-winning film, *The Power Of Community: How Cuba Survived Peak Oil,* recently released the highly acclaimed book, *Plan C: Community Survival Strategies for Peak Oil and Climate Change,* and has published fourteen groundbreaking *New Solutions* reports. The organization advocates for lifestyle solutions as opposed to technological solutions, and emphasizes the value of conservation and curtailment in reducing our energy use. Its mission is to teach people about the value and benefits of small local community and design solutions to the current unsustainable, fossil fuel based, industrialized and centralized way of living.

Contact: Jeanna Breza, Administrative Manager; Megan Quinn Bachman, Outreach Director

CATHOLIC NETWORK OF VOLUNTEER SERVICE (CNVS)
6930 Carroll Avenue, Suite 506   (800) 543-5046
Takoma Park, MD 20912   volunteer@cnvs.org
www.cnvs.org

General Information: Catholic Network of Volunteer Service connects full-time volunteers with Christian faith-based volunteer programs in all 50 U.S. States and over 100 international locations

There are currently nearly 200 programs in the network, offering full-time volunteer programs ranging from one week to several years. Volunteers offer their service in a variety of areas, including legal services, computers, social service work, medical fields, agriculture, education and more. CNVS programs average more than 10,000 volunteers per year. Many volunteers who work in the United States are eligible for an AmeriCorps Education Award. Some programs offer an opportunity to receive college credit and/or a master's degree.

CNVS is an ecumenical organization. Twenty-five percent of the programs are not Catholic, and many programs accept volunteers from other faith traditions. Most programs give volunteers an opportunity to integrate volunteer service with their Christian faith. Many programs that accept volunteers for periods of nine months or longer offer medical insurance as well as room and board to the volunteers.

Contact us to request a free copy of the *Response* directory and to complete a profile which helps match potential volunteers with programs that meet their needs.

Contact: Niki Shoemaker

CHINA SERVICES INTERNATIONAL (CSI)

Beijing Friendship Hotel   (8610) 689-48899 Ext 50114
Building #5, Room 50114   Fax: (8610) 689-47989
Haidian District   csiyx@163.com
Beijing 100873, People's Republic of China

Area: The cities of Beijing, Shanghai and Guangdong; the provinces of Jiangxi, Hebei, Gansu, Henan and other provinces in the People's Republic of China

General Information: China Services International (CSI), located in the Friendship Hotel complex in Beijing, PR of China, works to recruit and place English-speaking individuals to spend six months to a year teaching conversational English in primary and secondary schools in the poorer provinces of PR of China. CSI is a division of China Association for International Exchange of Personnel (CAIEP), a national non-governmental organization whose purpose is to promote technical exchange and cooperation between China and other countries in many fields, including education. Through a CSI placement you can help children and adults in China improve their English. CSI provides support services to foreign teachers and will assist with all the logistics of your stay. Most of the schools can offer free accommodations, food, medical care and some travel costs within China. We hope you will consider enriching our lives—and yours!

Skills: Degrees or teaching certificates are often required and for many of the positions you need at least a bachelor's degree. CSI will provide a brief training course before starting the assignment.

Contact: Ms. Yan Xin

COORDINATING COMMITTEE FOR INTERNATIONAL VOLUNTARY SERVICE (CCIVS)

UNESCO House   (33 1) 45 68 49 36
1 rue Miollis   ccivs@unesco.org
75732 Paris Cedex 15, France   www.unesco.org/ccivs

General Information: CCIVS was created in 1948 under the aegis of United Nations Economic, Social and Cultural Organization

(UNESCO) as an international non-government organization responsible for the coordination of voluntary service worldwide. The CCIVS Center provides information on voluntary service through publications, Internet, directories of organizations and research studies. CCIVS encourages individuals to volunteer through existing local, national and/or international programs, and encourages the development of new voluntary service programs on the local, national and international level. CCIVS provides information, studies and referrals to resource persons to assist individuals, public institutions and NGOs in setting up voluntary service activities.

Contact: Simona Costanzo, Directrice

NORTH AMERICAN STUDENTS OF COOPERATION (NASCO)

PO Box 180048   (773) 404-2667
Chicago, IL 60618   www.nasco.coop

General Information: NASCO is a membership association of campus and community co-ops. Founded in 1968, it encourages the growth of a socially responsible North American cooperative economic sector, and can provide ways for students to address needs in the local community. NASCO provides conferences, training courses, publications and other technical and educational services to its members and to the general public. Volunteer projects vary in nature, are open to all interested and may have a limited stipend available. People interested in cooperatives and/or social change are welcome.

Contact: Chicago office for more information

SOUTHWEST RESEARCH AND INFORMATION CENTER (SRIC)

PO Box 4524, 105 Stanford SE   (505) 262-1862
Albuquerque, NM 87106   admin@sric.org
                                 www.sric.org

Area: New Mexico and the Southwest

General Information: Southwest Research and Information Center (SRIC), founded in Albuquerque in 1971, focuses on effective citizen action as the means to a healthy environment and social, racial and economic justice. SRIC's mission is to provide timely, accurate information to the public on matters that affect the environment, human health and communities in order to protect natural resources, promote citizen participation and ensure environmental and social justice now and for future generations. Technical and organizational assistance is provided to communities affected or threatened by pollution or resource exploitation; empowering people with information; conducting research and advocating in the public interest. Our main program areas are: Community Development and Economics; Energy and Natural Resources; Nuclear Waste Safety; Uranium Impact Assessment; Environmental Information and Education. We also publish *Voices from the Earth*, our quarterly publication.

Contact: Annette Aguayo, Office Manager/Editor

UNITED NATIONS/DEPARTMENT OF PUBLIC INFORMATION NGO RESOURCE CENTER

760 United Nations Plaza   (212) 963-7233
Room GA 37   dpingo@un.org
New York, NY 10017   www.un.org

General Information: The NGO Resource Center, run by the UN's Department of Public Information (DPI), is responsible for providing the public and NGOs with information and documents, or information about how to obtain them, about the work of any department, committee, council or organization of the UN, including the General Assembly. The Department of Public Information also maintains calendars of UN-related events and programs open to NGOs and to the public.

VOLUNTEER REFERRAL CENTER

161 Madison Avenue, Suite 5 S/W   (212) 889-4805
New York, NY 10016   info@volunteer-referral.org
                                 www.volunteer-referral.org

Area: New York City

General Information: The Volunteer Referral Center (VRC) is a New York City-based nonprofit agency that connects people who are interested in volunteering with agencies that need volunteers. Through personal, one-on-one interviews, the VRC provides prospective volunteers with information on volunteer opportunities that are best-suited to their interests, skills, and availability. Volunteers may choose from opportunities at over 200 nonprofit agencies; volunteer commitments range from one-time opportunities to year-long placements, and beyond.

Contact: Patricia Girardi, Executive Director

GEOGRAPHIC LOCATION INDEX

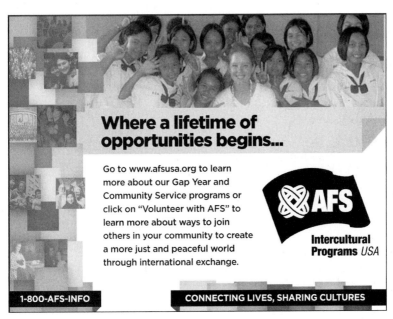

Invest Yourself

*Organizations interested in being included
in the next edition of INVEST YOURSELF,
see form on page 11.*

COMMUNITY AND LABOR ORGANIZING

COMMUNITY SERVICE: FAITH-BASED

DISABLED: CARE/ADVOCACY

Volunteer...
and enhance a life

How can I provide support to the dying and their loved ones?
How can I improve end-of-life care in my community? How can I make sure everyone has access to information and services they need?

Whether it is volunteering at your local hospice or end-of-life coalition or working at the state or national level to improve care at the end of the life, **Caring Connections** can help connect you to volunteer opportunities!

Contact the HelpLine at **800.658.8898**
Email us at **consumers@nhpco.org**
Or go to our Web site at
www.caringinfo.org

Caring Connections
a program of the
National Hospice and Palliative Care Organization

HEALTH CARE/MEDICAL SERVICE AND ADVOCACY

HOMELESSNESS: AID/ADVOCACY/AFFORDABLE HOUSING POLICY

HOUSING: CONSTRUCTION/REPAIR

HUNGER RELIEF/FOOD PRODUCTION & DISTRIBUTION

INDIGENOUS RIGHTS AND DEVELOPMENT

INTERCULTURAL AND INTERNATIONAL

LEGAL/JUSTICE/PRISONS

PUBLICATIONS/PRESS/MEDIA

Special Thanks

The production process for this catalogue is itself a testimony to the power of the non-government voluntary service and action movement. We thank the volunteers who contributed many hours to collect the information and do all the typing, copy-editing and proofreading. We also thank these companies for their part in making this edition possible.

1 Applegate Drive
Robbinsville, NJ 08691

Fine Paper
P.O. Box 253, 875 County Route 60
Newton Falls, New York 13666
info@nffp.com   866-738-5844